Painting And Decorating Furniture

Painting and Decorating Furniture

Sheila McGraw

Firefly Books

A FIREFLY BOOK

Published by Firefly Books 1997
Copyright © 1997 by Sheila McGraw

Cataloguing-in-Publication Data

McGraw, Sheila
Painting and decorating furniture
Includes index.
ISBN 1-55209-137-6

1. Furniture painting.   I. Title.

TX199.4.M33   1997   749   C97-930865-8

Text by Sheila McGraw
Photography and cartoon illustrations by Sheila McGraw
Edited by Sarah Swartz and Dan Liebman
Design by Sheila McGraw and Counterpunch/Linda Gustafson
Page production by Counterpunch

Published by
Firefly Books Ltd.
3680 Victoria Park Avenue
Willowdale, Ontario
Canada M2H 3K1

Published in the U.S. by
Firefly Books (U.S.) Inc.
PO Box 1338, Ellicott Station
Buffalo, New York 14205 USA

Printed and bound in Canada by Friesens
Altona, Manitoba

For Swee'pea

ACKNOWLEDGMENTS

Thank you to everyone who worked with me on this book: Lionel Koffler for making the book possible; Pamela Anthony, Melanie Siegel and Pauline McGraw-Pike for their assistance, and for lending their hands for photography. Also to Max Piersig and Jason Wing for their strong backs and sharp minds. Thank you to all who lent their furniture to this project and let me go to town on it, and to those who opened their homes to me for photography. Special thanks to The Paint Depot in Toronto for their excellent advice, their cheerful enthusiasm and their patience. Thanks to designer Linda Gustafson for gleefully knocking heads with me to get it all on paper, and to my editors, Sarah Swartz and Dan Liebman. My appreciation to all the people who work behind the scenes producing and printing this book and to the staff at Firefly Books.

CONTENTS

Introduction
■ 8 ■

A Brush with Destiny   10
Using This Book   11
Choosing Your Furniture   12

Tools and Materials
■ 14 ■

Adhesives   16
Deglossing Agents   18
Manual and Power Tools   20
Metallics   22
Painting Tools   24
Paint Products   26
Paint Removers   30
Specialty Products   32

Painting Basics
■ 34 ■

Preparation   36
Priming and Painting   38
Brush Painting   40
Roller Painting   42
Spray Painting   44
Staining Wood   46
Varnishing   48

Cabinets
■ 50 ■

Cupboard Love   53
   A Traditional Quebec Treatment
   for an Unusual Folk Art Cupboard

Prints Charming   57
   Fluid, Fast Block Printing
   Adds Bedside Appeal

Crackle   63
   Aging Artfully with a
   Simple Recipe for Crackle

Gold Standard   69
   Gold Leaf Glamorizes a
   Tiny Bathroom Cabinet

Victorian Secrets   75
   A Dramatic Recovery with Pretty
   Printed Fabrics and Soft Hues

Awash in History   81
   Washed in Stucco and Sepia, a Pine
   Cupboard Turns Classic Treasure

Bedtime Reading   87
   Eclectic Images and Personal Prose
   Create Contemporary Bedstands

Botanical Design   93
   Grapevines and Sophisticated Color
   Produce a Crafted Cabinet

Natural Tendencies   99
   Bedstands Go Country with
   Natural Branches and Rich Color

The Cupboard Was Bare   105
   A 1930s Baker's Pantry Is Stripped
   to Rich Wood and Finished with
   Traditional Hand-Painted Panels

Chairs
■ 114 ■

Country Folk   117
   A Country Chair Is Charmed with
   Decorative, Effortless Hand Painting

Keeping Time   123
   A Charming Rocker Reveals
   Its Pastel-Painted Past

Wrapture   129
   An Inglorious Group Goes
   Glamorous, Wrapped in Splendid
   Fabrics

Floral Arrangements   135
   Twin Bentwood Armchairs Are
   Romanced with Paint and Fabric

Mix Masters   141
   Fabric-Dye Stains Generate
   Glowing Color

Art Attack   147
   Adornments and Fanciful Paint
   Concoct a Work of Art

Seating   153
   Sitting Pretty with Professionally
   Crafted Cushions and Seats
     Basic Seat Cushion   155
     Piped Seat Cushion   158
     Woven Seat   161
     Backrest Cushions   164

Desks

■ 168 ■

A Subtle Distinction   171
Understated Texture Polishes
a Streamlined Desk

Letter Perfect   177
Découpage Transforms a Writing
Desk into a Fanciful Treasure

Office Romance   183
From Ordinary to Stunning – a Desk
Is Clad with Glorious Fabric

Art in Craft   189
Attention-Grabbing Layered Color
Is Offset by Crafted Copper

Dressers

■ 194 ■

Band Aid   197
Bold Bands in Neutral Shades
Redefine a Simple Highboy

Vanity Flair   203
Give Them the Moon and the Stars
with Unique Reverse-Stencils

Posterity   209
Playful, Historic, Romantic – Posters
Add Mood and Drama

Peaches on Cream   215
A Hand-Painted Trifle of Berries,
Bees and Bric-a-Brac

Heaven Sent   221
Divine Cherubs Are Framed by
Gilt-Edged Decorative Plasterwork

Tables

■ 226 ■

Lasting Impressions   229
A Simple, Striking School of
Block-Printed Fish

Times Tables   235
Simple Stenciling Creates
a Timely Classic

Basketry   241
Baskets Add Frivolity to Tiny Tables

Tabletop Rose Bower   247
Misty Stencils Bedeck a Wooden Table

Material Pleasures   253
Fabric Panels Add Drama with
Texture and Color

Sheer Delight   259
Gauzy, Printed Floral Vines Entwine
Over Painted Trellis

Ivy League   267
Set an Amber-Stained Table with
Ivy Trimmed in Copper

Sterling Qualities   273
Silver and Mica Put Fire into the Iron

Mineral Rights   279
Faux Marble, Granite and Gold
Forge a Miner's Palette

Mad for Mosaic   285
Crazy Paving Dishes Up
Three Fascinating Tabletops

Turning the Tables   293
Folk Painting Creates a Versatile
Seasonal Scene on a Dropleaf Table

Index

■ 300 ■

INTRODUCTION

Walk down the street. Go into an office building, a mall, or your own home. Art, painting, design and decoration surround us, reflecting current styles and messages through a universal visual language of texture, color and pattern. The need to creatively claim one's environment by marking it with personal art is well documented throughout history. The desire to paint your furnishings, imprinting a personal style, is a natural human urge. Furniture has unique properties that make it ideal for self-expression. Less intimidating to tackle than a wall or a full room, the scale of a piece of furniture is what makes its painting so appealing. Furniture offers a manageable area — much like an artist's canvas — in which fast, expansive wall-painting treatments can be mixed with the embellishments of artists' techniques for inspired results.

A Brush with Destiny

Many a furniture painter sets out with the simple intention of slapping a fresh coat of paint over a time-worn piece of furniture, only to have inspiration strike. The surprise result is a beautifully hand-painted work of art, a family heirloom to be cherished for generations. The flat planes of furniture – tabletops, drawer fronts and the like – present endless opportunities for decorative and pictorial techniques, while the three-dimensional form is sculptural in nature, offering many angles for viewing. Painting and decorating furniture is creativity in the round. Often the busy grain of wood, an unsuitable finish, or simply the familiarity of a piece of furniture can obscure these qualities until you stand before it, paint and brush in hand.

If you feel indecision creeping up as you try to decide on the right treatment, determine which type of decorator you are.

If you prefer furniture to be outstanding without standing out, think in terms of soft pastels or neutral colors and understated, tone-on-tone textures and treatments.

If you embrace the attitude that anything worth doing is worth overdoing, consider bright color, over-the-top decorative embellishments and a mixture of treatments for serendipitous results.

It's no longer necessary to use slow-drying oil-based paints to achieve professional results.

Using This Book

Whether you're a beginner or an advanced painter, this book will guide you through the maze of paints and tools available and show you how to manipulate and combine materials and techniques for wonderfully creative results. Check the *Tools and Materials* section (page 14), to acquaint yourself with the many easy-to-find and easy-to-use materials available at paint, craft and art supply stores. Unless absolutely unavoidable, only low-toxicity, water-based products are used and recommended. Water-based paints have evolved into easy-clean-up, simple-to-use, durable products.

Painting basics such as brush painting, roller painting, spray painting, staining wood and varnishing are covered, as is performing a basic paint job for those who simply wish to paint their furniture a solid color. You'll also be referred by your project instructions to these sections as required. They provide a goldmine of basic, common-sense advice and time-saving tips.

When choosing your treatment, turn to the section featuring the piece of furniture you wish to paint or decorate – cabinets, chairs, desks, dressers or tables – and examine the treatments. If you don't find a suitable finish,

Reading through the instructions before starting a project is like examining a road map. It helps you anticipate what's around the corner.

The toy penguin who appears in the Before pictures is 9 inches (22.5 cm) tall.

look through other sections. A crackle finish shown on a cabinet may be perfect for your table. Check the *Read This First* portion of the project to find out if there are restrictions in applying the technique on other pieces. To find special techniques and treatments such as sponge painting, dragging or stenciling, look at the *Index* at the back of the book. You'll be directed to the appropriate project. Within each section, projects are arranged in order, from elementary to more advanced skills. But don't be intimidated by the more complex treatments. All projects are broken into basic steps that are easy to follow.

Measurements are listed in imperial units, with metric conversions following them. To make the instructions less cumbersome, the conversions are often rounded. A quart-sized can of paint is listed as a litre, for example; a yard is converted to a metre. The projects work whether you use the imperial or the metric measurements. Finally, don't let the toy penguin who appears in the *Before* pictures throw you. This little fellow is working for scale, providing a point of reference. Without him, the size of a cabinet or some other piece of furniture could be hard to judge from the photo.

Test all moving parts of the furniture.

Choosing Your Furniture

Perhaps Aunt Flossie left you a four-legged monster. It's probably a sturdy, well-built, solid piece of furniture – better quality than you can purchase today. And it's free. Instead of relegating the monster to landfill, transform it to suit your decor and get ten or possibly a hundred years of use from it. If you don't have an Aunt Flossie, garage sales and flea markets are often treasure troves of old furniture. Another possibility is unpainted furniture – especially the knockdown variety, which is ideal for painting or staining in multiple colors. And don't throw out that plastic laminate furniture. Even recently manufactured melamine-over-chipboard furniture can be transformed with specialty melamine paints.

Just as the world is divided into cat lovers and dog lovers, it is also divided into furniture painters and furniture refinishers. Refinishers feel that wood and its grain are sacred, and that every stick should be stripped and refinished. Painters, meanwhile, believe that wood is simply nature's plastic, to be transformed into painted masterpieces. The truth is somewhere in between, and this book should help balance

Interesting lines and curves can be accentuated to advantage in refinishing.

Even a piece this severely damaged has renovation potential.

Simply constructed wooden tables suggest antique, Victorian or rustic treatments.

the two points of view. Virtually any style, type and finish of furniture can be painted, including wood, metal, melamine and all previously painted, lacquered and varnished pieces. But please: don't paint over genuine antiques or other pieces that have historic or architectural integrity, including classics from as recently as the 1960s and 70s. If you suspect your furniture has value, have it appraised. Often, you can simply take or send a snapshot to an appraiser or an auction house. If it turns out that you own a classic, but the style is unappealing to you, sell the item rather than paint it. Antiques with original paint should be left intact. Original paint on an antique, no matter how worn, adds to its authenticity and value.

If you wish to cut down on preparation time, look for a well-proportioned piece that is solid and has a stable finish. Beware of furniture with worm holes, especially if you see sawdust on the floor around the piece – a sure sign of bugs. When they move in, these boring guests will literally eat you out of house and home. And while you can't expect perfection – the furniture is *supposed* to be old and worn — try out all moving parts to determine the aggravation factor of drawers that bind or doors that stick, especially if the vendor has them taped shut. Remove drawers to check that dovetailing is intact and that the bottoms don't sag. If chairs or tables have wobbly legs, check that they can be fixed. Bypass the item if the legs have already had surgery but are wobbling a second time.

If you are planning to apply a smooth high-gloss treatment, choose a piece with a solid, even finish in good condition. Try the

Many new pieces, like this poorly finished jam cupboard, can benefit from refinishing.

fingernail test. Scratching with your fingernail should not lift the finish. Pieces with dents, scratches, cigarette burns and water or other surface damage require a busy-looking, low-luster finish to distract from the imperfections. You may wish to steer clear of pieces with water damage that has lifted veneer. Loose or raised veneer must be removed and the scars repaired, a job that requires some skill. And take a tape measure to be sure the piece fits its final destination and can be maneuvered through doors and up stairwells.

When choosing a treatment, look for finishes that will enhance the intrinsic style and accentuate the lines of the piece.

It is said that good design is form following function, and that real style is the appreciation of simple things. The art of painting furniture captures both elusive qualities.

Choose a finish in harmony with the mood of the furniture: rustic finishes for simple planklike constructions, Victorian treatments for decorative pieces, and glossy subdued finishes for simple modern furniture.

■

TOOLS
AND MATERIALS

Renovating furniture with paint and decorating techniques has never been more user-friendly. If several years have gone by since your last excursion to purchase paint, you are in for a pleasant surprise. Advancements in the technology of water-based paint have led to long-wearing products with low odor, smooth texture, a huge color range, dense coverage and fast drying times. Brushes, rollers, sandpapers and many other tools and materials for applying these paints have been redesigned to keep pace. And alongside the paints and brushes, you'll find innovative supplies, kits and other materials for a huge range of treatments. This section explains the properties and functions of the tools and materials used most frequently in furniture painting, and tells you where you can find them. Other, less common specialty items are covered in the projects that require them.

Adhesives

STICKY SITUATIONS CALL FOR GENTLE TAPES, SUPERTACKY GLUES AND DEPENDABLE PASTES

GLUE White carpenter's glue dries clear and is extremely strong. Use white carpenter's glue for bonding wood when joining or repairing pieces of wooden or painted furniture. Apply a generous amount to the join and connect the two pieces. (If repairing a piece, first clean out the join with a utility knife or sandpaper before gluing.) Wipe away excess glue and clamp the pieces tightly overnight, cushioning the clamps if necessary to prevent them from denting the furniture. If clamps aren't available, bungy cords can often be tightly wrapped around the pieces. When staining a piece of furniture, stain pieces before gluing, since the glue can act as a sealer on the wood, resisting the stain.

HOT GLUE With its fast drying time and good holding ability, a hot-glue gun is ideal for tacking decorative crafts. On furniture, it can be used for adding decorative detail or for finishing, but is not strong enough for gluing structural pieces of furniture. *When using a hot-glue gun, be careful.* This glue sticks to skin and can produce nasty burns. Some glue guns do produce a lower heat, but also a weaker tack.

MUCILAGE Mucilage is the amber-colored glue used in grade school. It comes in a slim bottle with a rubber nipple on top. Mucilage is the inexpensive magic ingredient used for creating crackled paint – the type that looks like flaking paint. The mucilage is painted onto a dry base coat of paint. While the glue is still wet, another color of paint is brushed over the glue. The different drying times of the glue and paint create the technique called crackle, which works best with latex paint. (See *Crackle*, page 63.)

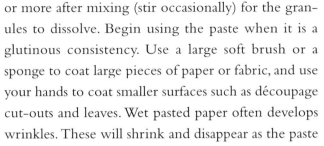

TAPE Isolating areas to be painted by taping around them is called "masking." Ironically, masking tape is not a good choice of tape for this purpose. Easy-release tape, available in a light and medium tackiness, has two major benefits over masking tape. Easy-release tape is smooth and gives a crisp edge; masking tape tends to be slightly crinkly, permitting paint to ooze under its edge. Easy-release tape peels off most surfaces without disturbing the underlying finish, while masking tape often lifts paint. The only drawback of easy-release tape is its tendency to live up to its name by spontaneously falling off. The trick is to use small pieces of masking tape to tack the ends in place. Remove all tape as soon as possible after painting, preferably as soon as paint is dry to the touch. Any tape left on for long periods will leave gummy deposits or will fuse to underlying paint, tearing it off when the tape is removed.

(1) easy-release painter's tape; (2) masking tape; (3) white carpenter's glue; (4) mucilage; (5) C-clamps; (6) hot-glue gun; (7) cellulose wallpaper paste.

WALLPAPER PASTE Clear-drying, easy-to-work-with water-based wallpaper paste is the adhesive of choice for mounting large flexible materials, such as paper and fabric, to furniture. Purchase cellulose-based paste in dry form from your paint store and mix the required amount with water. This paste needs to sit for fifteen minutes or more after mixing (stir occasionally) for the granules to dissolve. Begin using the paste when it is a glutinous consistency. Use a large soft brush or a sponge to coat large pieces of paper or fabric, and use your hands to coat smaller surfaces such as découpage cut-outs and leaves. Wet pasted paper often develops wrinkles. These will shrink and disappear as the paste dries. Paper can also stretch and will then require trimming when it has dried.

SPRAY GLUE Available at hardware, paint, office supply, craft and art supply stores, this relatively new product is versatile and fast and offers a choice of temporary or permanent bond. Apply spray glue to the backs of stencils to make a light, long-lasting tack for holding the stencil in position. Spray glue can be used as a permanent adhesive for mounting fabric and posters, although it allows only one attempt at positioning. If this prospect causes anxiety, use wallpaper paste. In upholstery work, use spray glue for laminating foam to plywood, and batting to foam. Spray glue is also used for gluing block prints to a roller for continuous-printing jobs. The down side of spray glue? The overspray you get, and the amount of glue that sticks to your fingers.

When using spray glue, be careful to avoid becoming stuck on your project. This glue is tenacious. It sticks like, well, glue!

Deglossing Agents

NEW SANDPAPERS AND SANDPAPER SUBSTITUTES MAKE DEGLOSSING QUICKER AND CLEANER THAN EVER

COMPOUNDS Furniture with a lustrous finish must be deglossed before being painted, to ensure that the paint will adhere to the surface of the furniture. Very high-gloss or melamine finishes require a light sanding, but furniture that has a stable, non-flaking, low- or medium-luster finish can be deglossed with liquid deglossing agents. TSP or another liquid sandpaper can be used to dull the gloss and remove all grease and dirt. Mix the TSP with water according to the package label. Then, wearing rubber gloves, wash the piece with the solution and rinse well with clean water. Allow to dry overnight before painting.

SANDPAPER To promote the best adhesion possible between the furniture's surface and the primer or paint, lightly sand surface areas that will be getting a lot of wear, using fine sandpaper (220 grade). High-gloss or plastic laminate finishes must be lightly sanded. This is a fast job. Remember, you're only deglossing the surface, not sanding down to bare wood. Sand the surface evenly until it has a dull surface texture. When sanding raw wood, always sand *with* the grain. Sanding lightly across the grain can leave deep permanent scratches. Sanding between coats of paint with fine sandpaper (220 grade or finer) will give a smoother, lacquerlike

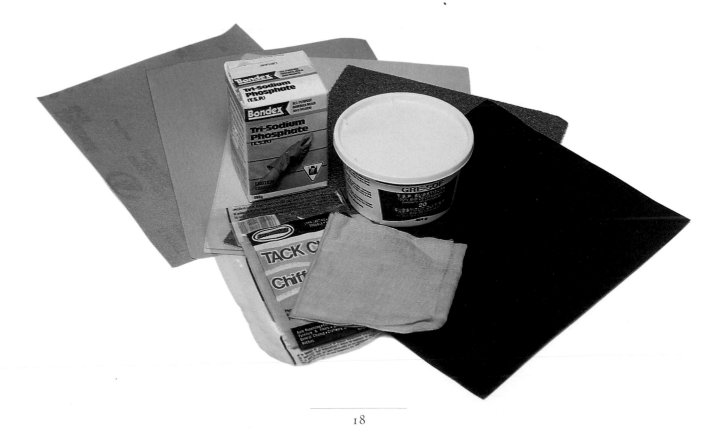

top coat. When varnishing, sand lightly with fine sandpaper (220 grade or finer) between coats. Don't be alarmed by the cloudy effect the sanding has on the varnish. The next coat will be smooth and clear. After sanding any surface, wipe away every trace of dust with a tack cloth.

Choose the right sandpaper for the job. The grit or grade, printed on the back, indicates grains of sand to the inch. The lower the number, the coarser the texture.

EMERY CLOTH

Emery cloth – black sandpaper with cloth backing, and gray-black sandpaper with green paper backing – is produced only in very fine grades. Both varieties can be used wet for sanding metal or dry for wood and metal.

GARNET PAPER

Brown in color, garnet paper is the most commonly used sandpaper. Use garnet paper for sanding wood, painted surfaces or plastic laminates. Available in very coarse to very fine grades, it is ideal for virtually all sanding requirements, except for sanding metal.

(1) fine garnet paper; (2) sandpaper for latex paint; (3) TSP deglossing compound; (4) coarse garnet paper; (5) biodegradable deglossing compound; (6) emery cloth; (7) tack cloth.

GREEN SANDPAPER

Recently developed for use on latex paints and varnishes, green sandpaper won't gum up like other sandpapers do. It is available in fine to coarse grades.

TACK CLOTH

A tack cloth looks like a slice of cheese in a plastic bag. Usually it comes with no instructions, one of the mystery materials sold at hardware and paint stores. Tack cloths are an absolute necessity for furniture painting and decorating. Composed of cheesecloth impregnated with a tacky substance, its purpose is to pick up all traces of dust. These cloths work so effectively, you may want them for dusting around the house.

Vacuum up any large quantities of dust. Then, remove the tack cloth from the package, but don't unfold. Instead, use the outside surfaces for wiping, until they are completely caked with dust. Then fold the tack cloth inside out and keep wiping. Continue wiping and refolding the cloth until it is completely used. Between uses, keep the cloth tightly packed in plastic so that it doesn't dry out.

You hate sanding, so why not just skip it? No one will know. Right?

Manual and Power Tools

TOOLS PLUS COMMON-SENSE PROTECTION
EQUAL PROFESSIONAL RESULTS

MANUAL TOOLS If you are putting together a basic toolbox, the following tools are recommended. Start with a screwdriver, the type that stores several interchangeable bits in the handle. (Some of these have a ratcheting device that saves time, energy and wrist fatigue.) Next are the screws. Old furniture that has been repaired will often have mismatched screws, and no two pieces of new furniture seem to use the same type of screw. In a perfect world, there would be one type of screw, and it would be a Robertson – the square-slot type that stays on the screwdriver. A small hammer is handy for attaching wood trim and hammering in loose nails. Small- and medium-sized C-clamps, for clamping glued pieces, are a good toolbox staple. So are small and large paint scrapers for scraping loose finish, spreading adhesive and lifting stripped paint. A small, lightweight, fine-toothed hand saw is often needed for cutting various wood trims. A staple gun is also useful. Choose one that takes ⅜ in. (1 cm) staples. If you have a lot of stapling to do, consider a power stapler. (See Power Tools, below.) Acquire additional tools as you need them. Reduce frustration by storing tools in a toolbox that keeps them visible or has shallow drawers, as opposed

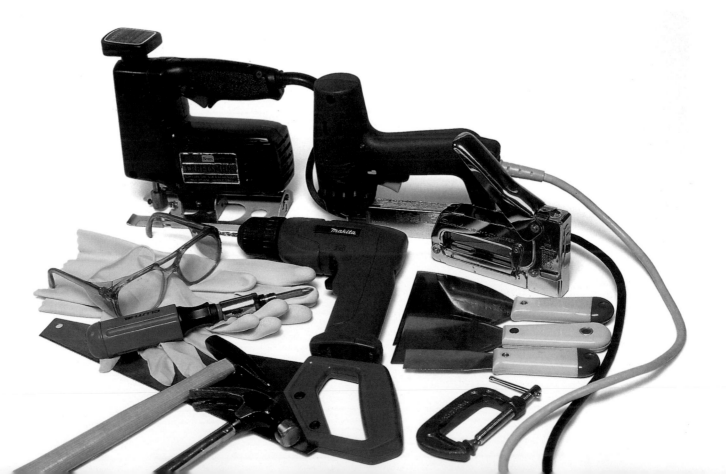

to the type with one deep box where tools become buried and difficult to find. There's a catch, however. For the toolbox to be effective, you have to put the tools back in when you're through.

Very few power tools are required for furniture painting and refinishing. A small vibrating sander can be a handy substitute for manual sanding. Occasionally, a power drill will be required for drilling holes for hardware and leader-holes for screws. A cordless, lightweight drill with a keyless chuck is preferable. Purchase the appropriate drill bits for whatever you are drilling, wood or metal, and in the required size. A drill can also take the elbow grease out of screwing in screws. You'll need screwdriver drill bits to fit your drill. To cut plywood for tabletops or chair seats, use the appropriate saw: a table saw for straight cuts, and a jigsaw or scroll saw for curved cuts. No need to skip a project because you don't have a power saw. Many lumberyards will custom cut wood. If cutting metal, use a specialty blade. *When cutting with any type of saw, wear the necessary protective gear and watch those fingers.* If you have a big stapling job, such as a set of six chair cushions, consider springing for a power stapler.

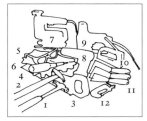

(1) 9 oz. hammer; (2) tacking hammer; (3) hand saw; (4) screwdriver; (5) safety goggles; (6) rubber gloves; (7) jigsaw (scroll saw); (8) power drill; (9) power stapler; (10) manual stapler; (11) paint scrapers; (12) C-clamp.

Unlike hand-held staplers, most power staplers take all staple sizes. The ease of operation makes the job breathtakingly fast.

PROTECTIVE GEAR Always wear safety goggles when cutting metal, smashing tile for mosaic, or tackling any other task that can produce flying debris. When sanding, spray painting or using other materials that can produce airborne particles of paint or dust that could be inhaled, wear a paper mask that filters particles. To block both particles and fumes (or only fumes), wear a charcoal mask. For some jobs, like applying paint stripper or other toxic materials where the symbol of a hand turning into a skeleton appears on the label, gloves are an absolute necessity. Choose the heavy rubber kitchen-style gloves for these jobs. Gloves are not a necessity for most paint jobs, but many painters won't paint without them.

Latex gloves – the ones that are disposable, stretchy, lightweight and thin – are perfect for painting. Wear these gloves for jobs that can irritate your hands, such as sanding, painting, rolling paint, or tiling. No more farmer's hands and wrecked manicures. If you develop a rash or hayfever-like symptoms, discontinue wearing latex gloves. You may have an allergy.

Buying tools needn't break the bank. Buy only what you need for each job, and consider renting one-job-only tools such as tile cutters or power saws.

Metallics

ANTIQUED AND PATINATED METALLICS ADD RADIANCE

METALLIC LEAF The rich patina of gold leafing is no longer the exclusive domain of the highly trained sign painter or the refinishing specialist. Imitation gold and other metallic leaf, and the necessary components of adhesive and sealer, are available at art supply and craft stores. For genuine gold, try a framing supplier. Purchase compatible products all made by the same manufacturer. Incompatible products can cause chemical reactions that ruin the finish.

Applying metallic leaf is straightforward and simple, and the results are professional looking. The adhesive is applied to the surface area and allowed to cure for several minutes. It remains extremely tacky. The metallic leaf is laid over the adhesive and burnished to make contact with it. Excess leaf is brushed away with a small paint brush. Then the leaf is protected with a coat of sealer. Leafing is available in gold, silver, pewter and copper, all of which can be antiqued or left bright. To antique the leafing, purchase an-

tiquing paint or use artist's acrylics. (See *Sterling Qualities,* page 273, step 3; *Mineral Rights,* page 279, step 3.)

METALLIC PAINT As an alternative to metallic leaf, paint-on metal (made from ground ore suspended in a liquid medium), available at art supply stores, provides a dense, convincing metallic finish. Don't confuse these paints with small jars of gold and silver hobby-type enamels. You'll know the right ones if they are displayed with the compatible patinas, sealer and etching fluid. Choose instant iron, gold, copper or bronze. The labels on the jars of paint include instructions for using each product. A clear sealer, which acts as a primer, is brushed on first, followed by two coats of the metal. The metallic paint can be patinated or sealed as is. (See *Ivy League,* page 267, for copper; *Sterling Qualities,* page 273, step 6, for rust.)

PATINA Patina is the thin sheen on a copper or other surface, produced by age. Patinating metallic paint gives an aged and refined quality to a piece of furniture.

These treatments are usually applied to molded or carved-looking decorative pieces such as pedestals; however, they are also effective on flat surfaces. Blue and green patinas are available for copper metallic paint, and rust is available for iron. Purchase the patinas wherever you buy the metallic paint. All the patinas are very watery. When brushed onto the

(1) liquid copper; (2) sheet copper; (3) patina blue; (4) primer-sealer; (5) etching fluid; (6) mica gel; (7) artist's acrylic paint; (8) liquid iron; (9) instant rust; (10) patina green; (11) copper leaf; (12) gold leaf; (13) sealer for leaf; (14) adhesive for leaf.

dry metallic paint, they begin their work, almost immediately oxidizing the metal. Apply sparingly, adding more coats to achieve the desired effect. Once the patina has finished the oxidizing process, usually three days, clear sealer is applied. Clear sealer can tone down the effect of the patina and kill the sheen of the metallic paint. It's a good idea first to do a test on cardboard to examine the effects of the sealer on the finish. If you don't seal the patinated metal, the treatment may transfer or be damaged by use.

SHEET COPPER Try hobby shops as well as art supply and craft stores for finding sheet copper. This is the copper that hobbyists use for burnishing. The sheets are as thick as heavy paper and can be cut with heavy workshop or kitchen scissors. *When cutting this copper, be extremely careful.* The edges can be very sharp. Injuries are more painful and annoying than paper cuts. (Wearing a cast-off pair of leather gloves can help protect you.) The cut edges can be sanded dull with very fine sandpaper or an emery cloth. Sheet copper can be patinated with the same blue or green patina used on metallic paints. Before patinating the copper, treat it with an etching fluid, often called metal master, which is part of the metallic paint and patina family. Then follow the same steps for patinating metallic paint. (See *Art in Craft,* page 189, step 4.)

Metallics are most effective when used as an accent rather than as an all-over treatment.

Painting Tools

INGENIOUS NEW APPLICATORS COUPLED WITH TRADITIONAL TOOLS PERMIT CREATIVE TREATMENTS

BRUSHES Purchase good quality brushes. A cheap brush will shed hair on your paint job and fuzz up like a squirrel's tail, spraying paint as you work. A quality brush will hold paint better, paint cleaner lines and endure far more use and washing, returning to its original shape and condition.

For cutting-in on furniture, choose a brush about 1½ in. (4 cm) wide. For painting large, flat sections, purchase a 2 in. (5 cm) brush. Choose brushes made for water-based paint. These synthetic brushes, unlike their natural-hair counterparts, won't get bushy from contact with water. Buy brushes with fine bristles that won't leave grooves in the paint job. A brush with a diagonal cut on the bristles makes it far easier to paint the many corners and angles of a piece of furniture.

Tackle detail work with two basic artist's brushes: a medium-sized, fine-point brush, and a square-tipped brush about ½ in. (1.25 cm) wide. These don't need to be expensive. Just be sure the fine brush will hold a point and not resemble a small palm tree. Choose brushes compatible with water-based paint products.

To prolong the life of your brushes, don't allow paint to dry in the bristles. Wash brushes thoroughly with warm water and dish soap. Rinse well and wrap each brush in a paper towel to hold bristles in shape. Lay brushes flat to dry. Standing them on their handles spreads bristles, rusts the metal and rots the handle. Standing brushes on their bristles gives them a bad perm. (For more information on painting with a brush, see *Brush Painting,* page 40.)

ROLLERS

The small, flat surfaces of furniture are perfectly suited to a small roller, eliminating brushstrokes and imparting a smooth, even texture to a paint job. Rollers are available in many sizes and materials. A small, short-pile roller is ideal. Foam rollers can hold air, creating bubbles in the paint job. (New "velvet" foam rollers have tiny hairs that pierce the air bubbles as you paint.) Bargain or high-pile roller sleeves can also make air bubbles. These can be eliminated (along with lint from the roller) by dampening the roller sleeve and rubbing it as dry as possible on a paper towel before slipping it on the handle. Choose a tray to fit the roller. A tray provides a reservoir of paint and a ramp to roll out the excess, preventing runs, sags and uneven application.

Roller sleeves can be washed with soap and water, but most lose their soft texture. Save them for applying primer, not the finished paint job. (For information on painting with a roller, see *Roller Painting*, page 42.)

SPONGES

Sponging paint onto a surface has become the staple texturing technique for all levels of painters. Sponges, both synthetic and natural, produced especially for use with paint, are available at paint, craft and art supply stores. Synthetic sponges are formed into a half-sphere shape and have consistent, small pores. Sea sponges have large, erratically spaced pores and are irregular in size and shape. Sponging onto furniture is unlike sponging onto a full wall. Large prints produced by a sea sponge, pleasing on a wall, look crude on a piece of furniture. The scale makes the difference. Either a synthetic or a sea sponge can be used, but try to get a sea sponge with small pores. When sponging, tear off a section about the size of a tennis ball. Holding it between your fingers and making a pouncing motion, sponge sections,

(1) synthetic sponge; (2) square-tipped artist's brush; (3) fine-point artist's brush; (4) brushes for latex paint; (5) broom for texturing paint; (6) small roller; (7) combing tool; (8) wood-graining tool; (9) natural sponge.

layering and blending colors for a suedelike effect.

TEXTURING MATERIALS

The creative painter can achieve many unique textures simply by layering paint and etching it with unexpected household items. Most texturing treatments lift a wet top coat of paint from a dry base coat with a texturing tool such as a crumpled plastic bag (smooshing), an inexpensive feather duster, or a twisted rag (ragging), or by dragging a brush through the wet paint (dragging). Shadowing is created by taping and painting stripes in two finishes — matte and glossy — in the same shade. Paint stores sell many texturing devices, including textured rollers for creating wood grain prints and combs for making even-textured stripes and basketweaves.

BLOCK PRINTS

Block printing is an effective method of creating multiple images for both the accomplished artist and the artistically challenged. You can purchase precut block prints made of foam, or you can hand cut your own prints. Purchase the thin, flexible foam used for children's cut-out crafts, or use a foam insole. After cutting out the block print, score details into the foam. These will hold more paint and print darker, giving the print added interest. Block printing can be done singly, or several identical prints can be laminated to a roller for continuous printing. Apply glazes, acrylic paint or latex paint onto the foam block (or laminated roller) and impress it onto the surface of the furniture, applying even pressure. Then lift it off. (See *Prints Charming,* page 57; *Sheer Delight,* page 259.) Potato printing is a form of block printing using a carved potato. Potato prints produce a naive, weathered print in keeping with many rustic and antiquing treatments. (See *Crackle,* page 63; *Lasting Impressions,* page 229.)

Paint Products

FAST-DRYING, LOW-ODOR, EASY-CLEAN-UP PAINTS, ADDITIVES AND VARNISHES ADD TO THE PLEASURE OF PAINTING

LATEX WALL PAINT Although the experts at the hardware store may insist you need oil-based paint, just keep in mind that they're probably not computer geniuses either. Times have changed. It is no longer necessary to endure the noxious fumes, glacial drying times and tedious clean-up of oil-based paints. The technology of water-based paint products means long-wearing paint in finishes from flat matte to high gloss; low odor; very fast drying and recoating times; and easy soap-and-water clean-up.

Whether you purchase a can of acrylic paint (plastic emulsion) or latex paint (synthetic rubber emulsion) at the paint store – both types are popularly referred to as latex – expect to apply two coats for solid coverage. Don't be alarmed that the paint is a light color in the can. It will dry darker. Choose a low-luster to glossy finish for furniture. Avoid flat finishes, which show fingerprints and scuff marks. Any water-based paint should be well stirred or shaken before using. Latex paint dries quickly to the touch – usually an hour – but it should be allowed to dry several hours before recoating. Consult the label for precise drying times. Water-based paints remain vulnerable and need to cure for at least thirty days before being washed or subjected to wear and tear.

ACRYLIC WALL PAINT

This paint can be bought by the can at paint stores. Because it is water based, it is generally (but improperly) referred to as latex. Check the label for the actual contents. More expensive than latex paint, pure acrylic wall paint is considered the highest quality of most paint lines. But the reality is that when it dries, it has a rubbery finish that tends to stick to objects that come in contact with the surface for any length of time, lifting the paint (a problem on furniture). A better bet is a combination of acrylic and latex. You'll get the best qualities of both types of paint. Like latex paint, acrylic needs to cure for thirty days.

ARTIST'S ACRYLICS

Originally intended as an alternative to artist's oils, acrylic paint has developed as a versatile medium in its own right. Available in a huge range of premixed colors and incredibly fast drying, their compatibility with latex paint makes artist's acrylics ideal for creative furniture treatments. Artist's acrylics can be used straight from the tube for an oil-paint texture or thinned with water for watercolor washes and glazes. They can also be used for stenciling, freehand painting or texturing. Generally sold in small pots and tubes, these acrylics offset the need to buy a large can of latex paint, which is too much paint for detail work.

MELAMINE PAINT

The popularity of plastic laminate, particleboard furniture and countertops has helped create a generation of new high-adhesion paints, referred to as melamine paints. Unlike most other paints, which lose their grip and peel,

(1) artist's acrylics in tubes; (2) artist's acrylics in pots; (3) colored glazes; (4) latex paint; (5) glaze; (6) extender; (7) shellac; (8) spray paint; (9) primer; (10) acrylic mediums; (11) varnish; (12) gel.

The versatile, durable quality of artist's acrylics, and their compatibility with other paints, allows creative expression on furniture.

these cling tenaciously to plastic surfaces. Always degloss the melamine surface by sanding with fine sandpaper (220 grade or finer) before applying the paint. Melamine paints vary from store to store. If a label indicates that a primer is necessary, use an ultra-high-adhesion, white-pigmented, shellac-based primer for best results. Allow melamine paint to cure for two to four weeks before subjecting to wear and tear or washing. If melamine paint is not available, latex paint can be substituted – so long as the melamine surface has been de-glossed by sanding and a coat of ultra-high-adhesion, white-pigmented, shellac-based primer is applied first.

SPRAY PAINT

Spray paints are ideal for painting pieces of furniture with spindles or intricate molding. Spray painting imparts a dense, smooth, even coat in a range of finishes from low luster to high gloss. It also eliminates the drips, gaps and sags usually associated with brush painting.

While graffiti may have given spray painting a bad name, this art form created a demand for spray paint that has benefited the furniture refinisher with a wealth of low-odor, low-toxicity acrylic spray products in a huge range of colors. Purchase spray paint at hardware, art supply and craft stores. Also available in spray form are textured treatments such as granite and marble; paints for covering metal or rust; varnishes; and fast-drying, crystal clear lacquers. (See *Spray Painting*, page 44, for more information on the application of spray paint.) For the avid spray painter, special nozzles giving narrow to wide coverage are available at art stores that cater to the graffiti trade.

EXTENDER Extender is added to paint to slow the drying time. Use extender when working on a painstaking technique, such as marbling, or when applying a texturing technique, such as sponging, over a large area.

Add water-based extender to latex or acrylic paint in the proportions specified on the label. Both extender and glaze can be mixed into paint at the same time. Extender is available at art supply and craft stores in smaller quantities than what you may find at paint stores.

GLAZE Glaze, a milky-looking viscous liquid, is added to paint to make the paint more transparent, while maintaining the original consistency. Add glaze for texturing and layering techniques, such as ragging, sponge painting or dragging, when you want the underlying coat to show through to a certain degree. Some painters are comfortable adding water to paint to achieve the transparency desired for sponging or similar treatments. Other texturing treatments, such as dragging, require the paint to maintain its viscosity; otherwise the paint, if too liquid, can run together and destroy the intended effect. Add water-based glaze to latex or acrylic paint in the proportions specified on the label. Both glaze and extender can be mixed into paint at the same time. Glaze is available at paint stores in larger quantities than what you may find at art supply and craft stores.

Premixed tinted glazes are available at art supply and craft stores. These are paint and glaze mixtures sold in small jars, saving you the trouble of mixing your own colored glazes. Use these glazes for small projects such as block printing, where a decorative, overlapping, sheer quality is desired.

MEDIUM AND GEL Mediums and gels are acrylic-based cousins of the glaze and extender family. They are available at art supply and craft stores in smaller quantities than what you may find at paint stores. Mediums are milky-looking viscous liquids that dry clear and are used as varnishes. They come in a variety of finishes, from flat to glossy, and many contain ultraviolet protection to help keep underlying paint from fading or otherwise breaking down under exposure to UV rays.

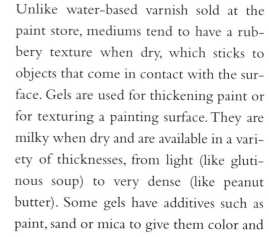

Heavy gels, which are malleable when wet and cementlike when dry, can be used for a textured tabletop, as shown here.

Unlike water-based varnish sold at the paint store, mediums tend to have a rubbery texture when dry, which sticks to objects that come in contact with the surface. Gels are used for thickening paint or for texturing a painting surface. They are milky when dry and are available in a variety of thicknesses, from light (like glutinous soup) to very dense (like peanut butter). Some gels have additives such as paint, sand or mica to give them color and texture. (See *Sterling Qualities,* page 273, for using gel on a tabletop.)

PRIMER/SEALER *Primer* is more than just a first layer of paint. It adheres more tenaciously than any paint, providing a painting surface that won't peel and an even skin over the surface to prevent patchiness on uneven and absorbent surfaces. Apply primer before painting or decorating, unless you are antiquing with sandpaper (see *Cupboard Love,* page 53) or staining. Stain must be applied directly to bare wood.

Many types of primer are available. Water-based, high-adhesion primers are ideal for most furniture. Primers that are not high adhesion are good for walls, but not for furniture. If you are using a water-based primer on unpainted wooden furniture, the primer may raise the grain of the wood. If this happens, sand lightly with fine sandpaper (220 grade) when the primer is dry. Furniture with a high-gloss finish should be deglossed by washing with TSP, or by sanding before priming.

For plastic laminate finishes, degloss by sanding, then paint with a melamine paint; or use an ultra-high-adhesion, white-pigmented, shellac-based primer before painting with latex paint. These ultra-high-adhesion primers require chemical solvents for clean-up (consult the label). Or simply use a cheap disposable brush and roller sleeve. Shellac-based primer is not recommended for varnished or lacquered furniture because it can eat into the finish.

Use spray primer for furniture with spindles or intricate detail.

Sealers have two uses. First, when painting (not staining) unpainted, wooden furniture, use shellac or another sealer recommended for this purpose to seal all knots in the wood before priming or painting. Otherwise, the knot will discolor the paint. Shellac requires a chemical cleaner for brushes (consult the label). Alternatively, you could use a cheap disposable brush. Second, you'll find that clear sealers are sold with specialty treatments such as gold leaf and paint-on metallics. These are used not only as a sealer to be painted over the treatment for protection, but often also as a primer. Purchase a sealer compatible with the products being used.

Whatever type of varnish you use, always apply it with a paint brush. Rollers, especially foam rollers, leave bubbles in varnish.

VARNISH

Water-based varnishes, often called urethanes, are fast drying, with low odor and easy soap-and-water clean-up. They come in a range of finishes, from low luster to glossy, and many are non-yellowing. Varnish enriches color, somewhat like wetting down your car does, and protects your paint job against cleaners, scuffing and chipping.

Several coats give a rich glasslike finish. Varnish can make the use of unorthodox materials and treatments workable, stabilizing transient color and encasing fragile materials in a durable plastic coating. It is best to varnish a full piece of furniture, though varnishing only the areas that will receive wear and tear is acceptable if a non-yellowing formula is used.

Don't view varnish as the enemy. Work quickly, avoid overbrushing and apply several coats, sanding lightly between coats. (See *Varnishing,* page 48.) Oil-based varnishes can also be used. If you find that the very quick drying time of water-based varnish makes application difficult, you may prefer oil-based urethanes. They take overnight to dry and tend to impart an amber tone to the finish. Oil-based varnish is used to create crackled varnish. (See *The Cupboard Was Bare,* page 105.)

Many a paint disaster has started on the Sale shelf — a quart of paint with a gallon's worth of tint . . . paint in the wrong color or finish . . . and paint that mysteriously never dries.

Paint Removers

NOT LIKE THE OLD DAYS – GENTLE STRIPPING AGENTS AND EFFECTIVE TOOLS MAKE PAINT REMOVAL FUN (ALMOST)

PAINT STRIPPERS If the idea of paint strippers conjures up visions of vats of steaming toxic waste, it's been a while since you tried stripping paint. There are strippers that smell like citrus fruit, and some are non-toxic enough that wearing gloves is optional. Welcome as these advancements are, stripping furniture is still a messy job, especially if the piece has intricate detail or many layers of paint and varnish. A piece of furniture with either historic or design integrity is, however, worth the journey into slime. Stripping a good basic piece buried under several coats of badly applied paint is also worthwhile, because it cannot be repainted until the

many layers are removed. But you can also partially strip such a piece, allowing sections of layered color to show through. This treatment is not only interesting and attractive, but it reveals the history of the piece. (See *Keeping Time,* page 123.)

The old way of stripping was called dip and strip. The whole piece was placed in a trough of heavy-duty toxic chemical stripper. This procedure often unglued joints and had caustic effects on the underlying wood. Most strippers today are much more gentle. Choose a gel stripper, which will cling to vertical surfaces. Placing plastic wrap over the stripper can speed the curing time. Just check first that the stripper doesn't eat the plastic. (For more information on stripping paint, see *The Cupboard Was Bare,* page 105.)

PROTECTIVE GEAR Paint stripper will destroy the finish on your floor. Do the job over several layers of paper (newspaper is fine), with a layer of plastic or, even better (since some strippers dissolve plastic), an old bedsheet on top. Decant the stripper to paint it on. Pour it into crockery, not plastic. Wear heavy rubber gloves for this job, the kitchen type. Avoid latex surgical gloves unless you are certain the stripper won't eat through them. Safety goggles are also recommended. When you brush the stripper on and scrape off loosened paint, some particles can become airborne.

TOOLS Using the proper tools will make the stripping go much faster and easier. In the first stages of the stripping, a medium-

(1) stripping brush; (2) rubber gloves; (3) organic stripper; (4) gel stripper; (5) safety goggles; (6) paint scrapers.

sized paint scraper is needed for lifting the bubbled, loose paint. Next, a hard plastic stripping sponge, which resembles a block of petrified spaghetti, is ideal to use along with the stripper to help lift paint. When most of the paint has been removed, use a stripping brush along with the stripping sponge. This brush resembles a barbecue-grill cleaner, with brass bristles (they won't rust) on one side and nylon bristles on the other. The nylon brush side is ideal for giving the piece a thorough rubdown. The brass bristles remove the last particles of paint and varnish from any carving and trim, and from the grain of the wood. When using scrapers and other sharp tools, remember to let the stripper do the work. Overly enthusiastic scraping can damage fine or soft wood, defeating the purpose of stripping, which is to reveal the natural, unspoiled beauty of the wood.

Hold it! Don't strip that antique! However worn and beaten-up the furniture may be, original paint on an antique adds greatly to its authenticity and value.

Specialty Products

FROM THE INSPIRED TO THE BIZARRE, NEW PRODUCTS ARE CREATED TO FULFILL THE PAINTER'S EVERY NEED

KITS A tremendous number of kits are available for techniques such as crackle, block printing, marbling, sponging and stenciling. Many of these kits are adequate for the painter, particularly if only a small area is to be painted, eliminating the need to buy large quantities of products that will go unused. However, some of the kits are pricey and don't live up to their promises, with poor instructions and materials that just don't work. Many of these techniques are actually quite simple to perform, require readily available ingredients and are demonstrated in this book.

SPECIAL APPLICATORS Manufacturers are scrambling to keep pace with the demand for innovative paint applicators. Aside from the usual brushes and rollers, there are combs (for creating striping and basketweave effects) and raised wood-grain patterns to be rolled and dragged. Most unusual are rollers that have plastic floral shapes riveted to them, reminiscent of a 1960s-era bathing cap. These rollers are used to create texture by layering similar paint colors, thinned with glaze, with the plastic attachments producing a subtle, semiregular pattern. Various sponges, rags and texturing brushes are available too, as are foam applicators for painting edges, corners and flat areas.

SPECIALTY PAINT

Fashion designers like Ralph Lauren and Laura Ashley, who have become lifestyle/interior designers, have come out with signature lines of top-quality water-based paints in painter-inspiring rich colors. These paints are created to complement the housewares that the designers also produce. Although this approach to choosing a paint color may seem excessive to some, others find it reassuring and exciting, trusting that the results will be exactly as expected and that the decor and paint will be tasteful and will harmonize perfectly. Other paint manufacturers are producing innovative paints with unlimited possibilities for application. There are very thick iridescent paints, which are applied in layers with a trowel, sanded and glazed to a glasslike sheen. There are paints with tiny flecks of suspended color, which are made to be layered with similarly toned glazes to produce wonderful depth and suspended texture. There are also a variety of spray-paint effects, including a granitelike composition that comes in kit form. There is

(1) stencil cream paints; (2) stencil brush; (3) texturing brushes; (4) marbling spray; (5) flecked paint; (6) marbling kit; (7) texturing roller; (8) spray granite; (9) texturing paint; (10) synthetic sponge; (11) colored glazes.

even spray-on marble veining, although it looks rather like a mix of hair and mushy spaghetti. Instead of trying to create marble veins with it, the creative painter could have fun with the effect in other unusual ways.

STENCILING MATERIALS

Purchase a precut stencil from the huge selection available, or design and cut your own.

To cut your own stencils, buy stencil plastic at an art supply or craft store — the lightweight, flexible blue plastic that is semitransparent for tracing designs — and use an X-acto or a utility knife or small, pointed scissors. Lightweight cardboard can be substituted for the plastic. To execute the stencil, use any type of paint you wish: spray paint for smooth even coverage, acrylic or latex paint applied with an artist's paint brush for a freehand look with brushstrokes, or stencil cream paint applied with a stencil (stipple) brush for dense smooth coverage. The spray and acrylic paints dry quickly, while the cream paint can take as long as a week to dry. Use spray glue to provide a tacky backing on the stencil. (See *Tabletop Rose Bower,* page 247.)

Don't be intimidated by the multitude of new products at the paint store. Many can add substantially to your creative pursuits.

Painting Basics

Most projects in this book will refer you to this section to prepare, prime and paint your furniture with a base coat of paint. This base coat is the groundwork for your decorative treatment.

Step one is the preparation. Virtually every piece of furniture needs some preparation before painting or staining, whether you're repairing wobbly parts, removing doors, hinges and hardware, deglossing a shiny surface, or sanding raw wood.

Step two is applying the primer. Most furniture – varnished or painted wooden pieces, melamine pieces, or unpainted wooden furniture – requires priming before painting. Exceptions include unpainted wooden furniture that will be stained, and furniture to be painted and then antiqued by sanding. See brush, roller and spray painting information in this section to determine the method of application most suitable for your piece of furniture.

Step three is the painting. Paint is applied (usually two coats) over the primer in the same manner as the primer was applied. After the base coat of paint has been applied, the creative and inventive stage of adding decorative effects and treatments begins.

Skipping the preparation stage now may haunt you later.

Preparation

In the final analysis, the preparation of the furniture – fixing loose parts and preparing the surface for painting – is more important than any painting or decorating. Avoid the temptation to skip the prep stage of painting. It will yield consequences (that mom warned you about) of the same variety as building a house on sand, eating dessert before the main course, or sleeping in an unmade bed. Different varieties of furniture will require different types of preparation. Read through this section to determine how much and which types of preparation your particular piece of furniture needs. Although many painters dread this part of the job, once it is out of the way, the paint and decorative

Purchase new hardware if desired. If the piece has wooden knobs, consider painting them.

treatments can be done with a clear conscience.

Right at the start, set up a comfortable, well-lit work area. Keep the work space as flexible as possible, with moveable light sources and a convenient table on which to work. You may wish to call off the bridge game and abscond with the card table. It's ideal for putting all but enormous items of furniture at a comfortable working height. Its small scale makes furniture accessible from all sides, and it can be folded up and tucked away when not needed. Keep a supply of dropsheets handy. Old large, non-slip bedsheets are good. Plastic or paper can be used, but don't use newspaper. The printer's ink will transfer to your paint job.

MATERIALS

The following tools and materials may be required.

- screwdriver
- machine oil
- new hardware and screws
- wood filler
- small paint scraper (or putty knife), wide paint scraper
- fine sandpaper (220 grade)
- sanding block
- wooden matchsticks
- white carpenter's glue
- clamps or a bungy cord
- power drill
- deglossing compound (TSP or other liquid sandpaper), rubber gloves
- tack cloth

1 *Drawers*

Remove drawers, marking their position (top, center, bottom, etc.) on the back panel. As a result of wear and tear or how they were built, drawers will often fit properly only in their original slots.

2 *Hardware*

Unscrew and remove all hardware. This includes removing doors by unscrewing hinges. On a dropleaf table, remove the hinges and the contraptions that keep the leaves up. Hinges should be cleaned and oiled. If a tabletop is removable, the painting will be easier if the top is removed and painted separately from the base.

3 *Filler*

If holes left by old hardware don't correspond to the new hardware, use wood filler and a small paint scraper or putty knife to fill the holes. Also fill any gouges in the surface of the piece. Sand the wood filler smooth and level with the surface, using fine sandpaper.

Fill the screw holes of loose door hinges with the wooden ends of matchsticks and carpenter's glue. Allow to dry before replacing the hinges. Hinges can also be shifted when they are replaced.

4 *Fixing loose parts*

Loose desktops and dresser tops are caused by lifting the furniture by the top instead of the base. Reattach a loose dresser top by replacing the existing screws with fatter, not longer, ones. Reglue loose joins in a chair by levering the join apart, cleaning it as much as possible, then applying carpenter's glue to the join and clamping it shut. (If you don't own clamps, you can wrap tightly with a bungy cord.) Glue and clamp loose trim. Allow all glue to dry overnight.

Loose, wobbly table legs are caused by dragging the table instead of lifting it. There are many different constructions for table legs. Try to figure out how the table and legs are constructed. Glue and clamp all joins and tighten or replace all screws.

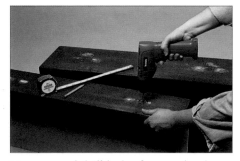

Measure and drill holes for new hardware, if needed.

5 *Preparing the finish*

Granny furniture – old, dark wood – should be given the fingernail test. Scratch the varnish with your fingernail. It should not be marked or lifted. If it is, this loose, crumbly finish will flake when painted, taking the paint with it. Scrape off the loose varnish with a wide paint scraper – a fast job. Then sand the surface smooth with fine sandpaper, either by hand or with a sanding block.

If the furniture has a high-gloss or plastic laminate finish, it will require light sanding to allow better adhesion between the paint and the furniture surface. Sand with fine sandpaper, in the direction of the grain on bare wood (sanding across the grain can create deep scratches), and lengthwise on painted pieces.

If you really hate the dust and the effort of sanding and your furniture has a medium- to low-luster finish, clean and degloss your furniture with a deglossing compound such as TSP. Mix the granules according to instructions on the label. Wearing rubber gloves, wash down all glossy areas, rinsing well with clean water. Allow the furniture to dry overnight.

Vacuum and clean the whole piece of furniture, both inside and out. Remove all remaining dust by wiping the piece with a tack cloth. If desired, wash the piece with a damp cloth and a gentle cleaner. Allow to dry overnight.

Cats seem to gravitate to the laps of those who want them least. Naturally, they're also drawn to fresh paint. Put puss out.

Priming and Painting

Applying a coat of primer before painting is a necessary step for most projects. Exceptions include furniture to be antiqued by sanding away paint to reveal bare wood, and unpainted wooden furniture to be stained. Primer adheres more tenaciously to the furniture's surface than paint does, to provide a strong bond and an even skin. The paint can then flow onto the primer without patchiness or an uneven texture.

Primer and paint should be applied by the same method. For instance, if the furniture is simple with flat surfaces, both primer and paint should be applied with brush and roller. If the furniture has intricate carving, trim, or spindles, spray primer and spray paint should be used. Don't be discouraged by the streaky, uneven quality of primer when you put it on. Apply primer swiftly and avoid the temptation to redo areas. Primer sets and dries quickly, and reworking will tear up the surface. Once the primer is dry, the furniture can be given one or two coats of water-based paint as a base coat. If your furniture has a plastic laminate finish, use melamine paint for the base coat. (See *Melamine Paint,* page 27.) Before adding other treatments, allow the coats of paint to dry for the time specified by the manufacturer.

Touching wet paint is a universal temptation, so devise strategies to keep yourself away while items are drying. Paint just before bedtime, for example. And remember, mistakes are the mother of inventive solutions.

MATERIALS

The following tools and materials may be required.

- small quantity of white shellac
- easy-release painter's tape or masking tape
- quart (litre) high-adhesion, water-based primer; or spray primer; or, for plastic laminate surfaces, if primer is suggested on the label, white-pigmented, shellac-based primer
- painting tools:
  -paint brush, 1½ in. (4 cm) wide, for water-based paint
  -roller handle, 4 in. (10 cm) wide, and short-pile sleeves
  -roller tray to fit roller
- quart (litre) eggshell or satin finish latex paint in the color of your choice
- quart (litre) non-yellowing, water-based varnish
- paste wax, buffing cloth

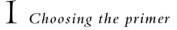

1 *Choosing the primer*

If your piece has molding, spindles or carved detail, you may wish to use spray primer. (Follow the instructions for *Spray Painting*, page 44.)

2 *Priming removable pieces*

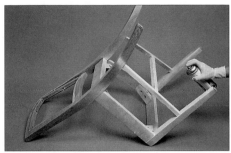

Seal any knots on raw wood with shellac before priming.

Stir primer thoroughly before applying it. Primer should be applied to all areas that will be painted.

Start with removable pieces, such as doors or drawers. Lay doors or other flat sections on supports and mask off any sections that are to remain unpainted.

If the drawers are clean, prime only the fronts and their edges. If the drawer interiors are grungy, paint them with primer.

Use the paint brush to cut-in with primer, painting all inside joins and corners that aren't accessible to a roller. (See *Brush Painting*, page 40.) Then use a roller to prime the flat areas up to the brushwork. (See *Roller Painting*, page 42.)

The exterior sides can be primed if desired, but make sure there is enough space between chest and drawer. (Adding coats of primer and paint to the sides can cause drawers to bind.) Water-based primers and paints dry quickly. Wash brushes when they're not in use.

3 *Priming the body*

Bottoms up. Whatever the type of furniture, from chairs to hutches to tables, start priming the body of the piece of furniture from the bottom. Lay chests and cabinets on their backs and turn chairs and tables upside-down. (If the furniture is heavy, get some help lifting it.) Using a brush, cut-in all corners and places that are inaccessible with a roller. Then roller paint the primer up to the brushwork on all surfaces that you can comfortably reach. Priming the backs and interiors of cabinets, desks and dressers is optional.

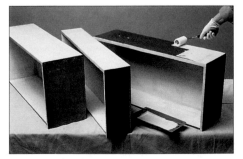

Stand the piece upright. Cut-in and roller paint all remaining surfaces. Wash all paint utensils with soap and warm water. Allow the primer to dry.

4 *Painting*

Repeat steps 1 and 2, now using latex paint. Allow to dry and apply a second coat if necessary.

5 *Varnishing and finishing*

Continue, painting and decorating your piece of furniture, or if the piece is to be left a solid color, protect the paint and enrich the color by applying a non-yellowing, water-based varnish. (See *Varnishing*, page 48.)

Attach the hardware.

Binding may occur where paint comes into contact with other paint. In such areas, apply one or two heavy coats of paste wax and buff.

Paint the hardest-to-get-at areas first. There'll be less paint on the painter and more on the furniture.

Brush Painting

In spite of the numerous advances in paint tools and products, the most necessary and versatile tool is still the paint brush. But don't get caught up in brushmania. It's not necessary to buy an arsenal of expensive brushes for painting furniture. Use a medium-width brush with an angled cut to the bristles for cutting-in and for painting flat sections; an artist's square-tipped brush for narrow areas and detail work; and a fine-point artist's brush for freehand, intricate painting. While full-coverage painting is usually executed with a combi-

Creating with a brush adds individuality and personality to an otherwise straightforward paint treatment.

nation of brush and roller, sometimes brush painting is necessary to produce brushstrokes, desirable in many antiquing and rustic treatments. (See *Painting Tools,* page 24; *Specialty Products,* page 32.)

There is no foolproof way to achieve a perfect paint job with a brush. There are, however, approaches to brush painting that will garner a smoother, more even coat with fewer drips and sags. Purchasing good-quality brushes, made to be used with your type of paint, either oil- or water-based, is a good start.

MATERIALS

The following tools and materials may be required.

- quart (litre) eggshell or satin finish latex paint in the color of your choice
- paint brush, 1½ in. (4 cm) wide, for water-based paint
- tube of acrylic paint in the color of your choice
- artist's brushes, medium square-tipped or fine point
- chalk or colored pencil

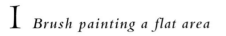

1 *Brush painting a flat area*

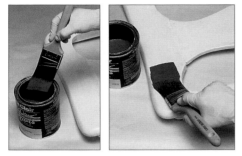

Stir the latex paint. Dip the paint brush into the paint to a level of about one-third to one-half of the bristles. Drag one side of the bristles against the lip of the can when removing the brush from the can.

Lay the wet side of the brush on an open part of the furniture, inside an edge. Brush the paint outward, brushing the length of the area, not the width.

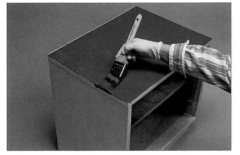

Brush toward and over edges, if possible. If the brush is dragged against an edge, as shown in the photo, the paint will form drips.

Continue brushing, quickly and deftly smoothing the paint. Reload the brush as needed. Keep a constant watch for drips, swiping them away with the brush. Water-based paint sets quickly. Avoid brushing over the same area several times.

Overbrushing will create deep brush-strokes in the setting paint. Finish painting one section of the piece at a time.

2 *Cutting-in*

When painting joins and corner detail, load a small amount of paint onto the brush and use the longer point of the brush's angled tip to coax paint into the corner, dragging the brush alongside the join. The angled cut on the brush suits this technique, especially when cutting-in on the insides of drawers and other pieces with many angles and inside corners. Watch for drips and sags, swiping them away with the brush.

3 *Painting details*

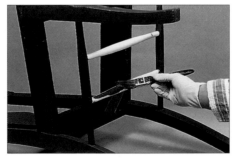

Though spray paint is usually best for spindles and other ornamental work, sometimes details must match the overall effect of a brush-painted piece. Load the brush with a small amount of paint. Holding the brush on an angle, drag it in a downward motion along the spindle, depositing the paint in a long bead.

Quickly brush out the paint to an even coat. Watch for any drips and sags, brushing them out.

4 *Freehand brushwork*

Freehand painting in contrasting colors is attractive on carved or turned details. Position at eye level the area to be painted. Use an artist's brush of a size suitable for the area, and artist's acrylics or latex paint. Thin the paint if needed so that it flows easily from the brush, but is not watery. Try to maintain a steady hand. Keep edges even and end the color at a natural break.

To paint freehand designs, such as curlicues or trailing vines, draw your design first with a piece of chalk or a colored pencil. Use a fine-point artist's brush and acrylic or latex paint, thinned if necessary to flow from the brush. Dip the point of the brush into the paint. With your hand raised (laying the heel of your hand on the table creates cramped shapes), apply pressure on the brush to obtain the thickness of the line desired. Paint the line, using the chalk line as a guide only. Following the chalk line too closely will cause hesitation, resulting in tentative lines.

Rollers are available in a wide variety of sizes. Choose one that fits the job.

Roller Painting

The roller is undoubtedly one of the most important painting tools, second only to the paint brush. It provides fast, even coverage and smooth texture without brushstrokes. A relatively recent invention, the roller has revolutionized painting. But until recently, roller painting was viewed only as a fast way to cover large areas. New, creative ways of using this versatile tool are now being explored to produce repetitive patterns and textured layering of color. For painting furniture, purchase a small roller handle with removable short-pile sleeves to fit. Buy two or

The smooth texture of a roller-painted surface provides an excellent base for creative treatments such as dragging.

more sleeves, because most are good for only one application of paint. Choose a paint tray to fit the roller. A paint tray is better than a paper plate or other disposable substitutes, because its reservoir and textured ramp provide more even distribution and better control of the paint. First, with a brush, cut-in on far corners and other hard-to-get-at places. Then use the roller to apply primer or paint, but not varnish. Varnish should always be brushed on.

MATERIALS

The following tools and materials may be required.

- quart (litre) eggshell or satin finish latex paint in the color of your choice
- roller handle, 4 in. (10 cm) wide, and short-pile sleeves to fit
- roller tray to fit roller
- fine sandpaper (220 grade or finer), tack cloth

1 *Ready to roll*

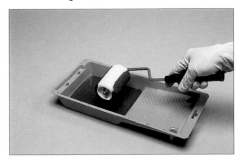

To prevent air bubbles from forming in the paint and to remove any loose roller-sleeve lint, dampen the sleeve and rub it as dry as possible with a paper towel.

Pour paint into the reservoir of the tray, filling it about half full. Dip the roller sleeve into the tray and roll it so that the full sleeve is coated in paint.

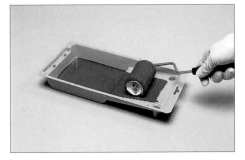

Roll excess paint from the roller on the ramp of the tray, but don't overdo it. The roller should still hold a good quantity of paint.

2 *Applying an even coat*

Position the roller on a surface of the furniture, inside the edges. Beginning at this central point, roll the paint outward in a triangular fashion, criss-crossing previous lines. This technique will give even texture and prevent a grid from appearing. Don't try to achieve full coverage in only one coat. Excessive paint that isn't rolled out will create stretch marks – an undesirable texture.

Apply moderate, even pressure. Let the roller do the work. It is better to reload the roller with paint than to squeeze more paint from it. Heavy pressure will create railroad tracks – a double line of heavy paint formed along the sides of the roller.

3 *Roller logic*

Roll toward and over edges, instead of pulling the roller against an edge. Rolling against an edge creates drips. As you roll, be on the lookout for drips and either swipe them with a brush or roll them out.

Continue rolling, overlapping each new roller of paint over the edge of the last, until the full surface is covered. Avoid the temptation to reroll a wet section. Water-based paint sets quickly, and rerolling will tear up the surface. Instead, allow to dry and apply another coat. For an ultrasmooth finish, lightly sand the first coat with fine sandpaper when it is completely dry and wipe clean with a tack cloth before applying the second coat. Between coats, keep paint wet by placing the tray and roller in a plastic bag, squishing the bag to eliminate air.

Block printing with a roller creates beautifully rendered, consistent, multiple prints for borders or all-over patterns. (See Ivy League, page 267.)

Be sure to check the direction of the nozzle.

Spray Painting

Spray painting gives smooth, dense coverage to furniture with ornamental carving and texture. The invasive nature of spray paint allows it to go where a brush can't reach, quickly and without drips or sags from brushing. Wherever you spray paint, large dropsheets are required to avoid home-and-garden decorating by default. Only a small portion of the paint coming from the nozzle connects with your furniture. The overspray really travels, settling on surfaces and in tiny crevices. So tape dropsheets together and cover everything that might catch drifting paint. Also make sure you work in a well-ventilated environment to avoid asphyxiating the canary. Spray painting outside is fine, unless it is too breezy. A garage with an open door is

The glossy lacquerlike quality of spray paint provides the perfect foil for painterly brushwork and crisp fabric treatments.

best. Indoors, several open windows, or an open window with a fan, will help. Inevitably, a certain amount of fumes and spray will be inhaled, simply because of the painter's proximity to the spray can. A paper mask will screen out spray paint particles, while a charcoal mask will filter out both paint and the fumes of the paint.

Most sprays don't require primer. But if your furniture has a patchy, uneven finish, spray with primer first. Acrylic-based sprays, available in both low-luster and glossy finishes, are superb for most furniture. Choose a specialty spray paint to cover rust or to add texture. If the local paint store has a limited selection of finishes or types of spray paint, try hardware outlets or art supply or craft stores.

MATERIALS

The following tools and materials may be required.

- dropsheets
- charcoal mask or painter's mask
- one or more cans of acrylic spray paint
- one or more cans of spray primer
- one or more cans of rust-covering spray paint
- steel-wool pad

1 *Getting started*

Attention allergy sufferers: a charcoal mask to eliminate fumes is recommended. If the label indicates flammable (inflammable) or explosive, do not work where there may be open flame, including a flame as tiny as the pilot light on a stove, furnace or water heater.

Using plastic dropsheets, old bedsheets or paper (not newspaper because the ink will transfer to the painted piece), cover every surface around your furniture piece that may catch some stray spray or over-spray.

Shake the can for at least two full minutes. Test by spraying paint on a piece of paper. The first few sprays may appear watery until the paint makes its way up the tube.

2 *Spray primer*

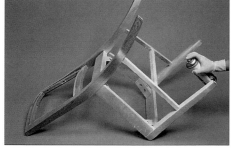

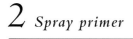

If you use a primer, apply one coat. Primer dries very fast. You should be able to turn the piece of furniture as you work, spraying all surfaces quickly. Allow to dry thoroughly.

3 *Rust-covering spray paint*

If using a special rust-covering spray paint, remove as much rust as possible from the furniture with water and a steel-wool pad. Rinse well and allow to dry. Follow the directions on the label for application and drying times.

4 *Spray painting, phase 1*

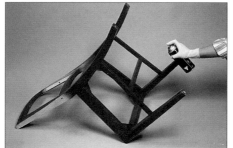

Position the piece of furniture upside-down on the dropsheet. (If the furniture is heavy, get some help lifting it.) Holding the can about 10 in. (25 cm) away from the object, depress the nozzle fully, spraying the furniture with a light, even coat. Spraying too heavily will create drips and sags. Several light coats are better than one heavy one. Spray all visible surfaces without moving the piece.

Recoat while the piece is in the same position. Check the label. The recoating instructions on most spray paints say to apply another coat within one hour. If you miss that deadline, you must wait three days to recoat. Apply as many coats as required for dense, even coverage.

5 *Spray painting, phase 2*

Allow the paint to become dry to the touch. Turn the piece of furniture upright and repeat step 4. Continue until all surfaces are covered. Allow to dry thoroughly.

The most beautiful stains can come from unexpected sources.

Staining Wood

The opaque density of paint invites creativity, but don't overlook the effect of stain on bare wood. Simple and very fast to apply, stains appear dark in their liquid form, yet are transparent when they dry. But transparent doesn't mean invisible. Stain not only provides color. As it is absorbed into the wood, it also accentuates the grain and markings. What was a bland, bare piece of pine five minutes ago is now a fascinating and intricate natural work of art. Most commercial stains for wood are natural brown wood shades. However, dramatic jewel

Paint treatments such as block printing add color and an extra dimension to stained wood. (See Ivy League, page 267.)

tones, rustic colors or rich shades can be had from berries or fabric dyes.

After applying a commercial stain, protect the surface with wax, oil or varnish. Many stains are available already mixed with varnish or oil – making staining and finishing a one-step process. Ask at your paint store about these mixes. Always varnish unorthodox or bright-colored stains to protect the finish and prevent transfer of color. (For bright stains, see *Mix Masters,* page 141.)

MATERIALS

The following tools and materials may be required.

- commercial stain in an appropriate quantity
- fine sandpaper (180 to 220 grade)
- sanding block
- tack cloth
- small quantity of white shellac or other sealer

- wooden stir stick
- paint brush
- rags
- quart (litre) non-yellowing, water-based varnish;or furniture oil or wax and buffing cloth

I *Getting started*

Start with completely bare wood, free of paint, varnish or glue. If the wood was previously painted and stripped it must be free of all paint residue, and the surface should be lightly sanded to open the grain. Unpainted wooden furniture is often sealed – the result of saws used to cut the wood – giving the wood a slightly shiny surface. Wood that is sealed will absorb stain unevenly, giving the surface a patchy appearance. Sand unpainted furniture lightly with fine sandpaper to open the grain.

Holding the sandpaper flat in your hand or using a sanding block, sand the surface lightly with fine sandpaper in the direction of the grain. (Sanding across the grain can create deep scratches.) Wipe the surface clean with a tack cloth.

End cuts – where the wood is cut across the grain – may absorb a large quantity of stain, becoming darker than the rest of the furniture. If you don't want this effect, dilute some white shellac or other sealer to half its normal strength and brush it onto the open grain. When the sealer is dry, stain the edge.

Using a wooden stir stick, stir the stain thoroughly. Wipe the stick on a rag and double check the color of the stain on the stick.

2 *Applying stain*

Lay the surface to be stained in a horizontal position to prevent runs. (If the furniture is heavy, get help lifting it.) Dip a brush or a rag into the stain and begin to spread the stain onto the wood. Most of the stain will be absorbed.

Follow the fresh stain with a clean rag, wiping away excess. Continue staining and wiping the excess, staining to the wet edge of the previous section.

When the full side is stained, allow to dry. Then turn it over and stain the other side. Continue until all sides of the piece are stained.

3 *Protecting the finish*

The finish of a stained piece must be protected. When the stained surfaces are dry, protect them by varnishing, oiling or waxing. Consult your paint store about the different applications available.

Clear thinking: Varnish in a dust-free setting.

Varnishing

Varnishing not only protects your paint job from scuffing, chipping and the effects of cleaning compounds. It also enriches color and gives a deep, glasslike finish. Some fragile materials such as paper and fabric, when protected by several coats of varnish, can be used in unexpected and creative ways. While it's best to apply varnish over an entire piece of furniture, you may opt to varnish only the parts that receive the most wear and need the greatest protection, such as a tabletop or the drawer fronts of a dresser.

Select a non-yellowing, water-based varnish in your choice of finish, from low luster to glossy. These varnishes are fast drying, skinning over within minutes, a quality that helps prevent dust from becoming embedded in the surface. Water-based varnishes have a relatively slight odor and are easy to

Applying water-based varnish is like wrapping furniture in plastic, making a finish as delicate as fabric tough and durable.

clean up with soap and water.

There are only two rules for achieving water-based varnish perfection. First, do it fast, quickly "floating" the varnish onto the surface with a brush, never a roller. Second, resist the urge to touch. Varnish begins to set immediately, and brush marks, fingerprints and kitty's paw prints are permanent. When the varnish is dry (usually a few hours), sand the finish lightly with fine sandpaper, wipe clean with a tack cloth and apply another coat. Don't be alarmed by the cloudy effect sanding has on the varnish. It will disappear when the next coat is applied.

Occasionally, a project with a special treatment, such as crackled varnish, will call for an oil-based varnish. These varnishes take much longer to dry than water-based ones, overnight compared with a few hours. They also lend an amber tone to the finish.

MATERIALS

The following tools and materials may be required.

- easy-release painter's tape
- tack cloth
- quart (litre) non-yellowing, water-based varnish
- paint brush, 2 in. (5 cm) wide, for water-based paint
- fine sandpaper (220 grade or finer)
- paste wax or car wax, buffing cloth

1 *Getting started*

Use easy-release painter's tape to mask around the area that you will varnish. Varnish must be stirred, never shaken. Shaking will create a multitude of bubbles that become trapped in the quickly drying varnish. While applying the varnish, stir it about every fifteen minutes.

2 *Applying varnish*

With a tack cloth, wipe the piece to be varnished, removing every particle of dust from the surface.

Using the paint brush, apply the first coat. Dip your brush to a level about halfway up the bristles.

Without wiping the excess off the brush, flow on a short, wide strip of varnish, starting near one corner or edge. Brush varnish out quickly and smoothly in the direction of the length of the surface, not

the width. Try to brush toward the edges. Brushing against edges causes runs and drips.

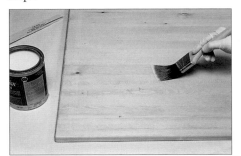

Repeat, brushing a second wide strip beside the first and connecting the strips. Continue until a section is complete. As you work, check for varnish that has slopped over edges and is creating drips. Wipe drips away with a brush, rag or finger. Continue across the surface, adding to the wet edge of previous strokes, until the surface is covered. Wash out the brush with soap and warm water.

Have a cup of tea and allow the varnish to dry.

3 *Additional coats*

When the varnish is thoroughly dry (usually about a couple of hours), sand the first coat lightly with fine sandpaper and wipe thoroughly with a tack cloth. The cloudy effect that the sanding has on the varnish will disappear when you apply the next coat.

Apply a second coat. Allow to dry. Sand again and apply a third coat, if desired.

Optional: Applying and buffing a coat of paste wax or car wax over the last, dry coat of varnish will produce a glowing, buttery finish.

Crackled varnish is created by layering oil-based varnish and gum Arabic. The resulting cracks are highlighted by rubbed-in paint.
(See The Cupboard Was Bare, page 105.)

CABINETS

Hold everything. The choice of cabinets is staggering. For large ones, check out hutches, wardrobes, armoires, chiffoniers that sport a closet plus drawers and vanity top, and large blank storage cupboards. Small varieties appear as bedstands, jam cupboards, and bathroom cabinets in all shapes and proportions. Cabinets are a godsend for those with a lack of closet space, and they can be more than simply functional. Their many doors and surfaces are ideal for inspired refinishing and decorating — adding personality, polish and warmth to a room. A cabinet, in short, makes a creative statement, bestows opulence or simply blends in nicely with its surroundings.

Cupboard Love

A TRADITIONAL QUEBEC TREATMENT
FOR AN UNUSUAL FOLK ART CUPBOARD

Judging from the elegant inset arches on each panel, this interesting cabinet

appears to have been assembled from a collection of old church doors.

Used as a garage storage cupboard it lost its grandeur as well as its floor,

and gained many mouse- and ant-sized cracks. Painting and antiquing the

cabinet in traditional Quebec colors disguises its flaws and accentuates

its elegant lines while keeping its folk integrity intact. Some of the

cracks were left, adding to the piece's farmhouse charm.

The overall effect is sturdy and rustic.

Read This First

The paint-and-antiquing technique demonstrated on this armoire can be applied to any piece of furniture – as long as the piece is made from solid wood, not particleboard or melamine. Unpainted furniture pieces are ideal for this treatment. If the piece is already painted, you will need to decide whether the existing color will work with your treatment. If it won't, you'll need to strip it partially or fully because areas will be sanded back to expose the undercoating. If the piece is varnished, sand it with a fine sandpaper or degloss the surface with TSP (see *Deglossing Agents,* page 18) for better paint adhesion.

BEFORE

A folk art cupboard? This neglected piece had varnish weathered to the wood, no floor and no feet. And in spite of its heavy weight and the thickness of the wood, it wobbled impressively. Strategic shoring with cut-and-nailed two-by-fours solved the disintegrating feeling and got it off the ground.

MATERIALS

- sandpaper or TSP deglossing compound, wood filler, scraper, other wood-repair materials and tools
- paint brush, 2 in. (5 cm) wide
- quart (litre) low-luster finish latex paint, barn red
- quart (litre) low-luster finish latex paint, deep linen blue
- medium and fine sandpaper (120 and 220 grades)
- amber stain
- rags
- paste wax, buffing cloth
- *optional:* rubber gloves

1 *Getting started*

Repair the piece, filling any cracks or holes as needed. (See *Preparation,* page 36.)

Sand or wash with TSP to degloss the surface for painting. If necessary, strip the piece to expose raw wood, as needed for the antiquing process (step 4). This cabinet was originally varnished, although most of the varnish had worn off. It was washed with TSP to clean the surface and degloss all remaining varnish.

Note: For photography purposes, the door was not removed from the cabinet. For best results, remove doors, drawers, etc., and paint separately.

2 *Painting the base coat*

Do not paint the cabinet with primer. Using the barn red paint and a brush (brushstrokes are desirable with this technique), paint the entire exterior of the cabinet, getting as much coverage as possible with one coat of paint. (See *Brush Painting,* page 40.) A second coat is not necessary, even if the first coat is not fully opaque. Paint the inside if desired. Allow to dry.

Though only some of the red will be exposed later, in the antiquing process, it is important to paint the full exterior. Eventually more aging will occur, and the red paint will show through the wear spots.

3 *Painting the top coat*

Using a brush, paint over the red paint with deep linen blue. Allow to dry. This color should be solid. Apply a second coat, if necessary.

4 *Antiquing*

When the paint is dry to the touch, use a medium-grade sandpaper to sand through the layers of paint. Sand wherever you feel natural wear will occur, exposing areas of red paint and some wood. Usually, wear occurs on all corners, on the high spots of trim and wherever a door or drawer would be pushed or pulled for opening and closing. Finish with a fine sandpaper.

5 *Staining*

Using a rag, apply amber stain to all areas of raw wood that have been exposed by the sanding. Wax and buff the stained areas with paste wax.

Attach the hardware.

Prints Charming

FLUID, FAST BLOCK PRINTING ADDS BEDSIDE APPEAL

A large-scale, bold pattern adds both decoration and repetitive interest to a piece of furniture. And when the pattern is created with a block print it takes on a charming, distinctive folk and country feeling. Block printing is like cloth woven from natural fibers: it's not completely uniform. Each print is subtly different, adding a hand-crafted feeling. Block printing with a roller is a fast way to achieve an overall pattern. This technique eliminates the usual endless measuring and planning involved in creating uniform patterns.

Read This First

This block-print treatment consists of two phases. First, the cabinet is painted with a base-coat color; then the print is applied with a roller. If your cabinet has a plastic laminate finish, use melamine paint for the base coat. (See *Melamine Paint,* page 27.) Purchase a small short-pile or foam roller and create the pattern to fit the roller. If the roller is much larger than the pattern, you'll find it hard to judge where the pattern should begin and end. The foam-printing blocks, which are laminated to the roller, can be cut from a foam insole. The insoles used for block printing should be the inexpensive kind, fabric on one side and perforated foam on the other. The small perforations will show up as tone-on-tone small dots. These dots give the design an additional decorative quality. Subtle changes occur from print to print as a result of variations in paint saturation and pressure. These slight differences should be viewed not as inconsistencies, but as desirable elements that create distinctive prints.

BEFORE

A 1960s-vintage bedstand that was acquired as part of a mismatched bedroom grouping. Its flat sides lend themselves perfectly to a block-printing treatment.

MATERIALS

- quart (litre) high-adhesion, water-based primer
- quart (litre) eggshell finish latex paint, cinnamon
- quart (litre) eggshell finish latex paint, cream
- painting tools: paint brush, small roller, roller tray
- paper (several large sheets), pencil, ruler, scissors
- pair of inexpensive foam insoles
- spray glue
- paper towels
- medium-sized artist's brush
- quart (litre) non-yellowing, water-based varnish
- *optional:* chalk or erasable pencil

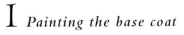

1 Painting the base coat

Refer to *Painting Basics* (page 34). Prepare and prime the cabinet before painting it with two coats of latex paint. The body of this cabinet is painted cinnamon and the doors cream.

2 Cutting the block print

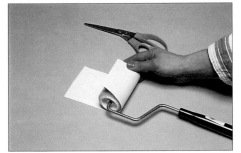

Begin making a pattern for the block print. Cut a strip of paper the width of the roller. Wrap the paper around the roller until the ends meet. Mark and cut the paper to this length. The paper should now fit neatly around the roller. Measure the piece of paper and set aside the measurements.

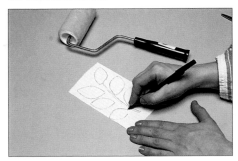

Trace the pattern from page 60, or draw a design, onto the pattern paper. A simple design is best.

Cut out the paper pattern pieces. One by one, lay a pattern piece onto the insole and cut around it until all pieces are cut out.

Note: Positioning the pattern for cutting on the fabric side of the insole will print the pattern as you drew it. Cutting from the foam side will print the image in reverse.

3 Laminating the block print

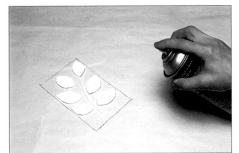

In the center of a large sheet of paper, draw a rectangle to match the pattern paper (from step 2). The excess paper is needed to catch ovesparay from the spray glue.

Lay the foam pieces *foam-side-down* within the rectangle's outline. Feel free to move pieces around and alter the original design.

Read the instructions on the spray-glue can for making a permanent bond. Usually the label states that the bond must be made when the glue is still "aggressively tacky," which means to spray, wait about two minutes, then bond the surfaces. Spray the fabric side of the foam pieces well with the glue.

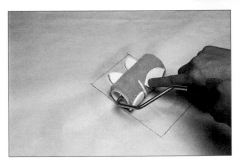

Position the roller on the paper at the base of the rectangle's outline, then begin slowly rolling it over the pattern pieces, lifting them and sticking them to the roller as you go. Don't worry if glue gets onto the roller fuzz. It will dry.

4 Test printing

Slightly dampen the foam pieces with a wet paper towel. With the artist's brush, apply paint onto the foam sections, using a color that contrasts with the painted background. Avoid getting paint onto the roller fuzz. The paint should flow easily, but it should not be watery. Before printing on the furniture, make some tests on paper to get the hang of the technique. Often, the foam prints better after several passes.

5 *Printing furniture*

Position the cabinet so that the side to be printed is horizontal. (If the cabinet is heavy, get some help turning it.) Before printing the furniture, you may wish to draw a chalk line to follow for printing. Or you can visualize a line, such as corner to corner (as was done on this cabinet). Follow the line with either the side edge or the center of the roller. Apply paint to the foam patterns. Position the roller at the beginning of the chalk (or imaginary) line, making sure the base of the pattern is at the starting point. Smoothly roll the image to the end of the line, applying even pressure.

Repeat a second line of patterns. Subsequent lines of pattern can be staggered, or the roller can be flopped (flipped over) to produce alternate upside-down rows. Allow to dry. Wash out the foam patterns, pat dry and print a second color if desired.

6 *Finishing*

Enrich the color and protect the paint by applying one or more coats of non-yellowing, water-based varnish. (See *Varnishing,* page 48.)

Attach the hardware.

PATTERN FOR

BLOCK PRINT

Roller block printing works well in combination with other techniques. Shown here, block printing over stained wood with a border of patinated copper. (See Ivy League, page 267.)

Crackle

AGING ARTFULLY
WITH A SIMPLE RECIPE FOR CRACKLE

Crackle is reminiscent of weathered barns and farmhouse kitchens.
Like pouring time from a bottle, applying this technique creates instant
antiques. Furniture treated to a crackle finish (also called crackleure)
immediately takes on a convincingly aged and distressed look. This time-worn,
rural treatment of overlaid and crackled traditional colors, accented by simple
potato block-printing, holds its own in any rustic setting.

Read This First

There are two types of crackle. One type has the effect of severely weathered paint. In the other, only the varnish is crazed into spiderweb-like cracks, while the underlying paint is intact. This project demonstrates the weathered-paint type of crackle. (For the second type, see *The Cupboard Was Bare,* page 105, steps 8 and 9.) Pass over the pricey crackle kits sold in paint, art supply and craft stores. The inexpensive foolproof method demonstrated here creates incredibly authentic-looking crackle, quickly. To produce the crackle, a base-coat color of latex paint is applied to the furniture. If your cabinet has a plastic laminate finish, use melamine paint for the base coat. (See *Melamine Paint,* page 27.) This color will show through the cracks. Mucilage glue is brushed on over the paint. Then, while the glue is still wet, a coordinat-

ing top coat of paint is applied. This top coat will begin cracking within minutes. Latex-based paint cracks much more effectively than acrylic-based paint, although a latex-acrylic blend can be used. For this cabinet, strongly contrasting colors of paint were used to demonstrate the effect dramatically. Similar colors crackled overtop each other produce a subtle, intricate result.

Potato printing is a perfect complement for crackle. Potato prints are by nature simple and imperfect, uneven and semitransparent, with an aged look. Potato printing is as simple as it sounds – stamping with a cut-out potato, like a rubber stamp. Crackle, because it is so busy, can often obscure proportions and details. Potato printing or block printing accentuates details and restores order.

BEFORE

An intriguing cabinet of plank construction with a garage paint job of dull cement gray. Crackle and block printing will accentuate its 1920s vintage and its handsome proportions.

MATERIALS

- latex paint in two coordinating colors, 1 quart (litre) each (Choose a low-luster finish for authenticity.)
- mucilage glue, the amber type used in grade school (One bottle will cover a surface just larger than two of these books lying open.)
- inexpensive medium-sized paint brush (for glue)
- paint brush, 2 in. (5 cm) wide
- paper, pencil, scissors
- large potato
- sharp paring knife
- medium-sized artist's brush
- tubes of acrylics for potato print: cadmium red deep, mars black, yellow ochre
- ruler or tape measure

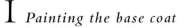

1 *Painting the base coat*

Refer to *Painting Basics* (page 34), and prepare and paint (priming is not necessary) the cabinet with the base-coat color. Apply two coats if necessary to achieve good coverage. This is the color that will show through the cracks. Allow the paint to dry. Place the area to be crackled in a horizontal position. (If the cabinet is heavy, get help moving it.) Decant some mucilage glue into a container.

2 *Applying crackle*

Apply the crackle in sections about 2 square feet (.2 m square). Using a medium-sized paint brush, spread the mucilage on the surface, brushing it out to a thin layer. The crackle will occur naturally along the direction of the brushstrokes. For busy, intricate crackle, brush in overlapping, multiple directions. Brush in straight lines for more even crackle. Place brush in glue and set aside.

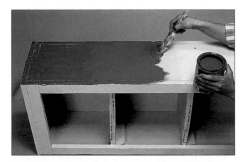

Without allowing the mucilage to dry, use the 2 in. (5 cm) paint brush and brush the second color of paint over the wet mucilage, almost to the edges of the glue. Flow the paint on without overbrushing. The largest crackles will be formed on the wettest glue, with the size of crackles diminishing as the paint is applied over damp glue. No crackles will be formed on dry glue.

Paint another section of glue, overlapping the still-wet edges of the first section, and apply more paint over the wet glue. Continue until the full side is covered. Cracking will start in minutes. Allow the side to dry. Continue crackling the cabinet until all sides are finished.

3 *Cutting the potato print*

Trace the pattern on page 67, or create your own pattern.

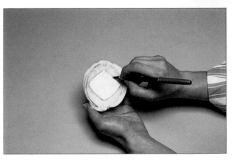

Cut a large potato in half, lengthwise. Cut out the design elements of the pattern and position them on the cut side of the potato-half. Trace around the pattern pieces with a pencil or a felt pen. (Retain the other potato-half.)

Using a sharp paring knife, cut away the potato surrounding the pattern outlines to a depth of about ¼ in. (.5 cm) or greater. On the uncarved side of the potato, carve two notches as a handle.

4 *Potato printing*

Using a medium-sized artist's brush, apply acrylics, in the desired colors, to the raised sections of the potato. (Shown here: cadmium red deep, mars black, and yellow ochre.)

It's a good idea to do some test prints on paper before printing the cabinet. Carefully position the potato print, paint-side-down, onto the paper. Apply pressure so that the print makes full contact. Carefully lift the potato print off without sliding it. The print should be uneven and semitransparent, and it may have gaps.

Now place the surface to be printed in a horizontal position, so that you can apply pressure. Begin printing the cabinet, forming a border or a center design.

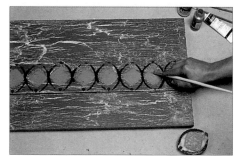

Continue printing with the potato, replenishing paint as needed, about every two or three prints. When finished, stand back and examine the prints. You can touch up any gaps or areas that are too transparent for your taste. Patting the paint on with a brush or your finger gives a block-printing effect.

5 *Sawtooth border*

To create a block-printed sawtooth border, cut an equilateral triangle (Geometry 101: all sides equal length) from the other potato-half. Measure and mark the center of the border. Apply mars black paint to the potato.

Position the first print on the center of the border, where marked. Work out from the center, with triangles just touching, until one edge of the border is complete.

Continue the border along adjoining sides, if desired.

Optional: Paint small motifs or dots in the open Vs of the sawtooth.

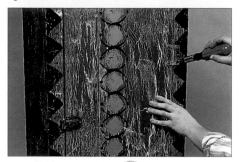

Attach the hardware.

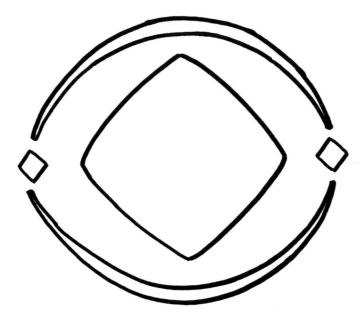

PATTERN FOR POTATO PRINT

For a more subtle, refined look than crackled paint, try creating crackled, antiqued varnish. (See The Cupboard Was Bare, page 105.)

Gold Standard

GOLD LEAF GLAMORIZES
A TINY BATHROOM CABINET

Typical of most small cabinets, the door is the focus of this miniature
hanging cabinet. Its plain, blank, vertical format and simple buttonlike knob
beg for a rich treatment. The antiqued gold leaf background glows against
the color and historical pageantry of découpaged postage stamps.
Juxtaposed against a dramatic black border, the door looks
like a miniature piece of art.

Read This First

This project consists of four straightforward phases. The body of the cabinet is painted a base coat of black. If your cabinet has a plastic laminate finish, use melamine paint for the base coat. (See *Melamine Paint,* page 27.) Then the door is gold leafed, the stamps are laminated onto the gold leaf, and the door is antiqued. Gold leafing is a simple treatment with glowing results. It is available at art supply and craft stores. Purchase the compatible adhesive and sealer made by the same manufacturer. Other adhesives and varnishes can cause chemical reactions that will ruin the finish.

Stamps, with their classic proportions and recognizable subject matter, are a natural element for découpage treatments. Purchase stamps for découpage at a post office or hobby shop. Choose from new stamps, packages of unsorted used stamps, or specialty theme picture stamps. Specialty stamps are not expensive, if you choose carefully. Finally, the door is antiqued with a sponged layer of thin umber-toned paint.

BEFORE

A new, unpainted, wall-mounted cabinet with interesting proportions and a tiny centered knob. The body is made of Masonite, with a natural wooden door. Functional, but bland.

MATERIALS

- quart (litre) eggshell finish black latex paint or acrylic paint; or a can of black spray paint
- gold leaf with compatible adhesive and sealer
- ½ in. (1.25 cm) wide square-tipped artist's brush or a small foam brush
- small house-painting brush
- postage stamps
- ruler and pencil
- glue stick, craft glue or spray glue
- tube of acrylic paint (burnt umber), or substitute latex paint (deep brown)
- sponge or rag
- *optional:* non-yellowing, water-based varnish

1 *Painting the base coat*

Remove the door from the cabinet, if possible. Paint the outside of the body of the cabinet using black latex, acrylic or spray paint. Painting the inside is optional. (This cabinet, constructed of Masonite, was painted with black acrylic paint. Applied with a rag, the acrylic was absorbed like a stain.)

Paint the back of the door. The back and edges of this door were spray painted.

Optional: When the paint is dry, apply non-yellowing, water-based varnish. (See *Varnishing,* page 48.)

2 *Gold leaf adhesive*

With the door right-side-up, use the square-tipped artist's brush or small foam brush to paint the surface with the gold leaf adhesive. Do the edges of the door, unless the door is a tight fit. This adhesive is quite thick, and brushstrokes will show in the gold leaf. Let the adhesive set according to the directions on the label. Apply a second coat, if suggested on the label.

3 *Applying gold leaf*

Lift a full sheet of gold leaf from the folio. It is very thin and may crinkle, which is okay.

Beginning at one edge of the door, lay a sheet of gold leaf onto the adhesive, wrapping it over the edge (if you are doing the edges).

Burnish the gold leaf with your fingers, or lay a piece of paper overtop and burnish it with your hand to make sure the gold leaf adheres firmly. Cracks are desirable in the gold leaf.

Using a small house-painting brush, whisk away all excess bits of gold leaf that are not stuck. This is a surprisingly messy job that creates fairy dust in your work area. Place a scrap piece of gold leaf on any missed areas and burnish. Continue until the full surface is covered.

4 *Découpaging stamps*

Position and mark the postage stamps on the door.

Glue the stamps in place using a glue stick, craft glue or spray glue.

5 Sealing

Using the compatible gold leaf sealer, paint over all of the gold leaf surfaces, including the stamps. Allow to dry.

6 Antiquing

Antique the door. Mix burnt umber artist's acrylics or deep-brown latex paint with water, to achieve a thin consistency. Using a sponge or rag, apply the paint over the surface of the door, wiping away excess with a damp rag. Allow to dry and apply another coat of the sealer over the antiquing.

7 Finishing

Attach all hardware and the door.

Découpage does not have to be limited to pasting small pieces of paper. **Above,** fabric is laminated to plywood for a table insert. **Left,** dried leaves are découpaged on a wardrobe. All forms of découpage must be sealed. (See Material Pleasures, page 253; Botanical Design, page 93.)

Victorian Secrets

A DRAMATIC RECOVERY WITH PRETTY PRINTED FABRICS AND SOFT HUES

Victorian treatments create the most impressive transformations,
taking the bland and the broken-down to new heights in a glorious melange
of muted florals and classic filigree. A wardrobe lends itself well to a
Victorian makeover. The various surfaces present options for mirror and
glass, fabric details, and a myriad of hardware selections: drawer pulls,
knobs and hinges in porcelain, brass and painted wood.

Read This First

The splendidly decorative results of this project are the product of a few elementary techniques — paint and découpage, plus an added shirred curtain. Select the fabric for the curtain first. Then make color photocopies from the curtain fabric. The photocopies will be découpaged onto drawer fronts. Paint the body of the wardrobe in one shade. Paint the drawer fronts and other areas to be découpaged in a color that matches the background color of the photocopies, not the fabric. (The copying process can alter colors.) These paint colors are the base coat. If your wardrobe has a plastic laminate finish, use melamine paint. (See *Melamine Paint,* page 27.) The curtain requires minimal sewing — only four straight seams. New hardware and a purchased wooden craft bow add sparkle and polish. The results are astounding.

MATERIALS

- fabric for shirred curtain (steps 6 and 7)
- color photocopies of the fabric to fit drawer and door fronts
- quart (litre) high-adhesion, water-based primer
- quart (litre) eggshell finish latex paint for doors and drawers of wardrobe (Choose a paint color to match the background color of the photocopies.)
- quart (litre) eggshell finish latex paint for body of wardrobe (Choose a paint color to match a color in the print of the fabric.)
- painting tools: paint brush, small roller, roller tray
- small, sharp scissors
- tracing paper, pencil, tape
- small quantity cellulose-based wallpaper paste
- quart (litre) non-yellowing, water-based varnish
- sewing materials
- hardware for shirred curtain (consists of 2 rods, 4 hook brackets, 8 screws)
- *optional:* glass or mirror cut to fit (screen or chicken wire, wire cutters and a stapler can be substituted), wooden trim, hammer and finishing nails
- *optional:* wooden decoration, such as a bow, from a craft store

BEFORE

Can this severely water-damaged and weathered wardrobe be saved? Rehabilitation was worth a try. Loose varnish was scraped off. Panels were glued and nailed, and separated veneer was reglued and covered with trim.

1 *Painting the wardrobe*

Refer to *Painting Basics* (page 34) and prepare the wardrobe, repairing it but not yet replacing the glass or mirror.

Prime the full wardrobe and allow to dry. Paint the doors and drawers of the wardrobe to match the background color of the photocopies of the curtain fabric.

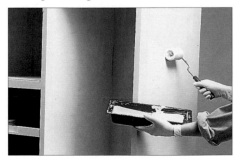

Paint the body of the cabinet in the second color.

2 *Cutting for découpage*

Using small, sharp scissors, cut out the photocopies for découpage, cutting as close to the images as possible.

Make a template to help center the découpage cut-outs on drawer fronts. Position one cut-out image onto the center of a drawer front. Position a sheet of tracing paper to cover the bottom half of the drawer front and half the image. Tack the paper in place with tape. On the tracing paper, trace around the half-image and mark the sides and bottom of the drawer front.

Cut out the traced half-image from the tracing paper, along your lines, discarding the cut-out and reserving the background.

3 *Découpaging*

Mix a small amount of wallpaper paste in a bowl, following the manufacturer's instructions. Position the tracing paper template on one drawer, lining up the sides and bottom as marked. Using your hands, apply wallpaper paste to both sides of the image. Make sure there are no dry spots.

Lay the image onto the drawer front, fitting it to the template cut-out. Lift off the template. Smooth the photocopy from the center to the edges. Don't rub too hard or the surface image of the photocopy may rub off.

Allow the découpage to dry. Though small wrinkles may appear in the photocopy while it is wet, these will flatten out (honest!) as the paper dries and shrinks. Do not touch.

Repeat on all remaining drawers. Découpage any other areas as desired.

4 *Varnishing*

When the découpage is thoroughly dry, protect the paint and enrich the color by varnishing the full wardrobe. Varnish all découpaged areas with at least two coats of non yellowing, water-based varnish. (See *Varnishing,* page 48.)

5 *Installing a window*

Install new glass or mirror panels where needed. Lay the door flat, upside-down. Place the cut glass into the window-well on the wrong side of the door.

Screen or chicken wire suits rustic wardrobes. It was originally used instead of expensive glass and allowed air circulation while keeping out bugs and mice. Place the screen in the window and staple it in the window-well. Keep the screen/chicken wire taut and even. Trim any excess with wire cutters.

Cut lengths of narrow trim to fit the top, sides and bottom. Paint the trim to match the door. Position the trim tightly against the glass, and nail it in place with finishing nails. For a professional-looking job, sink the nail heads, fill holes with wood filler and touch up with paint.

6 *Sewing the curtain*

Make the shirred curtain. Measure and attach two hooks (the hooks point upward) to the inside-top of the door. Place the hooks slightly wider than the window and at least 1 in. (2.5 cm) above the glass. Placing the rod on the hooks can help with positioning.

Cut fabric twice the width of the window.

Cut the top end square. Cut the length of the fabric at least 6 in. (15 cm) longer than the window.

Sew narrow hems along each side. Check if the fabric has a pattern that has a right-way-up, such as vines climbing a trellis. Sew a 1 in. (2.5 cm) channel along the top edge.

7 *Hanging the curtain*

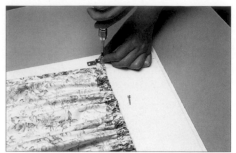

Gather the top channel onto the rod and place the rod onto the hooks. To determine the length of the fabric, mark with a pin, 2 in. (5 cm) below the bottom of the window. Remove the curtain from the rod. Add 1½ in. (4 cm) beyond the marker pin, and cut across the fabric at this measurement. Sew a 1 in. (2.5 cm) channel across the bottom.

Gather the fabric back onto the top rod and place the rod onto the hooks again. Gather the fabric onto the remaining rod through the bottom channel. Position the remaining hooks through the rod (hooks pointed downward). Pull the rod gently, positioning the hooks and screwing them into place.

Note: If you wish to remove the curtain easily from the rods, move the bottom hooks high enough to allow the rod to be removed. The trade-off for this convenience is a baggy curtain instead of a taut one.

8 *Finishing*

Hang the doors and attach the hardware.

Optional: A suitable wooden decoration, purchased at a craft store, will add to the Victorian effect. This bow was painted in the wardrobe colors and attached to the top-front with L-shaped brackets.

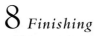

If you love the fresh effect of shirred fabric on furniture, consider halters instead of backrest cushions for chairs. (See Floral Arrangements, page 135.)

Awash in History

WASHED IN STUCCO AND SEPIA, A PINE CUPBOARD TURNS CLASSIC TREASURE

Create a tiny corner of ancient Greece or Rome with faux stucco, washed in umber and sienna and enhanced by ornamental plaster garlands or seraphims. Ordinary materials and quick treatments combine for a neutral color scheme and historical mood on a dresser, cabinet or hutch.

Read This First

Choose a boxy wooden cabinet with some simple trim or molding. It should have planklike construction, rather than Victorian opulence. If applying this technique to a hutch or a dresser, be sure there is clearance around doors and drawers for them to close when coated with the faux stucco. Otherwise, limit the textured faux stucco treatment to the fronts of doors and drawers. Reserve this treatment for cabinets, dressers or hutches. The faux stucco may not stand up to the wear and tear of a tabletop.

The first stage of this treatment, the stucco effect, is accomplished with gesso, a thick white primer available at art supply and craft stores. The second stage, the antiquing, consists of brushing very liquid brown paint over the gesso, then wiping it off the high spots and allowing it to pool in the depressions. Shop for a chunky, aged-looking plaster angel or plaster fruit, often available at flower shops. Steer clear of the detailed Victorian variety sold at craft stores. A power drill is needed to attach the plaster embellishment.

BEFORE

Not well constructed and not well finished, this jam cupboard, made of pine, was serviceable but very plain. Pour on the texture.

MATERIALS

- quart (litre) gesso
- paint brushes
- easy-release painter's tape
- medium-width paint scraper
- medium sandpaper (180 grade)
- cans or other containers for support
- plaster figure or fruit
- 2 wood screws (long enough to go through the door and into the plaster figure)
- power drill
- white carpenter's glue
- tube of dark-brown acrylic paint (or substitute latex) for antiquing
- paper towel or rag
- *optional:* small wood chisel

1 Getting started

Repair and degloss your cabinet if necessary and remove hardware, drawers and doors. (See *Preparation,* page 36, in *Painting Basics.*)

The backboard was removed from this cabinet because it has a Colonial flavor.

2 Priming

Mask off any areas that you don't want faux stuccoed. Using a paint brush, paint the cabinet overall with a thin coat of gesso. This coat of gesso will act as a primer for better adhesion of the faux stucco layer. Allow to dry. Painting the interior is optional.

3 Applying faux stucco

Stucco one section of the cabinet at a time with the gesso. Begin with the door, laid flat on cans or other supports. Using the paint scraper, scoop a blob of gesso out of the container and plop it onto the surface of the door. Move the gesso around, folding it with the flat edge of the scraper, until the gesso is in textured layers.

Different widths of paint scrapers give different textures. As you work with the gesso, it will become thicker and the texturing will become easier.

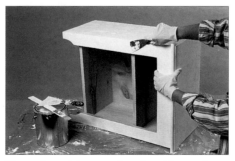

Place the cabinet so that the side you're working on is horizontal, to prevent dripping. (If your cabinet is heavy, recruit help turning it.) Do one side of the cabinet at a time, allowing it to dry before turning it to do another side. Allow the entire cabinet to dry.

4 Distressing news

Using a small chisel or the scraper, distress the cabinet by rounding off sharp edges on the trim and on corners. Be careful! Digging too deeply can produce splinters that become larger as you go on. Small chunks can easily be chipped out of the surface as well. Using medium sandpaper, smooth any rough or splintered sections.

5 Attaching the plaster figure

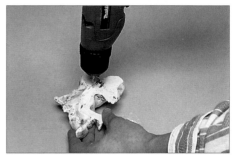

Drill two leader-holes (narrower than the screws) into the back of the plaster figure, in the thickest section of the plaster.

With the door right-side-up, position the plaster figure on the center panel. Check that both the door and the figure are in line (right-way-up) by verifying that hinge holes in the door and the cabinet match. Keeping the figure in position, lift it slightly and mark the position of the two predrilled leader-holes onto the door.

Remove the figure and drill leader-holes through the door.

Apply white carpenter's glue in the area of the plaster figure. Position the figure onto the glue. Attach the wood screws from the wrong side of the door, through the door and into the plaster. Do not overtighten.

6 Antiquing

Antique one section of the cabinet at a time. Mix dark-brown acrylic or latex paint with water to a very liquid consistency. With a paint brush, wash paint onto a small area. Allow the paint to settle for about a minute.

Using a moist (not wet) paper towel or rag, wipe across the painted area, picking up paint in the high areas and leaving the

paint in depressions and hollows. This technique will emphasize the texture. The cabinet will take on an antique sepia tone, with crevices and any exposed wood a deep brown.

7 Finishing

Attach the hardware and the door. Touch up any hardware with gesso and, when it has dried, antique the hardware following the technique used in step 6.

As an alternative to a rustic finish, achieve a decorative, intricate-looking faux plaster treatment with silicone caulking, découpage and paint. (See Heaven Sent, page 221.)

Bedtime Reading

ECLECTIC IMAGES AND PERSONAL PROSE
CREATE CONTEMPORARY BEDSTANDS

Individuality is what interesting decorating is all about. Add your own imprint with handwriting. It's as personal as a fingerprint and an ideal way to make your mark. Then push it over the edge with quirky, raunchy or retro images. These bedstands started as small office units. Their small size and multiple drawers make them ideal for the bedside. Their many flat surfaces lend themselves well to scattered, random images and quotations written by hand.

Sleep is when all the ....d stuff comes flying
out as from a dustbin upset in a high wind.
WILLIAM GOLDING

She's invented a ...... religion called
"Creative Sleep".
HENRY REED

... with her feet resting upon
.... rosy-dreams and a
.... amie hic.

Read This First

This project consists of only two techniques, handwriting and photo transfer, over a base coat of paint, but it looks like many more. If your furniture has a plastic laminate finish, use melamine paint for the base coat. (See *Melamine Paint,* page 27.) Choose quotations on any subject for the handwriting, perhaps from a book of modern quotations available at the local library or bookstore. If you have reservations about writing on a piece of furniture, keep in mind that it's not the perfection of your script that counts. On the contrary, your unique style is what makes the piece so personal and original.

As a counterpoint to the script, images are photocopied and then transferred onto alternating drawers and in open areas. The transfer is achieved by burnishing the wrong side of the photocopy with a broad nib marker, or turpentine. The chemicals melt the photocopy ink and release it from the paper. The marker color will bleed through the paper, so choose marker colors that are a close match to the paint colors. This technique imparts a soft, worn look to the transfers, not solid blacks. When choosing your transfer images, select small pictures and remember that they will print in mirror image. The two featured bedstands have six drawers each. If taking on two or more pieces, work on them at the same time, completing each step on each piece.

BEFORE

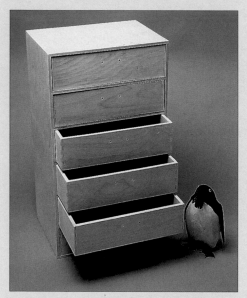

An unpainted small chest of drawers — not flawed, just bland. Furniture of modest proportions is ideal for busy, interesting treatments.

MATERIALS

- quart (litre) high-adhesion, water-based primer
- quart (litre) eggshell finish latex paint, taupe
- eggshell finish latex paint in three colors, 1 quart (litre) each: pale cinnamon, pale creamy yellow, pale blue-gray
- painting tools: paint brush, small roller, roller tray
- bond paper
- X-acto knife or scissors
- quill pen, calligraphy pen or waterproof marker
- black-and-white photocopied images (make a few extra for testing)
- easy-release painter's tape
- turpentine, or markers in colors similar to the paint (Take a photocopy along when purchasing markers and test the markers. Some new markers do not transfer the images.)
- non-yellowing, water-based varnish
- fine sandpaper (220 grade), tack cloth
- *optional:* can of non-yellowing spray fixative or varnish

1 *Painting the base coat*

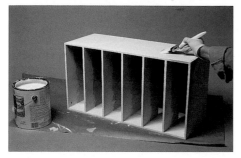

Refer to *Painting Basics* (page 34). Prepare and prime the shell and the drawers of the chest.

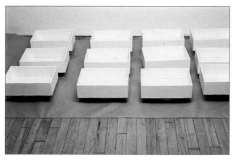

If working on two chests, as was done in this project, do both chests at once, rather than completing one, then starting on the next.

Paint the body of the chest with two coats of taupe latex paint.

Paint the drawers in pastel colors.

2 *Planning the quotations*

To transcribe the quotations, begin by cutting pieces of paper to fit the drawer fronts. Decide which drawer fronts (all, random drawers or alternating ones) you wish to inscribe. Mark the positions of the hardware onto the paper pieces.

Choose your quotations. Write the quotations on the corresponding pieces of paper, using the quill pen, the calligraphy pen or the marker, to get a sense of placement and how large you can write. Add borders – in zigzags, lazy S's, etc. Place the handwriting pieces and the photocopies in their approximate positions.

3 *Hand writing the quotations*

Line up the drawers, or place them in the chest and tip it onto its back. (Get help if the cabinet is heavy.) Remove a paper piece and copy the quotation onto the drawer front, using the pen or waterproof marker. Avoid the impulse to try writing perfectly. This approach will create hesitant, cramped penmanship. Just let the writing flow smoothly and quickly from the pen. Repeat for all quotations. Allow to dry. Don't throw out the written paper pieces.

Write quotations onto the body of the chest as desired. Allow to dry.

4 *Transferring photocopies*

Line up the drawers in order, as they fit into the chest, and position the photocopied images on the drawer fronts. Test the photocopy transfer technique on paper, to get the hang of it, before tackling it on furniture. Don't throw out the paper test pieces.

Lay a photocopy face-down onto the drawer front, taping it lightly in place. Cover the back of the image with the marker that matches the paint color. Work quickly, saturating the paper.

If using turpentine, brush it onto the back of the photocopy, saturating the paper.

Press your fingers firmly over the back of the image. Being careful not to shift the image, allow the marker to dry somewhat, but not completely. Peel off the photocopy. The image should be transferred onto the furniture.

5 *Varnishing*

Using the water-based varnish, check whether the handwriting ink and the photocopy images are indelible. Brush the varnish onto your paper tests. If the ink or images smear, purchase a can of non-yellowing spray fixative or varnish and spray the graphics with it. Allow to dry.

Using the non-yellowing, water-based varnish, apply two or three coats on all drawer fronts and the body of the chest. Sand lightly with fine sandpaper and wipe with a tack cloth between each coat. (See *Varnishing*, page 48.)

6 *Finishing*

Attach the hardware.

If your art store doesn't carry markers that will transfer photocopies, use turpentine, or apply a découpage treatment (as shown above) of random images or fully covered alternating drawers.
(See Letter Perfect, page 177.)

Botanical Design

GRAPEVINES AND SOPHISTICATED COLOR
PRODUCE A CRAFTED CABINET

Nothing creates style quite like the melding of a rich palette with the textures
and forms of nature. Earthy olive green paint and gray-stained natural wood
complement the controlled chaos of grapevines artfully arranged over
laminated, parchment-thin golden grape leaves. The marriage of city
and country flavors makes this armoire adaptable to virtually
any room in either environment.

Read This First

Part of the pleasure of finishing this piece of furniture is the experience of finding and collecting leaves and vines. If grapevines are not available in your area, collect leaves that are a suitable shape and buy the vines from a florist or craft shop. Leaves must be pressed and dried for at least two weeks. If you do collect your own vines, do it in the summer or fall when the vines are pliable. Wear boots, long pants, and gloves – and watch out for poison ivy. Pull out good long lengths, the thicker the stem, the better. As you pull the vine down, wind and tie it into a coil, small

enough to fit into a sink or laundry tub since the vines will later need soaking to rejuvenate them.

Collect leaves in the summer, if possible. By fall, grape leaves tend to be very fragile and thin. And fall colors aren't necessary because the leaves tend to change from green to a golden green-brown as they dry. While the leaves are drying, stain the cabinet's trim. Prime and paint the body with a base coat. If your armoire has a plastic laminate finish, use melamine paint for the base coat. (See *Melamine Paint,* page 27.)

BEFORE

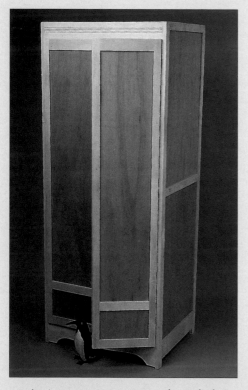

An inexpensive unpainted wardrobe made of pine with very thin mahogany board panels can become a one-of-a-kind horticultural presence. All it needs are the right touches.

MATERIALS

- 2 dozen grape leaves
- scissors and a thick phone book
- 20 to 30 yd. (20 to 30 m) grapevines (allows for two vines on each side and two on the front, plus a generous portion for top arrangement)
- fine sandpaper (220 grade)
- pale- to medium-gray stain
- rag
- fine-point artist's brush
- easy-release painter's tape
- quart (litre) high-adhesion, water-based primer
- quart (litre) eggshell finish latex paint, deep olive green
- painting tools: paint brush, small roller, roller tray
- quart (litre) non-yellowing, water-based varnish
- paper towels
- carpet staples, small hammer
- garden clippers
- small quantity cellulose-based wallpaper paste

1 *Leaves*

Snip stems off the leaves and press them in a phone book. Leave about twenty pages between each page of leaves. Allow leaves to dry for at least two weeks.

2 *Vines*

Place a coil of vines in a bucket or sink and cover them with water. Soak the vines while the cabinet is being painted or for two hours.

3 *Staining trim*

Stain can be applied only to raw wood. (See *Staining Wood,* page 46.) Using fine sandpaper, lightly sand all areas that will be stained.

Remove doors and hardware. Place the doors on a tabletop and work on them while you work on the cabinet.

Stir the stain thoroughly. Using the artist's brush, apply stain along recessed trim or other hard-to-reach areas.

Using a rag or a paint brush, apply stain to the trim. Allow to dry.

4 *Painting panels*

Mask off all stained trim. Prime the panels and paint them with the deep olive green paint. (See *Painting Basics,* page 34.) Allow to dry.

Apply one coat of non-yellowing, water-based varnish to the stained areas of the armoire. Allow to dry, then repeat. Varnish can also be applied over the paint if desired. (See *Varnishing,* page 48.)

5 *Attaching vines*

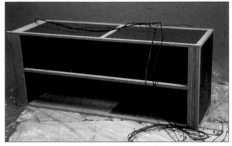

Unwind the vines and pat them dry with paper towels. When the armoire is thoroughly dry, lay it on its side. (If the armoire is heavy, recruit a helper.) Starting at the bottom of the armoire, arrange the vines onto the uppermost side.

Starting at the bottom edge of the armoire, hammer carpet staples into the trim, anchoring the vine. Use as many staples as necessary to keep the vine reasonably close to the surface of the armoire.

Using garden clippers, cut the vine cleanly at the bottom edge of the armoire. Continue stapling the vine in place on the full side of the armoire. Don't cut off any excess vine at the top of the armoire.

Stand the armoire up (get help if needed) and arrange any trailing vines from the side along the top edge, stapling them in place. Don't allow them to hang in the door space. Otherwise, the door won't shut. Staple vines to the other side of the armoire and work any trailing vines into the top arrangement. Staple vines to the door panels, keeping them within the trim and working from a bottom corner to the opposite top corner.

6 Laminating leaves

Follow the instructions on the package of wallpaper paste to mix a small quantity.

Coat both sides of a leaf with the paste, leaving no dry spots.

Lay the leaf onto the surface of the armoire, aligning it with the vine. Smooth it from the center, eliminating any air pockets. Continue, pasting leaves on both sides of the armoire. The leaves may become wrinkly. The wrinkles will disappear as the leaves dry and shrink. Avoid trying to stretch the leaves flat. You will only damage the leaves.

7 Doors

Reattach the doors. Laminate leaves onto the doors. Allow both the vines and the leaves to dry.

8 Varnishing

Brush two coats of varnish over the leaves to protect them.

Branch management. If natural ingredients and rich colors are your preference, provide your wardrobe with hardware fashioned from twigs. (See Natural Tendencies, page 98.)

Natural Tendencies

BEDSTANDS GO COUNTRY WITH NATURAL BRANCHES AND RICH COLOR

Bring the rustic indoors with natural tree branches — complete with bark, leaves and lichen — strategically installed as drawer pulls. Natural botanical properties such as leaves, twigs and branches lend personality and originality to furniture and accessories. Combined with rich traditional colors, these elements epitomize authentic style in country decorating. Antiquing is added for warmth and to soften the edges.

Read This First

Painting, antiquing and adding the natural-branch drawer pulls are the basics of this project. The branches should be collected, and their ends sealed, at least two weeks before beginning this project, so they have a chance to dry. Use a small pruning saw or hand saw to cut the branches. Branches should be about the thickness of a broom handle – the more gnarly, the better. Cut the branches from a mature living tree. Fallen branches or branches from a dead tree will lose their bark and can split.

This treatment best suits a piece of wooden furniture that is simple with a rustic sensibility. A knock-down cabinet is easier to paint in several colors than is one already assembled. Feel free to paint the cabinet one color instead of three. If it has a plastic laminate finish, use melamine paint and a primer if indicated on the label. (See *Melamine Paint,* page 27.) To antique the cabinet as shown, it must be made of wood. Attaching the branches so that they are cut, yet appear to be in one piece, takes patience, determination and a power drill. But the results are well worth the effort. If working on two cabinets at once, as was done here, work on them at the same time, completing each step on both.

BEFORE

Knockdown furniture, like this two-drawer bedstand, offers a good opportunity for a multicolor paint job. No masking needed to separate colors, and none of the usual touch-ups required.

MATERIALS

- branches cut from a living tree (Using a small pruning saw or hand saw, cut more branches – and cut them longer – than you will need for the cabinet.)
- varnish or clear nail polish
- eggshell finish latex paint in three colors, 1 quart (litre) each: burgundy, navy blue, forest green
- paint brush, 2 in. (5 cm) wide
- plastic containers or boxes for support
- medium sandpaper (180 grade)
- chalk or colored pencil
- power drill
- wood screws
- *optional:* quart (litre) high-adhesion, water-based primer
- *optional:* amber stain, small rag
- *optional:* clamp or pliers

1 *Sealing branches*

Paint two coats of varnish or clear nail polish onto the cut ends of the branches. This will force the branches to dry slowly through the bark, instead of through the ends, preventing the wood from splitting and the bark from falling off. Allow the branches to dry for at least two weeks.

2 *Painting the body*

Assemble the body of the bedstand without the top. If you wish to paint the back, assemble it too. If not, leave it off.

If your bedstand is assembled, prepare the piece for painting. (See *Preparation,* page 36.)

If your bedstand is wooden and you wish to antique it, do not prime. If you do not wish to antique it, prime before painting. (See *Priming and Painting,* page 38.) Using a brush, paint the body with burgundy. Subtle brushstrokes are desirable for this technique. (See *Brush Painting,* page 40.) Allow to dry. Apply a second coat, if needed.

3 *Painting the top and drawers*

Place the drawer fronts and the cabinet top onto plastic containers or boxes. Paint the back sides of drawer fronts forest green. Paint the underside of the cabinet top navy blue.

Allow to dry and apply a second coat if necessary. When surfaces are completely dry, turn over and repeat.

4 *Antiquing*

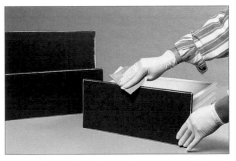

Antique the body of the cabinet with a medium-grade sandpaper. Sand off the paint in places wherever natural wear would occur, such as on corners and high areas of trim or detail.

Assemble and antique the drawers. The centers and edges of drawer fronts are also prime wear spots. Attach the top (and the backboard, if not already attached) onto the cabinet and antique the top.

5 *Staining*

Optional: The wood that you have exposed through sanding will eventually turn amber on its own. If you don't want to wait, touch up the raw wood with an amber stain. Dip a rag into the amber stain and rub it into the bare wood. Allow to dry.

6 Sizing branches

Get out your dried branches. Position a branch vertically on the front of the cabinet, across the drawers. Mark its length, indicating the angle of the cut. Using a small hand saw, cut the branch slightly longer than the correct length. Cut again to the correct length, making any corrections if necessary. Reseal the ends. Don't throw out the leftover branches.

Position the branch vertically on the drawer fronts. Using chalk or a colored pencil, draw a line centered under the branch.

On the branch, mark the horizontal cut between the drawers. Using the hand saw, cut the branch along the mark. Reseal the ends.

7 Positioning branches

Position the branch pieces on the chalk line. On the drawer fronts, mark the sites for screws. Mark at least two screws for each branch. Drill holes at the marks through the drawer fronts. Mark corresponding sites on the branches and check that the branches match up.

Then drill leader-holes (holes that are narrower than the screws) partway through the branches at the marks. Leader-holes will prevent the screws from splitting the branches.

8 Attaching branches

To keep the branches' natural curves and to allow them to be gripped like handles, they must be supported about ½ in. (1.25 cm) off the drawer fronts. Using the hand saw, cut several short coinlike pieces from the leftover branches to use as sup-ports between the drawer fronts and the branches. Assess which thicknesses you need by testing the wood coins under the branches. Drill a hole into the center of each coin. You may need to clamp the coins (or hold them with pliers) while drilling.

From the inside of the drawers, screw wood screws through the drawer fronts, through the wood coins, and into the branch. You may need several different screw lengths, if the branch bows away from the drawer front. The screw should be long enough to penetrate halfway through the branch.

Country-style folk painting makes a decorative addition to richly colored,
rustic treatments. To add a motif to your bedstand, see Country Folk,
page 117, for instructions on a simple, very effective
paint technique using templates.

The Cupboard
Was Bare

A 1930s Baker's Pantry Is Stripped To Rich Wood And Finished With Traditional Hand-Painted Panels

This old baker's pantry, with its tin-lined drawers (to discourage mice), its sliding tray-drawers, and its multiple doors, was buried under heavy layers of paint and gummy varnish. This piece was worth the effort of stripping to restore its original slab-style oak and rustic iron hardware. To offset the plain quality of the piece, hand-painted, crackled motifs were applied to the door panels and a ceramic-tile top was created to replace the mismatched, worn original.

Read This First

Just like other easy-to-use finishing products – such as latex paint and water-based varnish – non-toxic, low-odor strippers have been developed and are widely available. These are effective and easy to use. Once the piece is stripped, it can simply be sanded and varnished, or you can paint the traditional, homey design on the door panels. An easy crackle method is applied to the door panels with oil-based varnish and gum Arabic – a clear, viscous liquid normally used by watercolorists as a resist medium and available at art supply stores. (Water-based varnish can be substituted for the gum Arabic, although the results are much coarser and less pleasing. Do a test before applying.) This simple method is more effective than the expensive crackle kits sold in craft and paint stores. The crackle method shown here is subtle. Cracks appearing in the overlaying varnish are highlighted by a rubbed-in brown glaze. (For the type of crackle that looks like the paint is cracked and peeling, see *Crackle,* page 63.) Finally, a new tiled top created for the base adds polish and function.

The cabinet featured in this project is stripped to bare wood. However, a piece with many layers of paint can be partially stripped, as was done on this rocker, allowing various colors to glow through and reveal the history of the piece.

BEFORE

A vintage 1930s baker's pantry. Its age, charming proportions and various doors make it a worthwhile candidate for restoration.

MATERIALS

To strip the paint:

- plastic or fabric dropsheet (an old bedsheet is good), newspaper
- low-toxicity, gel paint stripper (Purchase enough for at least two coats.)
- heavy rubber gloves (not latex)
- inexpensive medium-sized paint brush
- wide and narrow paint scrapers
- hard plastic stripping sponge, stripping brush with wire bristles, bucket and water
- cardboard or heavy paper
- oil for hardware
- medium and fine sandpaper (120 and 220 grades), tack cloth
- extra-fine steel wool
- quart (litre) oil-based or water-based varnish
- quart (litre) eggshell finish latex paint for inside cupboard: Swedish blue or other color
- easy-release painter's tape or masking tape, paint brush, small roller, roller tray
- white carpenter's or craft glue, wooden matchsticks
- *optional:* plastic wrap, such as Saran Wrap
- *optional:* brass polish
- *optional:* wood stain

To paint and crackle the door panels:

- easy-release painter's tape or masking tape
- pint (.5 litre) latex paint, sage green (any finish)
- chalk or erasable pencil

- tubes of acrylics: raw sienna, Hooker's green, grass green, emerald, blue-green, olive green, apple green, cadmium red deep, Turner's yellow, cadmium red extra deep, off-white
- fine-point artist's brushes: large and medium width
- pint (.5 litre) oil-based varnish and a jar of gum Arabic (available at art supply stores)
- tube of burnt umber artist's oil paint and a small jar of turpentine, rag
- *optional:* small quantity latex or acrylic paint, cream
- *optional:* small quantity glaze, rag, cloth

To tile a countertop:

- plywood, ½ or ¾ in. (1.25 or 2 cm) thick, good one side (cut to fit cabinet, with overhangs for front and sides)
- primer and paint
- tape measure, pencil
- tile to cover surface of plywood plus at least 10% for breakage. (Small- or medium-sized tiles are more pleasing on a countertop than large tiles.)
- tile cutter (ask about renting from your tile shop)
- coarse sandpaper
- screws to attach countertop to base, screwdriver; or L brackets
- dropsheet
- tile adhesive (ready mixed or dry, mix-it-yourself), notched spreader
- yardstick or other straight edge
- wood trim for edge of countertop (For a substantial look, choose trim somewhat thicker than the plywood-plus-tile top.)
- finishing nails, glue, small hammer (to attach trim)
- paint for trim
- masking tape
- sanded floor grout in a color to coordinate with tile
- tile float
- plastic scouring pads or rags; sponge

STRIPPING PAINT

1 *Applying paint stripper*

Lay down several thicknesses of newspaper or plain paper. Cover the paper with a plastic or fabric dropsheet. On the dropsheet, place the first portion to be stripped. If possible, remove all hardware. If the screws are clogged with paint, remove the hardware later, during the stripping process. Put on rubber gloves. Pour a puddle of stripper onto the top surface.

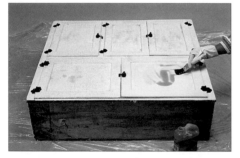

Use an inexpensive medium-sized paint brush to brush on the stripper. Continue brushing until the full area is covered. Paint all sides, the legs and other small parts with the stripper.

Some strippers melt plastic. Try this test. Paint some stripper onto a piece of plastic wrap. If the stripper eats through the

wrap, discard the plastic. If not, apply wrap over areas where the stripper may run off. The wrap will hold the stripper in place and allow it to work more effectively. If the stripper melts plastic, use only glass or ceramic implements, not plastic ones, and certainly do not use latex surgical-type gloves. The stripper may also devour the plastic dropsheet.

2 *Stripping paint*

Allow the stripper to work until the surface paint has bubbled. Check the manufacturer's instructions for a time estimate. It may take half an hour. This first coat of stripper may also begin to lift undercoats of paint.

Using a wide paint scraper, begin to scrape off the paint, discarding it onto an open newspaper or into a disposable container. Let the stripper do the work. Remove only the paint that comes away easily.

Use the stripping sponge to scrub hardware.

Remove any hardware as the paint becomes soft. To dislodge the paint from the groove of a screw, position the head of a screwdriver in the groove, on an angle, and tap the handle.

Place the hardware onto cardboard or paper and paint it with stripper. As the stripper gradually lifts paint from the hardware, scrub it with the stripping sponge and water. If there is still paint on the hardware, apply more stripper. When all paint is removed, dry thoroughly (a blow dryer is good for this). If the hardware is brass (lucky you!) polish it with brass polish. Oil the hardware and wipe off excess oil.

3 *Final stripping*

Apply additional coats of stripper. Allow it to work. Then scrape away loose paint. Don't get carried away with scraping. Too much scraping can damage the wood, especially on detail and trim.

As the natural wood appears, wash the surface with the stripping sponge and lukewarm or cool water. Decide how much paint you want to leave on the piece. Fine furniture should be completely clean of all paint residue, while rustic pieces, especially those that are well worn, are more interesting when they have some flecks of color remaining in corners, nicks and scratches.

When most paint is removed, use the stripping brush to clean the trim and the grain of the wood of all remaining paint. Wash the piece clean of all residue and allow the wood to dry thoroughly.

4 *Varnishing*

Sand the dry wood with medium-grade and then fine-grade sandpaper. Always sand in the direction of the grain. Follow the sanding with extra-fine steel wool, unless the stripper's instructions say not to.

Wipe away all dust with a tack cloth. If desired, stain the raw wood. (See *Staining Wood,* page 46.)

Apply two or three coats of the water-based or oil-based varnish. Sand with fine sandpaper, and between each coat wipe clean with a tack cloth. (See *Varnishing,* page 48.)

5 *Interior painting*

Paint the inside of the cabinet with the Swedish blue paint. Priming is not required. Mask off edges and areas that should not be painted. Use a paint brush and small roller for this job. (See *Priming and Painting,* page 38.) Apply two coats if necessary for full coverage.

Before attaching the hardware, fill screw holes by gluing the wooden ends of matchsticks in the holes. Allow to dry. Then attach the hardware.

PAINTED AND CRACKLED DOOR PANELS

6 *Brush painting the panels*

Decide which door panels will be painted. Mask around the panels and paint them with the sage green latex paint. Allow to dry.

Optional: To soften the effect of the paint, mix some cream-colored paint with a small amount of sage green and some glaze.

Color can be ragged on, or off. To rag on, dip a damp rag in the paint/glaze and squeeze out excess paint. Twist or crumple the rag and roll or pat it over the surface of the panels.

To rag off, brush the paint/glaze onto the panel. Using a rag slightly dampened with water, twist or crumple it and roll it over the wet surface, lifting paint and creating an irregular pattern.

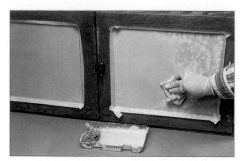

If the texture is too strong, wipe some paint off with a damp cloth to soften the texture.

7 *Painting trees*

If painting several door panels with the same motif or with accent designs in similar tones, paint them all at the same time. Using chalk or a lead pencil, lightly sketch the trees onto the door panels. This will help you to position the images.

Mix raw sienna and Hooker's green acrylic paints (or similar colors) to make an olive-brown tone. Thin the paint so that it flows from a brush. Using a large, fine-tipped brush, paint several long strokes for the trunks and branches of the trees.

Paint any branches on the accent designs.

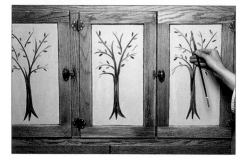

Paint leaves on the trees. Use several greens for this: grass green, emerald green, blue-green and olive. With more than one color of green on a medium-width fine-point brush, lay the side of the bristles onto the panel and remove the brush. This will give a painted leaf shape. Continue adding leaves to all trees and accent designs, but allow enough room for fruit.

Add apples by painting circles in apple green and highlighting areas in cadmium red deep.

Paint pears by painting pear shapes in apple green and highlight with Turner's yellow.

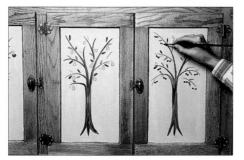

Create cherries by painting cherry shapes (like a valentine's heart without its point) in cadmium red extra deep. Highlight each cherry with a dot of off-white on its shoulder.

8 *Crackled varnish*

Crackle the surface of the panels. First, mask around the panels. Use masking tape or easy-release tape. Then paint the panels with a coat of oil-based varnish.

Monitor the dryness of the varnish by touching it lightly every half-hour. As soon as the varnish is *dry to the touch and no longer sticky* (this can take two to four hours or more), paint it with a layer of gum Arabic. If the gum Arabic is applied too early, it will form small pools instead of cracks. Too late and it will not crackle. Allow to dry. As the gum Arabic dries, it will form tiny subtle cracks that are difficult to see. Antiquing will show up the cracks.

Note: Water-based varnish can be substituted for the gum Arabic. However, the resulting crackle will be coarse and more uneven. Do a test on scrap wood or cardboard before applying.

9 *Antiquing the crackle*

Mix burnt umber artist's oil paint with turpentine to make a very liquid consistency. Oil paint must be used because the gum Arabic is water soluble.

Brush the paint over the gum Arabic and wipe off all excess paint with a rag.

The paint will remain in the tiny cracks and accent the crackle.

TILED COUNTERTOP

10 *Planning*

Cut plywood to fit the top of the cabinet, allowing for overhangs as required. The plywood can be primed on both sides or on the good side only, as desired. The good side of the plywood, which will be the exposed underside, may be painted a color.

Plan your tile pattern. With the good side of the plywood down, measure the length of the plywood, marking the center point. Draw a line across the width at your mark.

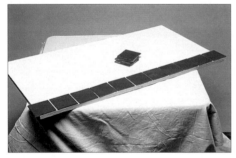

Starting on either side of the center line, with about a ³⁄₁₆ in. (.5 cm) gap between tiles, lay tiles across the front and down one side. If you wish, lay out the full top. You'll be able to determine how many tiles need to be cut, and by how much. The front row will be full tiles. Tiles to be cut will run along the sides and back.

11 *Cutting tile*

If you have rented a tile cutter, do a few test pieces to get the hang of the job. Tile cutters look intimidating, but are actually easy to use. Position a tile in the cutter, flush against the front edge. Draw back the handle, lower it, and score the tile as you push the handle forward. Scoring the tile twice often results in an easier, smoother cut. Lift the handle so that the "wings" attached to it are positioned over the score mark. Now apply pressure to the handle. The tile should snap along the score. Some tiles will, inevitably, break in the wrong places.

Buff the cut edge of the tile on coarse sandpaper to remove any sharp points. Continue cutting the tile until all necessary pieces are cut. Placing the tile in stacks – a stack of back tiles, a stack of side tiles – helps avoid confusion later. You will probably have two tiles that must be cut twice (for the corners where the back meets the sides).

12 *Laying tile*

Attach the plywood to the cabinet either by screwing it on from the top, or with L brackets from underneath. Drape the cabinet in a dropsheet for protection. Mix dry adhesive with water or use ready-mixed adhesive. It should be the consistency of peanut butter.

Apply tile adhesive to the countertop. Plop some onto the countertop, and spread it with a notched spreader. Continue until the top is completely covered with grooved adhesive.

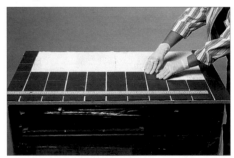

Start at the front. Beginning with a tile on either side of the center line, lay a line of full-sized tiles, flush with the edge and evenly separated. Position cut tiles where needed. Cut tiles should have the cut edge flush with the edge of the plywood. As you lay each tile, give it a small twist to ensure contact with the adhesive. Then lay a second row.

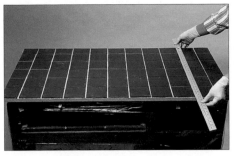

Use a yardstick or other straight edge to even up rows. While the adhesive is still wet, the yardstick can slide the tiles into position. Straighten the tile in both directions. Continue laying tile, until the full surface is covered. Allow the tile adhesive to dry at least 24 hours.

13 Adding trim

Cut wood trim to fit the sides and front of the top. The trim should be somewhat deeper than the thickness of the plywood-plus-tile top to provide a substantial appearance. If you have chosen very deep trim, position it and test that doors and drawers clear it when opened. Paint the trim and allow to dry. Glue and nail the trim in place, flush with the top edge of the countertop. Drilling small leader-holes (narrower than the nails) before nailing makes for an easier job, with fewer elephant's feet (hammer hits on wood). For a professional-looking finish, sink nailheads, fill the holes and touch up with paint. Mask the trim for grouting.

14 Grouting

Mix the grout according to package directions. The consistency should be like heavy sour cream with sand in it. If directions call for slaking, you must let the grout sit for the time specified. Slaking allows the chemicals in the grout to integrate.

Using a tile float, work the grout into the gaps between the tile. Hold the float with the back edge firmly on the tile and the front lifted slightly. Drag the grout diagonally across the tile, forcing it into the spaces. When all gaps are filled (including spaces between the tile and the edge trim) and the grout is level with the top of the tile, use the float to gather and remove any straggling bits of grout.

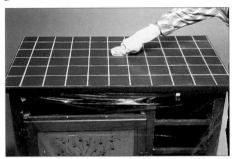

Using a *dry* rag or stiff plastic scouring pad, rub the tile to remove as much excess grout as possible. Water is the enemy of grout. Using water to remove excess grout will cause cracks to form in the grout when it dries.

To remove the final film of grout from the tiles, dampen a rag or sponge very slightly and wipe the tiles, avoiding the grout.

CHAIRS

The quest for seated comfort has inspired thousands of variations of chair designs, ranging in comfort from the Lazyboy to auditorium plastic seating, and in pomposity from spectacular thrones to simple wooden kitchen chairs. Reduced to basics, virtually every chair consists of four legs, a seat and a back. Yet the treatments and decorating techniques for covering and renovating chairs are endless. This section shows ideas for fashioning the best seats in the house.

Country Folk

A COUNTRY CHAIR IS CHARMED WITH DECORATIVE, EFFORTLESS HAND PAINTING

Not just any old chair, this sturdy, solid wooden one, with its turned spindles and legs and its subtly decorative backrest, elicits a simple, homey feeling. It was probably part of a kitchen set but, judging by the saw grooves, nicks and gouges, ended up as a workshop chair. First made with a natural wood finish, it was later painted off-white. This became its original paint. Original paint is considered untouchable by many antique aficionados — part of the furniture's history. Like many absolutes, this one must be tempered by reality. The owner of this chair wanted it repainted to suit her rustic yet refined decor.

Read This First

This project is quick and straightforward. First the chair is painted a solid deep-green base coat, either by spray painting or by brush. If your chair has a plastic laminate finish, use melamine paint for the base coat. (See *Melamine Paint,* page 27.) Then, with the help of templates, the floral pattern is applied. Templates look like stencil cut-outs, but instead of filling the cut-out areas with paint, you use them to trace an outline that's then filled in by brush painting. Stencils tend to give a smooth, even texture, while this technique achieves a hand-painted look with the brushstrokes and subtleties that give brushwork its appeal. Patterns for templates are provided on page 120. If the chair is wooden, you may wish to antique it. (See *Cupboard Love,* page 53.)

BEFORE

Lots of country character. The chair could be left as is, preserving its rustic and historic integrity, or painted in a style that complements its old world flavor.

MATERIALS

- can of low-luster acrylic spray paint, or quart (litre) satin finish latex paint, deep green
- 1½ in. (4 cm) wide paint brush (if using latex paint)
- paper, pen, scissors; access to photocopier
- white chalk or pencil crayon
- tubes of acrylic paint: cadmium red deep, yellow oxide, green gold, Prussian blue
- oval-tipped artist's brush, medium width
- fine-point artist's brush
- *optional:* can of spray primer or quart (litre) brush-on, water-based primer (The patchy finish of this chair required priming.)
- *optional:* medium and fine sandpaper (120 and 220 grades)
- *optional:* pint (.5 litre) non-yellowing, water-based varnish, or can of spray varnish

1 *Painting the base coat*

Following the instructions for *Preparation* (page 36), prepare the chair.

If the finish of the chair is patchy, paint the chair with one coat of primer, either by spraying or brushing it on. (See *Brush Painting*, page 40; or *Spray Painting*, page 44.)

If the chair is wooden and you wish to antique it, don't prime it. (See *Cupboard Love*, page 53.)

Spray paint or brush on two coats of deep green.

2 *Using templates*

Trace the patterns (page 120) onto paper, using a photocopier to enlarge or reduce them, if necessary, to the size appropriate for your chair. Cut out the centers of the templates, reserving the outer portion.

Lay the *Large Tulip* template onto the seat of the chair and run chalk or pencil crayon around the inside edge. Repeat three times, making a four-square pattern of tulips in the center of the seat. Draw symmetrical branches freehand, starting between the tulip shapes at the top and bottom and ending near the corners.

Draw smaller symmetrical branches between the tulip shapes at the sides.

Using the *Medium Tulip* template, trace flowers at each corner. Using the *Small Tulip* template, trace small flowers at the sides.

Using the same templates, draw a design onto both sides of the backrest of the chair. Especially pleasing is a design of tulips at the center, with branches extending to the sides.

3 *Hand painting*

Paint in the tulip outlines on the seat and both sides of the backrest with the oval-tipped brush and cadmium red deep paint. This job may require two coats.

Using the fine-point artist's brush and the yellow oxide, paint yellow centers onto the four-square tulips and the side tulips. Add lines to separate the petals, and create dots for stamens. Don't forget the backrest.

Using the green gold, paint lines along the chalk lines for the branches. Don't expect to follow the lines exactly. They are only a guide. Create small oval leaves by pressing the side of the fine-point brush against the surface.

With the Prussian blue, paint bunches of dots for a decorative element (like buds), where desired. You may also wish to add a decorative border of blue half-circles and dots. (Plan the border first, by sketching it with chalk.) Prussian blue can also be used to accentuate the edges of the branches and leaves.

Add these same elements to the backrest.

4 *Painting spindles*

Using any combination of colors, paint the spindles of the chair, keeping the edges as even as possible. (See *Brush Painting,* page 40.)

If you wish to antique your chair, sand wear spots onto it. (See *Cupboard Love,* page 53.) This can be done only on wooden chairs that have not been primed before painting.

5 *Varnishing*

Optional: Enrich the color and protect your paint job. Varnish the seat and backrest with two coats of non-yellowing, water-based varnish. Or use spray varnish to varnish the full chair. (See *Varnishing,* page 48.)

TEMPLATES FOR SEAT AND BACKREST

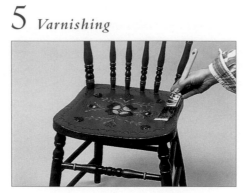

Large Tulip

Medium Tulip

Small Tulip

If you like the ease and predictability of working with stencils but want an interesting twist, try the reverse-stenciling technique used on this vanity. It involves laying decal shapes over painted areas, painting over the decals, and then peeling the decals off to reveal an exciting, random pattern.
(See Vanity Flair, page 203.)

Keeping Time

A CHARMING ROCKER REVEALS ITS PASTEL-PAINTED PAST

An old chair such as this well-worn rocker, or another piece of furniture with many layers of paint, can be refurbished imaginatively. Impressionist painters created radiant color by allowing layers of paint to glow through one another in a technique called *scumbling*. A similar quality is created in reverse by removing layers and partial layers of existing paint to produce a beautiful layered effect that reveals the furniture's history. In refurbishing the seat, the unexpected touch of woven wicking, normally used for oil lamps, adds texture and a neutral foil for the stripped paint.

Read This First

A piece of furniture with carved detail, clogged and obscured by layers of old paint, defies repainting. Painting over the drips and sags of a poor paint job guarantees another poor paint job. By stripping the piece only partially, you can eliminate lumps and bumps and reveal some of the furniture's history without the tedious finishing that stripping down to wood involves. Does stripping paint conjure up visions of vats of steaming toxic waste? Banish that image. You can now find new non-toxic, low-odor paint strippers.

The hand-crafted quality of a cane seat can be very attractive. If the cane is broken, however, that seat is a hazard and should be replaced. If you don't want the expense of recaning, try repairing the seat with webbing or with woven cotton wicking used in oil lamps. (See *Woven Seat,* page 161.)

BEFORE

Passed through many hands — most holding a paint brush — a small nursing rocker displays its last owner's handiwork: white oil-based enamel with nail polish hearts.

MATERIALS

- paint scraper
- newspaper; plastic dropsheet or old bedsheet
- rubber gloves
- low-toxicity paint stripper (Try to purchase a gel stripper.)
- inexpensive paint brush
- plastic stripping sponge
- fine sandpaper (220 grade)
- pint (.5 litre) acrylic or latex paint, in a color to suit your chair
- rags
- pint (.5 litre) non-yellowing, water-based varnish
- *optional:* tape and sheets of paper and plastic (for protecting the cane seat)
- *optional:* small hand saw or garden clippers (to remove cane seat)
- *optional:* plastic wrap, such as Saran wrap

1 *Seat preparation*

If you are planning to recane the seat, remove the old cane before doing anything else. A small hand saw or garden clippers are good for this surprisingly messy job. Cut as close to the rungs as possible and remove all pieces of cane that are wrapped around the rungs.

If you wish to retain the cane seat, protect it from the stripper by covering it in paper, then in a layer of plastic, taped securely closed.

If the chair has a cushion, unscrew it and remove it from the seat.

2 *Assessment*

Using a paint scraper or other sharp tool, scrape away a section of paint to investigate how many layers of paint there are and in what colors. You'll be better able to decide whether to partially strip and expose the layers, or to strip completely (and then stain or, possibly, repaint). (For more about complete stripping, see *The Cupboard Was Bare,* page 105.)

3 *Applying paint stripper*

Lay out several layers of newspaper covered with a large plastic, disposable drop-sheet or an old bedsheet. Put on rubber gloves. Using the low-toxicity paint stripper and an inexpensive paint brush, paint one area of the chair with stripper.

Some strippers melt plastic. Try this test. Wrap the area in plastic wrap to prevent the stripper from running off. The plastic keeps the stripper in contact with the paint, making the stripping process faster and more even. If the stripper eats through the wrap, discontinue using the plastic. Continue until the whole chair is covered.

4 *Stripping paint*

When the top layer of paint is bubbled (the time can vary from fifteen minutes to an hour, depending on the brand of stripper), remove a section of plastic wrap. Remove loose paint with the paint scraper or scrub with the plastic stripping sponge to reveal the layers beneath.

The effect should be uneven, with various layers and some raw wood showing through in different places.

5 *Deactivating stripper*

Inspect the chair to determine which areas are satisfactory and which ones need to be stripped some more. Wash the satisfactory areas thoroughly with dish soap and water and rinse well to deactivate the stripper. Repeat and dry the surfaces with a rag.

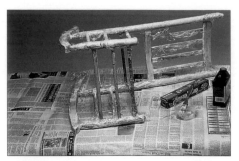

Apply a second coat of stripper and plastic wrap to areas that require more stripping. Repeat step 4. Wash the stripped area. Allow the chair to dry. Some paint may remain soft. These areas will harden in time.

6 Sanding

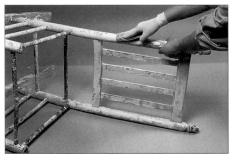

Give the chair a light sanding with the fine sandpaper.

Inspect the chair. Don't be dismayed if it is mottled and blotchy looking. The next step will help even out the color.

7 Color washing

Choose a color of paint to suit the colors that have been revealed. Blue, rose or violet are good bets. Thin the paint with water to a watery consistency. Dip a small damp rag into the paint and wash the paint over a section of the chair.

Allow the paint to set slightly, only a minute or two. Then use a second clean, damp rag to wipe off some of the paint to the level of opacity you desire. Try not to obscure the scumbled, layered effect of the stripping.

Repeat the color washing over other sections.

To enrich color and protect the paint, apply one or two coats of non-yellowing, water-based varnish. (See *Varnishing,* page 48.)

If you wish to make a woven seat, see *Woven Seat,* page 161.

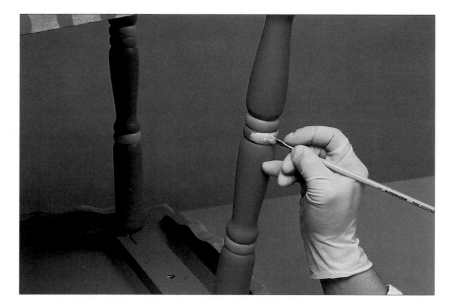

If your chair has turned legs and spindles, painting the details in coordinating, solid colors provides a decorative counterpoint to the soft washes of partial stripping. (See Brush Painting, page 40.)

Wrapture

AN INGLORIOUS GROUP GOES GLAMOROUS, WRAPPED IN SPLENDID FABRICS

Pattern, texture, color. These chairs are at once tactile, breathtaking, intriguing. The scrunching and wrapping of the fabric produces a potpourri of color and pattern, turning butterflies and flowers into abstract art with fantastic texture. The fabric's full pattern is displayed on the seat cushion, coordinating perfectly with the wrapping. Chair feet and knobs are treated to humorously puffy covers. Each seat is one of a kind, a serendipitous mixture of color and pattern placement. No two could ever be exactly the same.

Read This First

Small wrought iron tables or chairs, the rustier and more decrepit the better, are ideal for this treatment. The rust is covered with rust-coating spray paint. The damage is covered by the textured fabric. A bamboo chair can also be wrapped, although the job is somewhat more time-consuming because of the indigenous filigrees and fiddleheads. All chairs to be wrapped must be spray painted in a light color before wrapping. A dark color will show through light-colored fabric, giving it a dirty appearance. If you wish to apply this treatment to a table or desk, see *Material Pleasures* (page 253) and *Office Romance* (page 183) for information on covering a tabletop so that it will withstand wear.

Choose lightweight fabrics, which don't fray easily. These are easier to find in a dressmaker's fabric store than in an upholstery or a decorator's shop. Using a heavier cotton demands a more tailored approach, which is also shown. Tiny, repetitive patterns will look similar on the chair to how they appear on the bolt. Medium to large all-over prints make an interesting abstract pattern. Stripes will create sections of color. While the suggested quantity of fabric may seem excessive, it's difficult to assess the exact yardage needed for wrapping, plus cushions.

BEFORE

Left, three wrought iron chairs. The rust damage could be covered with paint, but why not go for originality? Right, a bamboo chair painted deep brown and well worn (see finished chair, page 133). Repairing bamboo is practically impossible.

MATERIALS

- screwdriver
- tape measure
- steel-wool soap pad
- packing tape or duct tape
- can of spray paint in a pale color that coordinates with the fabric (Choose rust-covering paint for wrought iron.)
- 2½ yd. (2.25 m) lightweight, patterned fabric, 54 in. (135 cm) wide, for a simple wrought iron chair (Purchase more fabric for intricate chairs.)
- scissors
- masking tape
- white carpenter's glue or craft glue
- scraps of terrycloth or similar fabric, 4 rubber bands
- *optional:* garden clippers (for cutting the cane of a bamboo seat)
- *optional:* small amount of coordinating paint for highlighting, artist's brush (step 2)
- *optional:* crochet hook
- *optional:* dressmaker's pins, iron-on interfacing, needle and thread, iron
- *optional:* fabric protector spray

1 *Removing cushions*

Remove the seat cushion by turning the chair upside-down and unscrewing the screws. If the chair has a backrest, remove it too. Don't throw out either piece. The plywood inside the cushion is needed for recovering. Remove the old covering and foam and clean up the plywood. Measure and replace the plywood for the seat, if desired. But keep the formed plywood from the backrest. It is difficult to replace.

If your chair is bamboo, the seat may be woven into the chair with cane in one or two spots. Remove the seat by cutting the cane with garden clippers.

2 *Spray painting*

Wash the wrought iron chair with soap and water. Use a steel-wool soap pad to remove as much rust as possible. Rinse well and allow to dry thoroughly.

On a bamboo chair, glue down any broken cane. Wrap loose areas very tightly in packing tape or duct tape.

Spray paint the chair in a pale color similar to your fabric, following the directions on the can. Apply two coats if necessary.

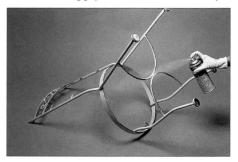

When spraying a wrought iron chair, make sure all rust is completely covered. (See *Spray Painting,* page 44.)

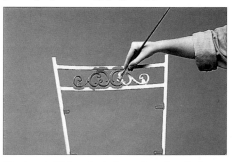

Optional: If the chair has nice detail that you want to leave exposed, then, before wrapping, paint the area with a color to complement your fabric. Use acrylic or latex paint.

3 *Cutting fabric*

Cutting across the width of the fabric, cut twenty strips of fabric, 2 in. (5 cm) wide. Set aside fifteen strips. Cut five strips in half lengthwise to give you ten narrower ones. These are for fine filigree.

When using a heavy fabric, press a narrow hem on one edge, folding and ironing it toward the wrong side.

4 *Wrapping*

Start wrapping on the finest filigrees or spindles. The fine filigrees inevitably run to bigger ones that, when wrapped, will hide any loose fabric ends.

Cut and reserve some small pieces of masking tape. Dab glue at the starting point of a fine filigree (where it joins a larger one). Lay the end of a fabric strip onto the glue and tape it in place. Start wrapping. Bunch lightweight fabric and begin winding it tightly on a diagonal, covering any visible glue or tape. Overlap each previous edge of wrapped fabric.

With a heavier fabric, wrap the fabric flat, tight and even for a tailored look instead of bunching it as you wrap. Make sure the pressed edge overlaps the previous raw edge. Snip into the raw edge of the fabric, as needed, to work around obstacles. Should the chair have filigrees that end in points midair (very unusual), see step 5 for finishing the ends.

5 *Wrapping, continued*

At the end of each filigree, glue and tape the fabric down and cut the fabric. Leave 1 in. (2.5 cm) of excess, to be tucked under and covered later.

As you work, prevent the fabric from slipping by dabbing glue onto the wrought iron and wrapping over it. You can use dressmaker's pins to hold fabric in place. A crochet hook can be helpful for pulling fabric through tight spots.

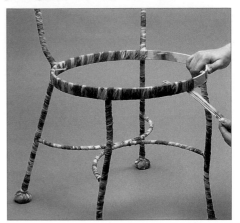

Wrap the next group of filigrees, according to fatness. When passing the junctions of previously wrapped filigrees, tuck any excess fabric under, gluing and wrapping over it. Avoid leaving any gaps at junctions.

Continue wrapping all filigrees and spindles.

6 *Covering feet*

Before wrapping the chair legs, cover the feet. Cut four circles of fabric, 6 in. (15 cm) in diameter, and four circles of padding (terrycloth will do), 4 in. (10 cm) in diameter. Center the padding pieces on the wrong side of the fabric circles.

Place a circle under a foot of the chair, padding-side-up. Apply glue near the edge of the padding, draw up the edge of the circle, and wind a rubber band around the leg to bunch and secure the fabric circle. Repeat with the three remaining feet and fabric circles.

This technique can also be used to cover knobs or the ends of chair arms.

7 *Final wrapping*

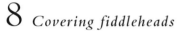

Wrap the final (largest) sections, the legs, the rim of the seat and the back. Begin close to the feet, gluing and taping the end of the strip and tucking it under the raw edge. As you proceed, cover any loose ends.

8 *Covering fiddleheads*

To cover floral decorations on wrought iron or fiddleheads on a bamboo chair, first press iron-on interfacing onto the wrong side of a piece of fabric to prevent fraying.

Cut 2½ in. (6.25 cm) circles from the fabric, large enough to cover the fiddle-

heads completely in the style of a draw-string purse. Hold the circle to the fiddlehead. Then cut into the side of the circle, fitting the cut around the area where the fiddlehead joins the chair.

Remove the circle of fabric. Beginning and ending at the cut, sew running stitches near the edge and gather slightly. Place the circle onto the fiddlehead and gather tightly so that the circle is snugly closed.

Optional: Spray with fabric protector.

9 *Cushions*

Cover any seat cushions or backrest cushions and attach to the chair. (For more about cushion covers, see *Seating,* page 153.)

Shown here, the finished results of wrapping a bamboo chair — with all its attendant filigree and frippery — in a heavy cotton using a tailored approach.

Floral Arrangements

TWIN BENTWOOD ARMCHAIRS ARE ROMANCED WITH PAINT AND FABRIC

A splash of fresh flowers on a crisp white cotton background is the perfect foil for glossy white lacquer. Mixing texture, color and pattern creates dramatic change for any worn-out furniture, especially when the original is dark and dreary. Painting the fabric's design onto the seat of the chair moves the treatment from predictable to original, adding an artist's touch while echoing the fabric's design and colors. Thoroughly modern gathered halters create both a cover-up and new interest, a unique approach to a slipcover.

Read This First

These chairs are unusual because the backs were broken, while the seats, which were in perfect condition, were covered with bulky cushions. If your chair has a broken cane seat and a good back, reverse the treatment by painting the back and adding a fabric-covered cushion to the seat. If both the back and the cane seat are broken, make a halter and a cushion. (See *Seating,* page 153, for more about cushions.)

This treatment is accomplished in three phases. First, the chairs are spray painted. Then a portion of the fabric design is traced and painted on the seats. For ease of copying, choose a fabric with a large, uncomplicated pattern that looks brush painted. Finally, the backs are covered with gathered halters. The halters require only basic sewing. Halters are the perfect solution for a chair with a broken cane or spindle back.

BEFORE

Tweed cushions compromise the elegant lines of a pair of bentwood chairs. Damaged finish and broken backs demand an imaginative renovation.

MATERIALS

- can of acrylic spray paint, gloss finish, in an appropriate color
- dropsheet
- fabric (To determine yardage, see step 5.)
- tubes of acrylics to match colors in fabric, artist's brushes
- access to photocopier, or tracing paper and pencil
- scissors for cutting fabric and canvas
- piece of canvas to fit chair back (To determine size, see step 4.)
- stapler and ¼ in. (.5 cm) staples
- sewing machine with thread to match fabric, or needle and thread; dressmaker's pins
- white carpenter's glue, small brass nails, small hammer
- hot-glue gun
- iron
- *optional:* heavy-duty scissors or garden clippers, chisel, wood filler, fine sandpaper (220 grade)
- *optional:* tape measure, power drill, two small knobs
- *optional:* shirring tape

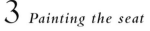

1 *Removing cane*

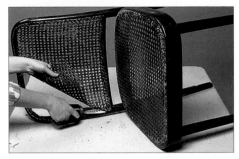

Remove the broken cane. Cut it away with heavy-duty scissors or garden clippers.

Then remove the stubble by cutting it off level with the wood, laying a chisel against the base and tapping it with a small hammer.

Fill any holes with wood filler and allow to dry. Sand smooth with fine sandpaper.

2 *Preparation and painting*

Optional: If your chair has round shoulders, create physical borders for the halter. Measure an equal distance both sides of center and drill holes for two knobs. Test that the knobs fit. Then remove them and set them aside.

Place the chair on a dropsheet and spray paint the chair. (See *Spray Painting,* page 44.)

3 *Painting the seat*

If the cane seat is in good condition, paint it as follows. Isolate an area of the fabric's design that will fit onto the seat of the chair. Photocopy or trace this area onto paper. Cut out elements of the design. Lay the cut-outs onto the seat and trace around them with a pencil. Using artist's brushes and the acrylics, follow the fabric as a color guide. Paint the shapes. Allow to dry.

If the cane is in poor condition, create a cushion. (See *Seating,* page 153.)

4 *Halter liner*

Without a canvas reinforcement, the finished halter will not support the weight of a seated person. Measure the height of the backrest and add 6 in (15 cm). Cut a piece of canvas to this length and to a width 2 in. (5 cm) narrower than the halter will be (step 5). Serge or glue along the sides to prevent fraying. Allow the glue to dry. Center the canvas onto the front side of the chair back. Wrap the end of the canvas around the bottom rail and staple the canvas to the rail. Pull the canvas very tightly around the top rail. Staple it securely in place.

5 Sewing the halter

Cut the halter fabric as follows. Measure the width of the halter. Cut fabric one-and-one-half times to twice the width. To determine the length of the fabric, measure the height of the backrest. Double the measurement and add 6 in. (15 cm) for finishing. Cut the fabric to this length.

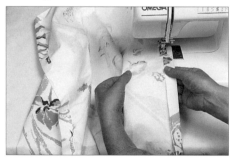

To hem both sides, fold the side edges under, ½ in. (1.25 cm) to the wrong side. Repeat. Press, then sew close to the inside fold. Do not hem the ends.

Measure the length of the fabric and

mark the center. Gather across the fabric at the mark, either by sewing shirring tape to the wrong side or by sewing large stitches.

6 Positioning the halter

If using the knobs, attach them now through the drilled holes. Position the fabric with the gathering between the knobs, adjusting the gathers to fit.

Determine if the fabric has a pattern that runs in one direction, such as vines climbing a trellis. The fabric's design should run up on the front of the backrest. Center the gathers along the bentwood back, gluing and/or nailing the fabric in place with small brass nails. Cover the heads of the nails with the gathers.

7 Attaching the halter

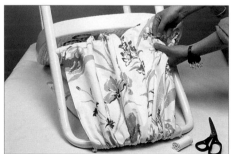

Turn the chair upside-down, so that you are working with the fabric on the back of the chair back. Pull the halter fabric snugly to the center of the bottom rung, marking it with pins. Sew a running stitch along the pin line for gathering. Cut away excess fabric ½ in. (1.25 cm) outside the pin line. Gather the stitching.

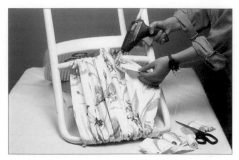

Centering the gathers onto the bottom rung, use the hot-glue gun to glue the gathers to the bottom rung, pulling the fabric taut. *Be careful not to burn your fingers, especially if you are not experienced with a glue gun.* The glue becomes hot enough to cause deep burns, and the glue sticks and keeps burning.

Stand the chair up. Measure and cut the front fabric as you did for the back, adding a 1 in. (2.5 cm) hem. Flip the front fabric over and iron the 1 in. (2.5 cm) hem to the wrong side. Sew and gather along the crease of the hem.

Pull the fabric taut and hot glue the gathered edge along the center of the bottom rail, covering the raw edge.

If replicating the pattern of the fabric seems like too great a challenge, consider using a
solid-colored fabric with coordinating stencils for graphics. Shown here, Victorian rose stencils.
(See Tabletop Rose Bower, page 247.)

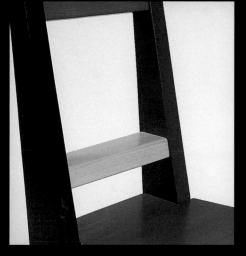

Mix Masters

FABRIC-DYE STAINS GENERATE GLOWING COLOR

Bright colors send spirits soaring. They grab your attention. They detonate a room and make it sparkle. Brights are more versatile than most people think. Use one piece as an accent, or use a roomful as a personal statement. How do you get those glowing, vibrant, incandescent brights? Paints won't do it, because they're not transparent. Wood stains for sale are uniformly neutral and soft. Try fabric dyes. They're available in virtually every shade, and they are very, very easy to use.

Read This First

Use fabric-dye-staining techniques on any un-painted or stripped and sanded piece of furni-ture. It must be applied to bare wood. Only knockdown furniture can be stained in multiple colors, piece by piece. Assembled furniture must be stained one color, because the stains will bleed into each other. Fabric dyes are available in eye-popping colors, as well as sub-dued and deep tones. The dyes are mixed with a small amount of hot water and rubbed into the open grain of the wood. Then the dyed pieces are varnished to seal in the color – and to prevent it from transferring to your guest's white designer jeans. If you are matching a color to your drapes or a piece of furniture, remember that the varnished color is often not the same as the stained color. Varnish can dramatically alter the inten-sity of the dye, enhancing and brightening colors. Do a stain-and-varnish test on scrap wood first. Knockdown furniture is assembled after varnishing.

BEFORE

This chair is straight out of the box. Knockdown and unpainted furniture is ideal for staining or painting multiple colors.

MATERIALS

- pencil and paper
- fine sandpaper (220 grade), tack cloth
- lightweight waterproof painter's gloves
- fabric dye (any brand that calls for dye to be mixed with water)
- disposable mixing pots (margarine or other sturdy plastic containers)
- kettle
- stir sticks or scrap wood
- paper or plastic dropsheets
- lint-free rags
- narrow-width artist's brush
- boxes or containers for elevating chair sections
- quart (litre) non-yellowing, water-based varnish
- paint brush
- *optional:* transparent or translucent artist's acrylics
- *optional:* X-acto knife or utility knife

1 Getting started

If you are staining more than one color, sketch a picture of the chair or use the picture on the assembly pamphlet and mark the colors for each piece as a guide.

Sand the raw wood lightly with fine sandpaper to open the grain of the wood. Wipe away all traces of dust with a tack cloth.

2 Mixing the dye

Wear painter's gloves for this staining technique. These dyes work very well on skin. Ignore the instructions supplied with the dye. Instead, pour the dry dye into a disposable mixing pot and add 1 cup (250 ml) boiling water. Mix well.

If you mix several colors of dye, wipe up any spilled dry dye. The smallest amount of airborne dye particles will contaminate other colors, especially light ones such as yellow or pink. Airborne particles can also bleed if they land on a damp surface, such as a piece in progress.

Test each color on a wooden stir stick or a scrap piece of wood. If you wish to strengthen or brighten the color, add acrylic paint to the dye. Purchase tubes marked transparent or translucent. These paints are concentrated and may appear dark in the tube. Mix a small amount into the dye and test again. Add more paint if necessary.

3 Applying stain

To begin staining, take the sanded piece of wood to be stained and position it onto a dropsheet. (Don't use newspaper. The ink will transfer.) Wearing the waterproof gloves, dip a rag into the dye-stain and spread the stain onto the wood. It will be absorbed. Continue spreading the stain, without stopping, covering the piece with an even coat. Use the artist's brush to paint stain into any recessed or hard-to-reach details.

The stain should penetrate the wood and accentuate the grain. It will feel dry to the touch almost immediately. Turn the piece over and stain the other side.

4 Avoiding color transfer

Move the fully stained piece, on its dropsheet, away from your work area, so it won't come into contact with any other pieces. Until it is varnished, the stain will transfer to anything that touches it.

5 Staining, continued

Wash your gloves with soap and water to remove as much stain as possible and prevent it from being transferred to the next piece. Lay down a new dropsheet. Repeat step 3 and 4 with another piece and a second color.

Continue until all sections have been stained. Allow them to dry.

6 *Varnishing*

Grouping them by color, elevate sections of the chair on boxes or containers. Pour a small quantity of varnish into a container instead of using the varnish straight from the can. Some of the stain will inevitably transfer to the brush and the pot of varnish. Brush a coat of varnish onto all sections that are stained the same color. Allow to dry.

Using fine sandpaper, sand the varnish very lightly. Don't be alarmed by the cloudy appearance of the varnish. Wipe clean with a tack cloth. Repeat the varnishing and sanding process once more, then apply a final coat of varnish so that all pieces have three coats of varnish.

Wash the brush thoroughly and pour a new pot of varnish each time you move on to a new color group. Continue until all of the pieces are varnished. Allow to dry.

When they're thoroughly dry, turn the pieces over and apply three coats of varnish to the other side, wiping clean between each coat.

7 *Assembly*

Assemble the furniture according to the directions. If the screw holes are clogged with varnish, carefully scrape them out with the point of an X-acto or a utility knife.

While the block-printed roses shown above are on a painted background, treatments such as stenciling and block printing add drama and texture when applied to stained wood. Florals over a pastel stain can produce a soft romantic effect. (See Sheer Delight, page 259, for information on block printing.)

Art Attack

ADORNMENTS AND FANCIFUL PAINT
CONCOCT A WORK OF ART

Putting the funk in functional, defying labels, this startling, heavily
ornamented chair is at once a gypsy's suitcase of beads and baubles, a
collection of folk wind chimes, a work of abstract art and a statement on the
creative kitchen. Lively freehand images, painted in primary colors, mix with
found pieces of beads and silver cutlery to give the ultimate
makeover to a sturdy old pantry chair.

Read This First

A time-consuming but not difficult job, adorning this chair takes some paint, beads, cast-off cutlery or other adornments – and a sense of humor. Hunting the silver cutlery is part of the adventure of finishing this piece. Stainless steel simply doesn't make the grade. Find silver-plated or solid silver mismatched and damaged pieces of cutlery at a Goodwill, Salvation Army or similar type of store. These shops usually have a box of single and broken pieces for as little as a dime each. Most antique or *junque* stores charge far too much for silver to be used in this way. A jigsaw and drill with attachments for metal must be used to cut and pierce the cutlery. If you are intimidated by power tools, substitute medallions or pieces from old jewelry or clockworks that have holes for attaching. Use beads with a center hole large enough for a sewing needle. (Beading needles are slimmer, but can't be threaded with a heavy thread.) Treat this project as a creative process to be done in st7ages, whenever the mood strikes.

BEFORE

Chunky, sturdy and pea-soup green, this chair is suitable for a wide range of treatments, including the outrageous.

MATERIALS

- quart (litre) high-adhesion, water-based primer or can of spray primer
- latex or tubes of acrylics in various colors: mars black, tangerine, turquoise, bubble gum pink, royal blue
- paint brush, 1 in. (2.5 cm) wide
- fine-point artist's brush
- random silver cutlery or similar found objects, appropriate metal polish
- jigsaw and metal cutting blade
- power drill and small-diameter metal-drilling bit
- needle-nosed pliers
- clear spray varnish or lacquer
- small screw-eyes
- miscellaneous beads (center hole should be large enough for a sewing needle), piece of velvet
- scissors, sewing needle, button-hole thread
- *optional:* small brass nails, hammer and nail
- *optional:* clamps, rags

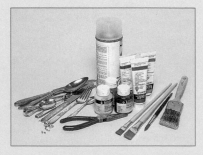

1 *Painting*

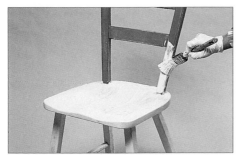

Refer to *Painting Basics* (page 34). Prepare and prime the chair. Allow to dry.

Start from the bottom of the chair. Using the 1 in. (2.5 cm) paint brush, paint sections of the chair in various colors with one or two coats of latex or acrylic paint. Wash the brush between colors.

When the paint is dry, turn the chair upright and paint the top and back. Allow to dry.

2 *Freehand painting*

Using the fine-point artist's brush, paint designs onto the large surfaces of the chair, particularly the seat and the back-rest. Add stars, curlicues, stripes, etc., to other parts as desired.

For best results, thin the paint so that it flows easily from the brush point. Draw the patterns freehand and quickly to avoid bunched-up, tentative lines. Realism is not a concern. Set the painted chair aside and allow to dry.

3 *Cutting the cutlery*

Polish the cutlery.

Using a jigsaw with a metal-cutting blade, cut the ends off several pieces of the cutlery. *Wear goggles for this job, and watch your fingers.* If the pieces require clamping to secure them while cutting, pad the clamped sections with rags to prevent the clamp from leaving gouges in the silver.

Drill holes in the silver for hanging. Place the pieces on a wooden board, and drill a hole centered at one end of each piece. Use a power drill fitted with a small-diameter drill bit designed for drilling metal. *Wear goggles for this job.*

4 *Bending the cutlery*

Make the fork tines expressive by bending them into a variety of tight and loose curls in different directions. Grasp the tip of a tine in the point of a pair of needle-nosed pliers and turn it to the desired curl. If you wish, pad the pliers to prevent marks on the silver. Handles can also be bent or curled. The ease of bending will vary greatly from piece to piece. Some cutlery may be too stiff to bend.

5 *Sealing*

When you've completed all polishing, cutting, drilling and bending, spray all sides of the cutlery with a clear varnish or lacquer. This will prevent tarnishing. Allow to dry.

6 *Hanging silver and beads*

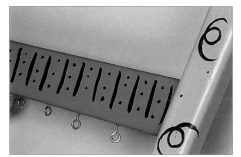

Decide on the best places to hang the cutlery and beads. Screw small screw-eyes into the chair in the locations selected. Creating a small hole with a hammer and nail can help you start the screw-eye. A nail through the screw-eye can help provide leverage to turn it.

Spreading the beads on velvet will help prevent them from rolling away. Thread a small- to medium-sized sewing needle with thread, doubled. Thread one or more beads.

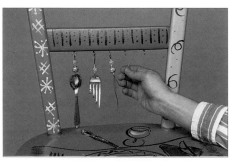

Slip the needle through a screw-eye, and then back through the beads.

Slip the needle through a drilled hole in one of the pieces of silver. Tie a tight square knot in the thread. Cut the thread close to the knot. You may be able to cover the knot by sliding a bead over it.

Repeat for the remaining silver pieces, creating whatever combinations of beads and silverware you desire.

7 *Finishing touches*

Pieces of silverware can be nailed onto flat areas of the chair by hammering brass nails through the drilled holes. But be sure your placement won't be a pain in the butt.

*If freehand brush painting isn't your strong suit, consider making photocopy
transfers or inscribing the furniture with handwritten quotations.
(See Bedtime Reading, page 87.)*

Seating

SITTING PRETTY WITH PROFESSIONALLY CRAFTED CUSHIONS AND SEATS

The seat of a chair is more than a place to park. Chair seats and cushions offer a design opportunity to add texture, color and pattern with fabric — along with a higher degree of comfort. Try to find an upholstery supplier that sells upholsterer's-quality high-density foam, batting, and dust-cover cloth. Dust-cover cloth is the non-fraying fabric that goes under the seat to cover raw edges and bare plywood. If you can, take along the plywood base from the old cushion as a pattern, and have the foam pieces cut to fit.

Following are instructions for a basic seat cushion, a piped seat cushion, and a woven webbing seat, along with two treatments for backrest cushions — tailored and shirred. Only the piped cushion requires sewing.

Above, the chair on the left has a basic seat cushion and a shirred backrest cushion. The chair on the right has a piped seat cushion. *Left,* both chairs have basic seat cushions and tailored backrest cushions.

Basic Seat Cushion

Read This First

This seat cushion is the type that looks like a large soft cookie. Use this treatment primarily on round chair seats. Square seats tend to look better with a straight-sided or piped cushion. Choose the thickness of the foam, between one and two inches (2.5 to 5 cm), depending on the style of the chair. If the thicker foam will obscure detailing or be ungainly in height, choose a thinner foam. It will look better, but the trade-off will be a harder chair and slightly less comfort for those sitting on it. Buy plywood that is good one side. This means that one side has a smooth finish, while the other is knotty and rough. The good side of the plywood will be positioned down on the seat. (Good both sides, which is much more expensive, is not necessary.)

MATERIALS

- plywood, ½ in. (1.25 cm) thick, good one side, cut to fit the seat of the chair
- high-density upholstery foam, 1 to 2 in (2.5 to 5 cm) thick, cut to fit plywood
- fabric, 8 in. (20 cm) larger than the plywood both in length and in width
- iron
- ruler and marker
- scissors
- batting, 6 in. (15 cm) larger than the plywood both in length and in width
- stapler and ⅜ in. (1 cm) staples
- non-fraying upholstery dust-cover cloth (enough to cover the plywood)
- screws (to reattach cushion to chair), screwdriver
- *optional:* jigsaw
- *optional:* spray glue; scrap paper or dropsheet
- *optional:* lining (step 5)

1 *Getting started*

Remove the fabric and foam from the underlying plywood. Clean the plywood as thoroughly as possible, removing any mold and staples.

If the old plywood is beyond salvation, have a new piece cut or cut one yourself with a jigsaw. The new plywood should be ½ in. (1.25 cm) thick, good one side.

Have a piece of high-density upholstery foam cut to match the size and shape of the plywood.

2 *Cutting fabric*

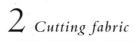

Iron the fabric.

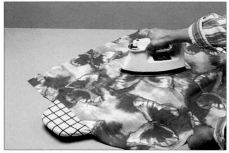

Lay the foam or the plywood onto the wrong side of the fabric. Measure and mark the fabric 4 in. (10 cm) from the edge of the foam. Do this at regular intervals around the perimeter of the foam. Join the marks to make a continuous solid line.

Cut along the line.

3 *Laminating foam to plywood*

Optional: Gluing the foam to the plywood can reduce slippage. Lay down some scrap paper or a dropsheet and place the foam onto it. Check the directions on the spray-glue label for making a permanent bond. Spray the foam with glue.

Lay the rough side of the plywood on the gluey foam, centering it.

4 *Batting*

Lay the plywood/foam onto the batting. Lift the batting up, against the side of the foam, marking the batting at the top edge of the foam. Do this all the around the foam.

Cut the batting along the marked line.

Optional: With the plywood/foam centered on the circle of batting, foam-side-down, spray-glue a section of the overhanging batting. Fold the glued section up onto the foam. Repeat until the batting is glued to the perimeter of the foam.

5 *Stapling*

If the cushion fabric is lightweight, cut a lining from a woven material such as broadcloth. Lay the fabric face-down, with the lining on top.

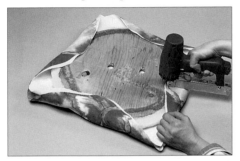

Position the plywood/foam/batting sandwich, batting-side-down, onto the center of the fabric. Gently but firmly, pull and staple the fabric to the plywood in four places, equal distances apart.

Gently but firmly, pull and staple the fabric to the plywood between each of the four staples, keeping the pressure even.

Gently but firmly, pull and staple the fabric to the plywood between each of the eight staples, keeping the pressure even.

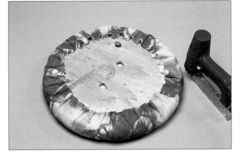

Gently but firmly, pull and staple the fabric to the plywood between the staples. Continue until the fabric is stapled evenly all around.

6 *Finishing*

Cut a circle of dust-cover cloth slightly larger than the circle of staples, but smaller than the bottom of the cushion. Staple it to the bottom of the cushion, starting with four equidistant staples. Then staple between them, as you did to staple the cushion fabric, until the full perimeter is stapled.

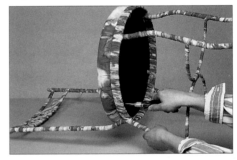

Reattach the cushion to the chair by screwing appropriately sized screws into the seat frame and the plywood of the cushion. Work from underneath the seat.

Piped Seat Cushion

Read This First

Making a piped seat cushion takes some planning and sewing ability, although the sewing is actually basic and straightforward. The piping gives the cushion an elegant, crisp finish. Piping is available in braids or wovens, and it comes in a wide range of colors, prints and finishes, from shiny to matte. Choose a piping that will coordinate with the fabric, yet stand out enough to accentuate the tailored edge. If you have never sewn piping with a piping foot on your sewing machine, here's a chance to try it and see how professional the results are. The sewing goes faster and is easier if a piping foot is used. It keeps the piping on track and the sewing uniform. If a piping foot is not available, use a zipper foot.

MATERIALS

- plywood, ½ in. (1.25 cm) thick, good one side, cut to fit the seat of the chair
- high-density upholstery foam, 2 in. (5 cm) thick, cut to match the plywood
- paper, pencil, ruler
- fabric, approx. ½ yd. (.5 m) for each cushion
- scissors
- piping (measure perimeter of cushion and add 6 in. (15 cm))
- dressmaker's pins
- sewing machine with piping foot
- thread to match fabric
- batting, 6 in. (15 cm) larger than the plywood both in length and in width
- stapler and ⅜ in. (1 cm) staples
- non-fraying upholstery dust-cover cloth (enough to cover the plywood)
- screws (to reattach cushion to chair), screwdriver
- *optional*: jigsaw
- *optional*: zipper foot
- *optional*: spray glue; scrap paper or drop-sheet

1 Getting started

Remove the fabric and foam from the underlying plywood. Clean the plywood as thoroughly as possible, removing any mold and staples.

If the old plywood is beyond repair, have a new piece cut or cut one yourself with a jigsaw. The new plywood should be ½ in. (1.25 cm) thick, good one side.

Have a piece of high-density upholstery foam, 2 in. (5 cm) thick, professionally cut to match the size and shape of the plywood.

2 Drafting a pattern

Make a pattern for the top of the cushion cover. Lay the plywood onto paper and trace closely around it. Using a ruler, measure and mark a ½ in. (1.25 cm) seam allowance from the plywood edge all around the perimeter. Then join the marks to create a cutting line.

3 Cutting fabric

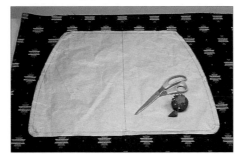

Cut out the pattern and lay it onto the fabric, centering it carefully onto the fabric's design. If the design printed on the fabric is directional (vines climbing a trellis, for example), it should run from the front of the cushion "up" to the back.

On fabric with a geometric pattern, the placement should match for all cushions. Pin the pattern in place and cut out the fabric for all cushions.

For the sides of the cushion cover, cut strips of fabric, 6 in. (15 cm) wide, across the width of the fabric. Cut the strips to match up with the fabric design of the cushion tops, taking into consideration the width of seam allowances. Usually, one width of fabric will circle one cushion.

4 Sewing

Starting at the center-back of the cushion top, pin piping on the right side of the fabric, matching the raw edge of the piping to the cut edge of the fabric. Check that the piping has a ½ in. (1.25 cm) seam allowance. If not, compensate. Pin well. At corners, clip into the seam allowance of the piping, allowing it to bend. At the start and the end, allow 2 in. (5 cm) extra piping, laying the ends across the seam allowance.

Attach the piping foot to the sewing machine. With matching thread, begin at the center-back and sew the piping in place, ½ in. (1.25 cm) from the cut edge.

Lay a cut strip of fabric onto the piped edge of the cushion, with right sides together, matching the pattern along the front edge of the cushion. The ends of the strip should join at the center back. Pin the strip to the cushion top, starting at the center-front and working out, until the strip is pinned to the full perimeter of the cushion top. Clip the seam allowance of the strip at corners, if necessary. If the strip is too short, sew an additional section to the strip.

With the piping foot still in place, sew the strip tightly against the piping. Join the ends of the strip. Turn the cushion cover right-side-out and inspect the seam. Resew any gaps.

5 *Batting*

Using the foam as a guide, cut a piece of batting 3 in. (7.5 cm) larger all around (or measure and cut batting as shown on page 156, step 4). Lay the foam onto the plywood and the batting onto the foam. Notch the corners, so they dovetail when bent down over the sides of foam.

Optional: Gluing the foam to the plywood and the batting to the foam can reduce slippage. (See *Basic Seat Cushion*, steps 3 and 4, page 156.)

If you opt not to glue the plywood and the batting to the foam, lay the foam onto the rough side of the plywood and center the batting over the foam.

Slip the piped cushion top over the batting.

6 *Stapling*

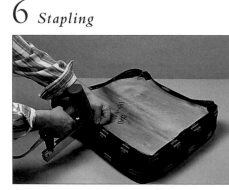

Turn the cushion upside-down. At the center of each side, gently but firmly pull the fabric to the back of the cushion and staple in place.

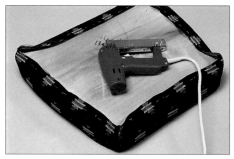

Continue, adding staples equally to all sides, keeping the tension even. Don't staple one full side before going on to the next. This will cause uneven tension and ripples.

Finish corners by stapling the center of the corner, then folding and stapling the excess down, like a fan, on both sides. Do several small folds to avoid puckering.

7 *Finishing*

Cut a piece of dust-cover cloth to fit the bottom of the cushion. It should cover the staples but be within the edge of the cushion. Staple it in place with one staple centered on each side. Work out from these staples, stapling all around the edge.

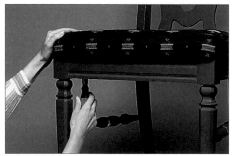

Reattach the cushion to the chair by screwing in appropriately sized screws from the bottom of the seat.

Woven Seat

Read This First

This technique is for replacing a worn-out web-bing or split-cane seat. The seat must have the necessary dowel-like four rungs: front, back and sides. Purchase webbing at an upholstery supply store or buy wicking for oil lamps. The wicking shown here was bought at a hardware store in a 25 yard (23 m) roll for a surprisingly modest price. The wicking is a flatly woven natural cotton of a pleasing width. But why stop here? Many cast-off items can be used to great effect. Layers of ribbon, bunched yarn, or ends of trims can be used. Torn rags, tied end to end, could give a folksy, rag-rug feeling to a seat. Once started, stick to this project until finished (it only takes a few hours), so you won't lose track of the weaving.

MATERIALS

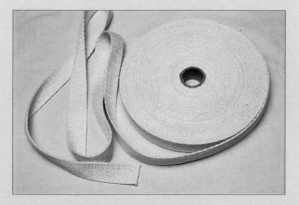

- approx. 20 yd. (20 m) wicking (the type used for oil lamps) or webbing about 1 in. (2.5 cm) wide (amount required can vary, depending on size of chair seat)
- stiff cardboard, 3 x 6 in. (7.5 x 15 cm)
- ruler and marker
- stir stick or other narrow stick, to fit the width of the seat
- white carpenter's glue and tape, or stapler and ¼ in. (.5 cm) staples
- *optional:* needle and thread for sewing webbing ends

1 *Getting started*

Cut a rectangle of stiff cardboard, about 3 x 6 in. (7.5 x 15 cm). Wrap the webbing around the length of the cardboard from end to end to make a shuttle. Don't cut the webbing.

Mark the center points on the front and back rungs of the seat. The markings will help you keep the weaving straight, especially if the rungs are different lengths.

2 *The first pass*

Stand in front, facing the chair. Begin on the left side. Glue and tape (or staple) the webbing to the left-side rung. (Glue, tape and staples will be hidden by the weaving.)

Slip the shuttle under the back rung, then bring it up and over the back rung and toward the front, keeping the webbing flat.

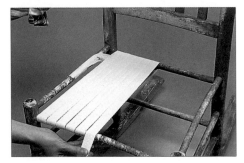

Bring the shuttle forward, passing over the front rung, then under the chair seat to the back, and over the back rung again.

Keep the webbing even, neat and tight.

Continue until the full seat is covered, ending on top at the front right corner.

3 *Weaving*

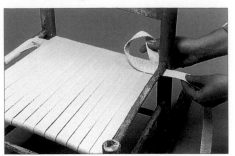

Slip the shuttle under the seat to the back right. Bring it up, over the back rung, then under the right-side rung.

Weave the first row by bringing the shuttle over the right rung. Pass it *over the first strip* of webbing and under the second. Continue this over-under motion across the full width.

Using a ruler (or stir stick, as shown here), prop up the alternating strips under which you will pass. When you finish a row, remove the stick and reposition it for the next row. This will make the weaving easier and help you to avoid errors.

Turn the chair upside-down and weave across the back of the seat, as you did for the front.

Turn the chair right-side-up again. Reposition the ruler or stick. Weave the second row by bringing the shuttle up over the right-side rung. Pass the shuttle *under the first strip* and over the second. Then continue across the full width of the seat.

4 Weaving, continued

Continue in this manner, alternating the over-under weaving pattern. Stop to check the pattern occasionally. Keep the weaving tight by pushing it together with the tip of the ruler or stick.

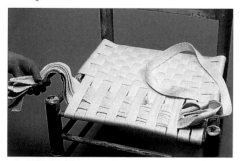

About halfway through the weaving, the shuttle may not fit through between the webbing. Take the webbing off the shuttle and pull it through in a loosely gathered bunch.

If the webbing isn't long enough and you need to join it, sew the ends together on the underside of the seat and tuck in any loose ends.

5 Finishing

Weave to the last row.

On the underside, weave halfway across the last row. Then cut the webbing and glue (or sew) the end down, tucking away any excess.

Backrest Cushions

Read This First

The decision to have a tailored or a shirred cushion on the seat's backrest is based on the style of the chair. A tailored cushion doesn't stand out. It is an integral part of the design of the chair. A shirred cushion, in contrast, commands attention. It makes a statement, giving the chair a showy, fashion-conscious sensibility. A tailored backrest cushion can be made from any type of fabric. A shirred backrest should be made from lightweight, finely woven fabric. The backrest can be finished decoratively with braid trim on the back side to hide staples, or by carefully gluing the finishing panel in place for a clean, crisp look.

MATERIALS

- plywood, ½ in. (1.25 cm) thick, good one side, to fit chair back (If the backrest is curved, reserve plywood from existing cushion.)
- high-density upholstery foam, 1 in. (2.5 cm) thick, cut to match the shape of the plywood
- fabric (To determine yardage, see step 2.)
- tape measure
- batting, 4 in. (10 cm) larger than the plywood both in length and in width
- stapler and ⅜ in. (1 cm) staples

- *for shirred cushion:* needle and thread
- hot-glue gun
- *for trimmed back:* 2 yd. (2 m) braid trim, 2 small pieces of tape
- dressmaker's pins
- screws (to reattach seat to chair), screwdriver
- small amount of paint to match fabric (for heads of screws)
- utility knife or X-acto knife
- *optional:* spray glue; scrap paper or dropsheet

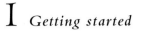

1 Getting started

For all cushions: Remove the fabric and foam from the underlying plywood. Clean the plywood as thoroughly as possible, removing any mold and staples.

Have a piece of high-density upholstery foam, 1 in. (2.5 cm) thick, cut to match the size and shape of the plywood. Although it is best to have the foam professionally cut, foam this thin can be cut with scissors.

2 Cutting fabric

For tailored cushions: Lay the foam (or the plywood) onto the wrong side of the fabric. If the design printed on the fabric is directional (vines climbing a wall, for example), it should run up, from bottom of backrest to top. Measure and mark a cutting line 3 in. (7.5 cm) from the foam. Do this around the full perimeter. Cut along the line.

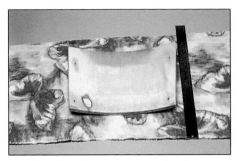

For shirred cushions: Measure the deepest section of the plywood backrest. Add 5 in. (12.5 cm). Cut fabric to this depth and to double the width of the backrest. Set the fabric aside.

For all cushions: Cut a piece of fabric 1 in. (2.5 cm) larger on all sides than the foam. This will be used to cover the back of the backrest cushion. If the design printed on the fabric is directional (vines climbing a wall, for example), it should run up, from bottom of backrest to top. Set the fabric aside.

3 Cutting batting, gluing foam

For all cushions: Cut batting 1½ in. (4 cm) larger on all sides than the foam. Notch the corners of the batting so that they dovetail when the batting is folded over the sides of the foam. Set the batting aside.

Optional: Gluing the foam to the plywood can reduce slippage. Lay down some scrap paper or a dropsheet and place the foam onto it. Check the directions on the spray-glue label for making a permanent bond. Spray the foam with glue.

Lay the gluey side of the foam onto the front side of the plywood.

4 Gluing batting

For all cushions. Optional: Lay the plywood and foam, foam-side-down, onto the batting. Using the spray glue, spray a section of the overhanging batting and fold the glued section up onto the side of the foam and plywood. Repeat until the batting is glued to the edges of the foam all the way around.

5 *Shirring*

For shirred cushions: By machine or by hand, sew along the top and bottom edges of the fabric and gather to the width of the seat back, plus 5 in. (12.5 cm).

6 *Stapling*

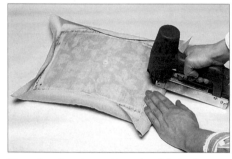

For tailored cushions: Lay the fabric face-down. Center the plywood/foam/batting section, batting-side-down, onto the wrong side of the fabric. Gently but firmly, pull the fabric onto the plywood and attach with one staple centered on each side.

7 *Stapling, continued*

For tailored cushions: Work around the cushion, adding staples equally on all sides. Keep the pressure even.

For shirred cushions: Don't staple the fabric at the sides yet, only at the top and bottom.

Occasionally turn the cushion to the front side and organize the gathers.

Staple the sides, with the fabric pulled taut. Pulling the fabric too tightly will disturb the gathers.

8 *Corners*

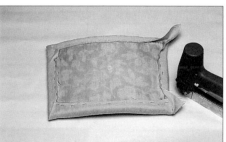

For all cushions: To make a neat corner, cut the point off the corner. Tuck one point into the overlap. Then fold the remaining point under. Staple in place.

9 *Finishing*

For all cushions: Find the fabric set aside for covering the back of the cushion. Fold and press the edges 2 in. (5 cm) to the wrong side.

To make a neat corner, notch the corner nearly to the crease. Fold one edge flat. Then fold the other edge over it, tucking the corner under.

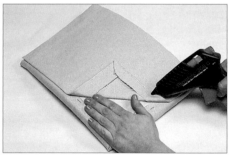

For a flat finish: Heat up the glue gun. *Be careful not to burn your fingers, especially if you are not experienced with a glue gun.* The glue becomes hot enough to cause deep burns, and the glue sticks and keeps burning.

Position the fabric, centered onto the back of the cushion, right-side-up. Pin at the corners. Unpin and lift one corner. With the glue gun at high heat, squeeze a narrow, neat bead just inside the folded edge of the fabric. Lay the corner down, allow the glue to cool and lift the next corner. Repeat until the back is glued on all the way around.

10 *Finishing, continued*

For a trimmed finish: Plug in the glue gun. Lay the fabric centered onto the back of the cushion, right-side-up. Staple the fabric to the back of the cushion, centering one staple on each of the four sides. Staples must be carefully placed at the edge of the fold of the fabric. Otherwise, they will not be covered by the trim. Work out from the positioning staples equally, stapling along the edges of the fabric on all four sides.

Wrap a small piece of tape around the end of the braid to prevent fraying. Carefully apply hot glue to the taped end of the braid, then slip this end under the edge of the fabric between two staples, hiding the tape. Working in sections, apply a bead of hot glue to the underside of the braid and lay the braid glue-side-down, hiding the staples and the folded edge of the fabric.

When the braid is glued on all the way around, cut it with 1 in. (2.5 cm) excess. Tape around the end. Apply glue to the end and tuck it into the gap with the other end, keeping the join as invisible as possible.

11 *Reattaching cushions*

For all cushions: In a color compatible with the fabric, paint the heads of the screws to be used for reattaching the seat.

Position the seat back into the chair. Mark where the screw holes will go.

Using a sharp utility knife or X-acto knife, cut a tiny hole at each of the marks. The cut should break only one or two threads, allowing the screws to pass through the fabric. If these holes are not cut, the fabric will bunch when the screws are screwed in.

Position the seat back in place and screw in the screws.

DESKS

Your desk defines your domain. Whether you use it for a home office, for homework or for the simple pleasure of writing a personal note, it should reflect your personal style. Make it country, avant-garde, English cottage or businesslike. Desks are somewhat like tables and dressers combined: lots of drawer fronts for finishing, and an expansive top to treat creatively. Older ones aren't properly designed for a computer, but don't throw out that elderly desk. Update it by adding a monitor holder and a keyboard tray, available at office furniture and computer stores.

A Subtle Distinction

UNDERSTATED TEXTURE POLISHES
A STREAMLINED DESK

Lacking trim, panels or other details that could draw the eye of the onlooker
away from peeling veneer, this understated desk demanded a treatment to
complement its clean lines, yet create visual interest with tone-on-tone
texture. As textural treatments go, dragging has become a classic — and
it's a surprisingly simple effect to achieve. The antiqued gold leaf
adds polish and finish.

Read This First

Texturing is based on a simple principle: wet paint is lifted off a background color with any tool that will produce an even, all-over texture. A crumpled plastic bag can be used in a technique called smooshing, a twisted rag used for ragging, a comb for combing. Even a feather duster can be used to produce texture. The dragging technique shown in this project is easy and can produce wonderfully subtle results. Paint, with glaze added, is applied over a base coat of a similar tone. A brush is then dragged through the wet top coat, producing bristle marks. The degree of subtlety depends on both color choice and brush choice. Similar shades and intensities of color create the most subtle contrast. A soft brush gives finer and more subtle texture lines than a stiff one. When you first drag the paint, the texture may not be very apparent. As the paint-glaze mixture dries, the paint will shrink somewhat, creating larger gaps in the bristle lines. This technique looks best when finished with one or more coats of water-based varnish. It produces a smooth, glasslike surface and provides richness and depth to the color.

MATERIALS

- quart (litre) high-adhesion, water-based primer
- quart (litre) eggshell or satin finish latex paint for base coat, taupe
- painting tools: paint brush, small roller, roller tray
- easy-release painter's tape, 1 in. (2.5 cm) wide
- yardstick or other straight edge and pencil
- plastic for cutting triangles (grocery bags are okay), masking tape
- pint (.5 litre) glaze, paint pot
- measuring tool such as a large serving spoon
- quart (litre) eggshell or satin finish latex paint for texture, olive green
- stir stick
- small whisk brush (Softer brushes can be used for a subtle effect.)
- quart (litre) non-yellowing, water-based varnish
- *optional:* extender
- *optional:* utility knife
- *optional:* fine sandpaper (220 grade), fine brush for touch-ups
- *optional:* gold leaf and compatible sealer and adhesive
- *optional:* tube of acrylic (for antiquing gold leaf), burnt umber
- *optional:* rag or paper towel

BEFORE

A fantastic 1950s desk, solidly constructed, with simple, pleasing lines. The veneer top was loose and flaking, however, requiring extensive filling and sanding.

1 Painting the base coat

Refer to *Painting Basics* (page 34). Prepare, prime and paint the desk with two coats of taupe latex paint. Allow to dry.

2 Masking

Each section of the design for dragging must be masked. Mask a border on the desktop. Using easy-release painter's tape, tape the perimeter of the desk, matching the edge of the tape to the edge of the desk.

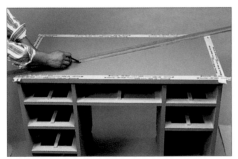

Divide the top into four triangles. Lay a yardstick or other straight edge diagonally across the desk, from one corner of tape to the opposite corner of tape, and lightly draw a line along the yardstick. Repeat, linking the other two corners.

The east-west triangles will be dragged first. Use the easy-release tape to mask inside, along the lines of the north-south triangles.

Cut plastic triangles to fit within the north-south triangles and tape them all around with masking tape, leaving no gaps. Check to be sure that no tape or plastic overlaps the east-west triangles.

Position the drawers in their slots. Decide on a pattern for the drawer fronts. This pattern can either match or be different from the top. Tape a border around the edges of the drawers and mask around the sections to be dragged, as you did for the top.

3 Dragging the desktop

Using a large serving spoon or similar measuring tool, scoop one part glaze and four parts olive green latex paint into a paint pot. Stir well. If you want to slow the drying time of the paint, giving you more time to work, add extender.

Using a paint brush, brush the paint mixture onto one of the east-west triangles on the top of the desk. Apply the paint thickly and evenly.

Stand at the end of the desk. Gripping the whisk brush firmly, reach forward, planting the whisk just beyond the triangle. Drag the whisk straight toward you and over the edge of the desk, scoring the paint with the bristles. Wipe excess paint from the bristles. Drag a second swath, overlapping the first grooves slightly so that there are no gaps.

Work quickly, dragging the full

triangle before the paint dries. Crooked or uneven drags can be redone easily, as long as the paint is still very wet.

Repeat with the opposite triangle. Remove the tape and plastic when the surface of the paint has set, but while the paint is still soft. Allow to dry.

4 *Dragging drawer fronts*

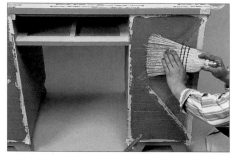

Repeat step 3 on the drawer fronts. Keep the drawers in place, to be certain the grooves in the dragging match from drawer to drawer. Laying the desk on its back can make the dragging easier. (If the desk is heavy, recruit a helper.) Allow to dry.

5 *Dragging remaining portions*

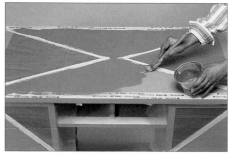

Repeat step 2, masking the east-west triangles on the dresser top and the dragged portions on the drawer fronts. Cover these areas with plastic.

Paint the north-south triangles with the paint mixture. Drag the north-south triangles at a right angle to the east-west triangles.

Remove the tape and plastic while the paint is still soft.

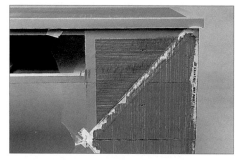

Drag the drawer fronts, dragging the remaining design section at right angles to the previous dragging. Remove the tape.

Note: If the drawers are stuck together with paint, use a utility knife (nice new, sharp blade, please) to separate them by scoring the paint where they are joined.

Lightly sand lumps and bumps smooth (where the drawers were stuck together) with fine sandpaper. Where necessary touch up with paint, using a fine brush.

6 *Gold leafing*

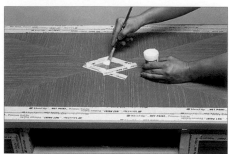

Optional: Gold leaf can polish and finish a textured treatment. Using the easy-release painter's tape, mask a narrow border around the dragged rectangle. Tape a square at the center, if desired. Repeat on the drawer fronts.

Using the gold leaf adhesive, paint the masked-off areas. Allow the adhesive to dry according to the instructions on the label. It will remain very tacky.

Lay a section of gold leaf onto the adhesive, burnishing it with your fingers. Tear off any large pieces of excess gilt. Repeat until all the masked areas are leafed.

Antique the gold leaf, if desired. Mix burnt umber paint with water to a thin consistency. Apply the paint over the gold leaf with a brush or rag. Before the paint dries, wipe it with a slightly moist rag or paper towel, leaving a thin film of paint on the gold leaf.

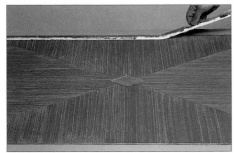

Remove the tape and paint the gold leaf with sealer.

7 *Varnishing*

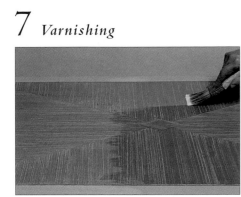

Enrich the color, smooth the texture and protect your paint job by applying two or more coats of non-yellowing, water-based varnish. (See *Varnishing,* page 48.)

Attach the hardware.

Texturing a background before applying a paint or decorating treatment adds subtle interest. Shown here, block printing over smooshing. (See Sheer Delight, page 259.)

Letter Perfect

Découpage Transforms A Writing Desk Into A Fanciful Treasure

Charming and inviting, découpage of wrapping paper and deep-forest green paint accentuates this desk's detail and molding, while providing a cozy English-country atmosphere. A lucky find of specialty wrapping paper with Sunday afternoon letter-writing motifs – postage stamps, typewriters, teapots and clocks – was used to découpage this desk. If similar motifs are hard to locate, real postage stamps mixed with old postcards from flea markets, or even old letters – positioned at random – make a quirky and eclectic substitute.

Read This First

The desk is painted with a color to coordinate with the découpaged materials. Areas to be découpaged are left white, because color, especially deep color, can show through the paper. If your desk has a plastic laminate finish, use melamine paint. (See *Melamine Paint,* page 27.) Then two types of découpage are applied. The drawer fronts are completely covered with sheets of paper, while the desktop is treated to traditional découpage, with carefully cut-out images pasted on in a random pattern. The background of the desktop is painted to match the background of the découpage paper, making the cutting-out stage fast and easy. The instructions call for wallpaper paste to adhere the découpage. Those who are brave can avoid this gooey step and use spray glue. Read the glue can's directions for permanent adhesion, and remember that spray glue allows only one chance to position the image, and no opportunity to remove it. Wallpaper paste is more forgiving. All découpage must be varnished for protection.

BEFORE

A well-built, solid wood writing desk with interesting feet and trim. The badly scarred top finish and loose base trim provide a good opportunity for a découpage cover-up.

MATERIALS

- for découpage: wrapping paper, or posters, or paper items such as stamps, postcards, pictures and letters
- quart (litre) high-adhesion, water-based primer
- easy-release painter's tape
- quart (litre) eggshell finish latex paint for base coat, to coordinate with découpage materials
- painting tools: brush, small roller, tray
- latex or acrylic paint for desktop, to match background of découpage pictures (step 2)
- small, sharp scissors
- small quantity of cellulose-based wallpaper paste
- small, soft paint brush; household sponges
- X-acto knife and ruler
- fine-point artist's brush
- quart (litre) non-yellowing, water-based varnish
- fine sandpaper (220 grade), tack cloth

1 *Painting the base coat*

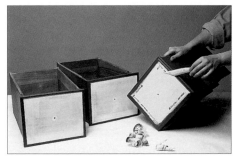

Refer to *Painting Basics* (page 34). Prime the desk with high-adhesion primer and allow it to dry.

Using easy-release painter's tape, mask off areas to be découpaged, such as the drawer fronts and the top, so that they will not be painted. Otherwise, the paint color could show through the découpage paper and give the découpage a muddy appearance.

Paint the desk with the coordinating color of latex paint. Allow to dry and remove the tape.

2 *Random découpage*

To découpage the desktop with small random images, mask around the edges of the desktop. Paint the desktop a color to match the background of the wrapping paper.

Here the background was painted a cream shade and sponged with a warm brick tone.

Using small, sharp scissors, cut out the images from the wrapping paper, cutting as close to the images as possible. Or use other paper images such as postage stamps and postcards.

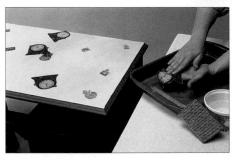

Position the images on the desktop. Mix some wallpaper paste. Follow the instructions on the container, but mix only a small fraction of the total package. Use the sponge or your hands to apply paste to both sides of an image, leaving no dry spots.

Lay the pasty image onto the desktop. Gently smooth the image from the center to the sides, using a damp sponge. Don't scrub – the surface printing could rub off. Paste all images down and allow them to dry. Sometimes the paper will wrinkle, but don't smooth it out. It will shrink and flatten as it dries. Lifting or rubbing will tear and crease the paper.

3 *Sheet découpage*

Découpage the drawer fronts. Since drawer sizes can vary, measure all the drawer fronts. Using a ruler and a sharp X-acto knife, measure, mark and cut out squares of wrapping paper to fit the drawers, keeping in mind the placements of images.

Mix some wallpaper paste. Follow the instructions on the container, but mix only a small fraction of the total package. Use the sponge or paint brush to apply an even coat of paste (avoid blobs) onto a drawer front, then onto both sides of the image. There should be no dry spots.

Position the paper onto the drawer front. Start at one corner, line up an adjacent side, and then lay the paper flat. Gently smooth the surface with a damp sponge, pushing out any air pockets. Start at the center and work out to the edges. Don't scrub. The printed image could rub off.

The paper may have stretched but that's normal, so don't be alarmed. Let it dry. It will be trimmed later. Attempting to trim it while wet will produce a ragged edge.

Although the paper has been smoothed, it may become wrinkly. The wrinkles will go away as the paper dries, shrinking and tightening in the process. Trying to stretch or smooth the paper will tear or crease it. Allow the paste to dry.

4 *Trimming*

If the paper stretched, or if your measurements were slightly off, the paper may turn out to be too big for the drawer front. When the paper is thoroughly dry, trim off the excess using the X-acto knife and ruler. Use a new, sharp blade. Instead of trying to cut through in one slice, make several light cuts along one line. The blade will be less likely to slip off course.

5 *Finishing*

Using a fine-point artist's brush, make any needed touch-ups.

Apply varnish to the découpaged surfaces of the desk. Découpaged surfaces must be varnished for protection. If you wish, varnish the full desk. Using the non-yellowing, water-based varnish, apply two coats. Sand lightly with fine sandpaper after the second coat. Wipe away dust with a tack cloth and apply another coat. (See *Varnishing,* page 48.)

Découpage on drawer fronts has tremendous impact when a full-sized art poster is used, straddling all the drawers. Use this technique on a dresser or cabinet with plain doors. (See Posterity, page 209.)

Office Romance

FROM ORDINARY TO STUNNING — A DESK IS CLAD WITH GLORIOUS FABRIC

Covering a piece of furniture with fabric is easier than the elegant results would have you believe. Unusual, daring, breathtaking — a desk or dresser completely covered in rich, tactile fabric has it all and more. Decorator fabric shops offer an infinite choice of patterns and color combinations, allowing complete customizing of a desk or dresser. The intrinsically romantic and delicate properties of the fabric are preserved and protected with a coating of crystal clear varnish.

Read This First

If your fabric is narrower than the combined front and sides of the desk or dresser, sew two widths of fabric together matching the pattern, and press the seam open. If the fabric isn't sewn, there will be an obvious join on the front of the unit. The desk or dresser you choose should be very simple, without lumpy trims or decorations. It should have drawers with overhanging fronts, not the type that are set in. Wrapping fabric onto the sides of set-in drawers will cause the drawers to bind; that is, if they'll even fit back into their slots.

The best fabrics for this job are decorator fabrics in stable weaves, not knits – neither too heavy nor lightweight, and without a nap (such as velvet or corduroy would have). Stripes and intricate patterns can create problems when matching the pattern for a stack of drawers. Best bets are large, somewhat random patterns or tiny repetitive patterns such as polka dots. Consider mixes. Many companies print fabrics in coordinating patterns of small and large prints in the same colors. These can be used in a complementary way. Cover the background with the small print, and the drawers and top with the large print.

MATERIALS

- screwdriver
- 3 yd. (3 m) decorator fabric, 54 to 60 in. (135 to 150 cm) wide (quantity may vary according to size of furniture)
- ruler and pencil
- scissors
- cellulose-based wallpaper paste
- plastic dropsheet
- large, soft paint brush
- household sponge
- X-acto knife
- dressmaker's pins
- quart (litre) non-yellowing, water-based varnish
- fine sandpaper (220 grade), tack cloth
- *optional:* quart (litre) each: high-adhesion, water-based primer; white latex paint (step 1)
- *optional:* painting tools – paint brush, small roller, roller tray
- *optional:* staple gun and staples
- *optional:* access to photocopier
- *optional:* hot-glue gun or carpenter's glue

BEFORE

A 1970s-vintage student desk with a melamine top. The flat, flush-fit drawers and lack of detail make it ideal for covering with fabric.

1 *Preparation*

If possible, remove the desktop by taking out all drawers and turning the desk upside-down. (Recruit help if the desk is heavy.) Unscrew all screws that hold the top in place.

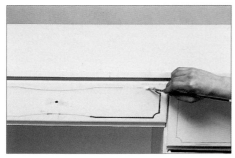

Remove all hardware and sand any lumps or bumps off the surface of the desk. Even very small bumps will pucker the fabric.

If the fabric has areas that are pale in tone, variations in the color of the desk will show through the fabric. To avoid this problem, use a water-based primer to paint any areas that are not pure white, covering stains and any printed decorations. If the imperfections show through the primer at all, recoat the areas with white paint. If the finish on the desk is a color other than white, prime the desk and paint it white. (Refer to *Painting Basics,* page 34.) Allow to dry.

2 *Cutting fabric*

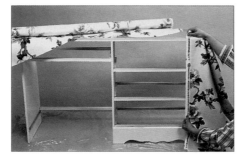

Hold the fabric against the front of the desk, measuring and marking the height plus a 2 in. (5 cm) allowance for both the top and the bottom. If the design on the fabric is directional (vines climbing a trellis, for example), position the fabric right-way-up. Cut straight across the fabric.

Check that the fabric is wide enough to cover the front (where the drawers go) and two adjoining sides. (See *Read This First,* previous page.)

3 *Wallpaper paste*

Following the manufacturer's instructions, mix a small bucket or bowl of the wallpaper paste.

Lay the cut piece of fabric wrong-side-up on a plastic dropsheet. Using the large, soft paint brush, spread an even layer of paste over the fabric, saturating it.

4 *Fitting fabric to the desk front*

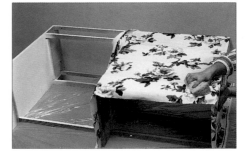

Tip the desk onto its back (drawers removed) and drape the pasted fabric over the body of the desk. The fabric should cover the front where the drawers belong, the outer side of the desk, and the adjacent side of the knee hole, with excess to wrap onto the back. Smooth the fabric with a moist sponge, eliminating air pockets and keeping the fabric damp. The principle of this technique is to keep surfaces smooth where they will be seen, and cut edges wrapped and pasted where they will not be seen.

Finish the bottom edges of the desk by pasting and smoothing the excess fabric and wrapping it to the inside of the desk.

This desk has a curvy bottom edge along the front. To make the fabric conform, multiple cuts were made along the edge. Then the fabric was smoothed and pasted to the underside.

5 *Finishing drawer openings*

Using a sharp X–acto knife, cut a small X in the center of a drawer opening. Using scissors, expand the X, cutting to the corners of the opening.

Trim the four V-shapes of fabric and smooth them over the edges, wrapping them to the inside of the desk.

Repeat for all drawer openings. If sections begin to dry, add more paste as needed and keep the fabric moist with a damp sponge.

6 *Fitting fabric, continued*

Stand the desk upright. Trim the fabric to a neat overlap along the top and back edges of the desk. Wrap it over the edge to the inside, and paste it down.

Keep corners neat by cutting away excess fabric, then folding and pasting in place. Corners that will not be seen can be stapled.

Check over the fabric, making sure it is pasted securely in place with no loose edges or air pockets.

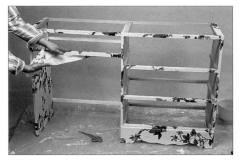

Continue pasting fabric to the rest of the desk, matching the pattern as you go. Where fabric joins, fold the edge under, like a narrow seam, to avoid a raw edge. Allow the paste to dry. As it dries, check that it doesn't lift. If lifting occurs, wet the fabric well with a sponge dipped in paste and smooth it down.

7 *Cutting for drawer fronts*

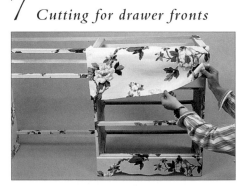

Because of the necessary wraparounds on each drawer front, the repeats on your fabric must be cut from three separate, repeat areas of fabric to match the pattern of the fabric already laminated to the desk.

Place the top drawer in position. Cut a generous piece of fabric, larger than the drawer front, that matches the section of fabric pattern already laminated to the body of the desk.

Drape the fabric over the drawer front, matching the pattern to the body of the desk. With the fabric in place, mark the four corners of the drawer front with pins.

Remove the fabric with the pins in place and trim some of the excess fabric away, leaving at least 1 in. (2.5 cm) as an overlap. Apply paste to the fabric.

8 *Laminating drawer fronts*

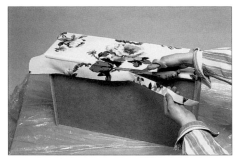

Drape the fabric onto the drawer front, placing the marker pins at the corners. Check that the drawer and the fabric are both right-way-up. Trim the excess fabric again, leaving enough to wrap over onto the inside edge of the drawer. Remove the pins.

To create a neat corner, clip the fabric to the corner of the drawer front. Smooth one side under, pasting it to the inside edge.

Then fold the point of the second side under. Smooth this side onto the inside edge.

9 Covering the desktop

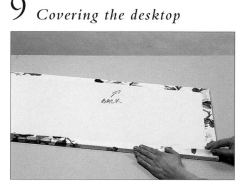

Cut fabric for the top as follows. Check that the fabric pattern matches the body of the desk and that it runs in the right direction, from front to back. Check also that there is enough overlap onto the wrong side for raw edges to be hidden when the top is reattached to the body. If the fabric isn't wide enough, try running the pattern lengthwise. Some large patterns are acceptable either way. As an alternative, consider painting the desktop a coordinating color. You could also photocopy the pattern of the fabric and

découpage it on the top at random. (See *Victorian Secrets,* page 75.) Paste the fabric to the desktop, folding and trimming to make neat corners. Allow to dry.

As the drawer fronts dry, check that the overlap onto the inside edge is stuck down. If it lifts, glue it with a hot-glue gun or carpenter's glue. *If using a glue gun, be careful not to burn your fingers.* The glue becomes hot enough to cause deep burns, and it sticks and keeps burning.

10 Varnishing

When the paste is thoroughly dry, all fabric areas must be varnished for protection. Apply a coat of non-yellowing, water-based varnish to all fabric surfaces. Allow the varnish to dry completely. Apply a second coat of varnish to all fabric surfaces. Allow to dry.

Using a fine sandpaper, very lightly sand the varnished surfaces. Don't be alarmed by a cloudy effect on the fabric's colors. Wipe all residue and dust from the sanding with a tack cloth. Varnish again. If the fabric is still porous, repeat the sanding and varnishing.

Reattach the desktop and the hardware.

Art in Craft

ATTENTION-GRABBING LAYERED COLOR IS OFFSET BY CRAFTED COPPER

Acid green, layered over brilliant blue paint and spiced with crafted and stenciled copper, renders an outdated desk a vibrant piece of contemporary art. This desk has aggressive texture, color and pattern — elements that create a novel, fast-forward piece. Not for the faint of heart, this combination of tactile materials, random stencils and vivid colors takes some nerve. But accolades from admirers will reward your daring decision.

Read This First

A cid and cool colors rub up against each other in this paint technique. The paint treatment consists of layering color, then lightly sanding the coats with a hard plastic stripping sponge to expose the underlying colors. If your desk has a plastic laminate finish, use melamine paint for the base coat. (See *Melamine Paint,* page 27.) Also demonstrated is dry brushing, a technique with an effect similar to sanded paint. The stenciling can be done in any contrasting color or in a metallic leaf – gold, copper or silver – with a purchased or homemade stencil. For metallic leaf, you'll need the compatible leaf, adhesive and sealer. For the copper cut-outs buy one or more sheets of copper, the type used for copper-burnishing kits. You will also need copper etching fluid and patina in blue or green. These chemical treatments, used to oxidize the copper and produce a patina, are available at art supply and craft stores.

MATERIALS

- quart (litre) high-adhesion, water-based primer
- eggshell finish latex paint, 1 quart (litre) each: brilliant blue, moss green, chartreuse green
- painting tools: paint brush, small roller, roller tray
- plastic paint-stripping sponge
- rag or scrap paper
- inexpensive square-tipped artist's brush, ½ in. (1.25 cm) wide
- purchased stencil, or stencil plastic or cardboard (step 4)
- spray glue; scrap paper or dropsheet
- copper leaf and compatible adhesive and sealer
- sheet of thin copper, heavy scissors
- etching fluid for copper (often called "Metal Master," and available at art supply and craft stores)
- rag or paint brush
- patina blue or green fluid (available at art supply and craft stores), soft paint brush
- sealer (made by manufacturer of the patina)
- small hammer and small brass nails
- quart (litre) non-yellowing, water-based varnish
- *optional:* needle-nosed pliers

BEFORE

Lacking personality, this mediocre desk deserves some zip.

1 *Painting*

Refer to *Painting Basics* (page 34). Prepare, prime and paint the body of the desk with two coats of brilliant blue latex paint. Paint the drawer fronts with two coats of moss green. Allow to dry.

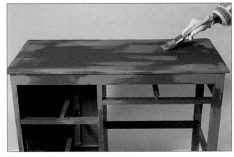

Paint moss green over the body of the desk, brushing it on at random. Allow to dry.

Paint chartreuse in random areas over the drawer fronts. Allow to dry.

2 *Painting and distressing*

Paint one coat of chartreuse over the body of the desk, with as much coverage as possible. When the paint is dry to the touch, firmly buff it with the paint-stripping sponge, removing layers of paint and exposing the undercoats in areas where the desk would naturally show wear, such as along all trim, on corners and in random spots on the top and sides. Try not to rub through all layers to the primer. If you accidentally do, however, you can touch up areas later.

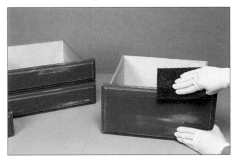

Paint the drawer fronts with the brilliant blue. Buff through the paint, exposing various layers.

3 *Dry-brush technique*

Using a dry-brush technique add more contrasting color to the surface, if desired. Dip the artist's brush into the paint. Wipe excess paint onto a rag or piece of scrap paper. Brush the remaining paint onto the desk surface. This is a lot like wiping out a used brush, leaving a thin, some-what transparent layer of paint on the surface. The paint will be dense where you start, becoming thinner the more you brush. Make any touch-ups as required.

4 *Stenciling copper leaf*

Add stenciled copper leaf designs onto the desk in a random fashion. Use a purchased stencil, or cut a design from stencil plastic (available at craft stores) or light-weight cardboard. For ease of stenciling, coat the back of the stencil with spray glue. Allow the stencil to sit for an hour or more until the glue is lightly tacky. Lay the stencil onto the desk and paint the image area with adhesive for the copper leaf. Remove the stencil. Repeat in all locations where a stenciled pattern is desired. Allow the adhesive to set. It will remain very tacky.

Lay a sheet of copper leaf onto the adhesive. Burnish it with your fingers.

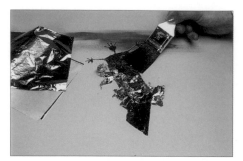

Using a small paint brush, brush excess copper leaf from the edges of the image. Repeat for all stenciled areas of adhesive. Using the sealer for the copper leaf, paint the stenciled copper leaf designs.

5 *Sheet copper*

Draw patterns and trace them, or cut shapes freehand from the sheet copper. *When cutting this copper, be extremely careful.* The edges can be very sharp. Injuries are more painful and annoying than paper cuts. (Wearing a cast-off pair of leather gloves can help protect you.)

Lay the cut-outs right-side-up on paper and paint them with etching fluid.

Using a rag or a paint brush, coat the cut-outs with either patina blue or green. Allow to dry and to turn color. Check the instructions on the jar of sealer to determine the length of time you need to wait before sealing (often three days).

Using a dry soft paint brush, brush away excess patina.

Coat the patina side of the copper with sealer. Allow to dry.

Using a small hammer and small brass nails, nail the copper cut-outs in place on the desk. If the nails are very short, use needle-nosed pliers to hold the nails while hammering.

Protect the paint, smooth the edges of the copper pieces and enrich color by painting the desk with two or three coats of non-yellowing, water-based varnish. (See *Varnishing*, page 48.)

Attach the hardware.

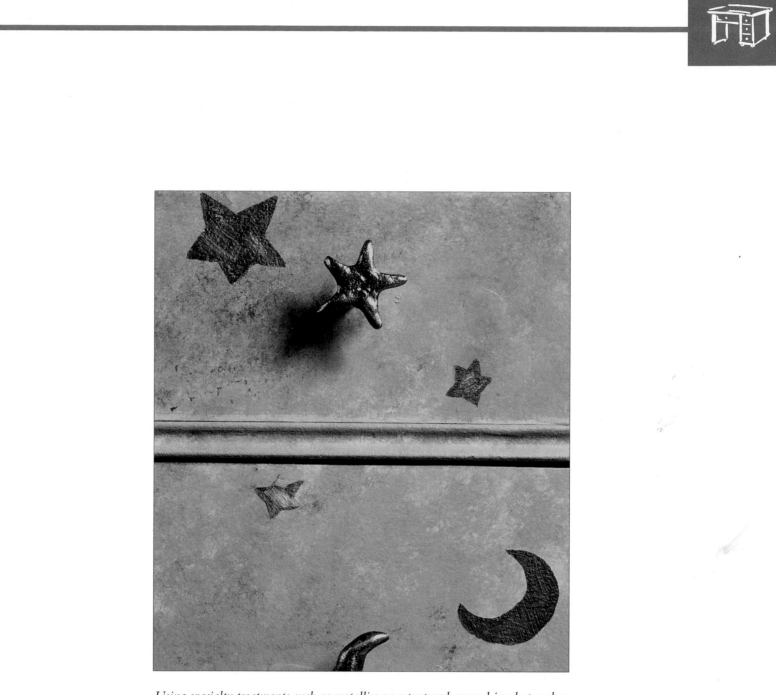

*Using specialty treatments such as metallics on a textured ground is what makes
the difference between painter and artist. Shown here, reverse-stenciling on a
sponge-painted background. (See Vanity Flair, page 203.)*

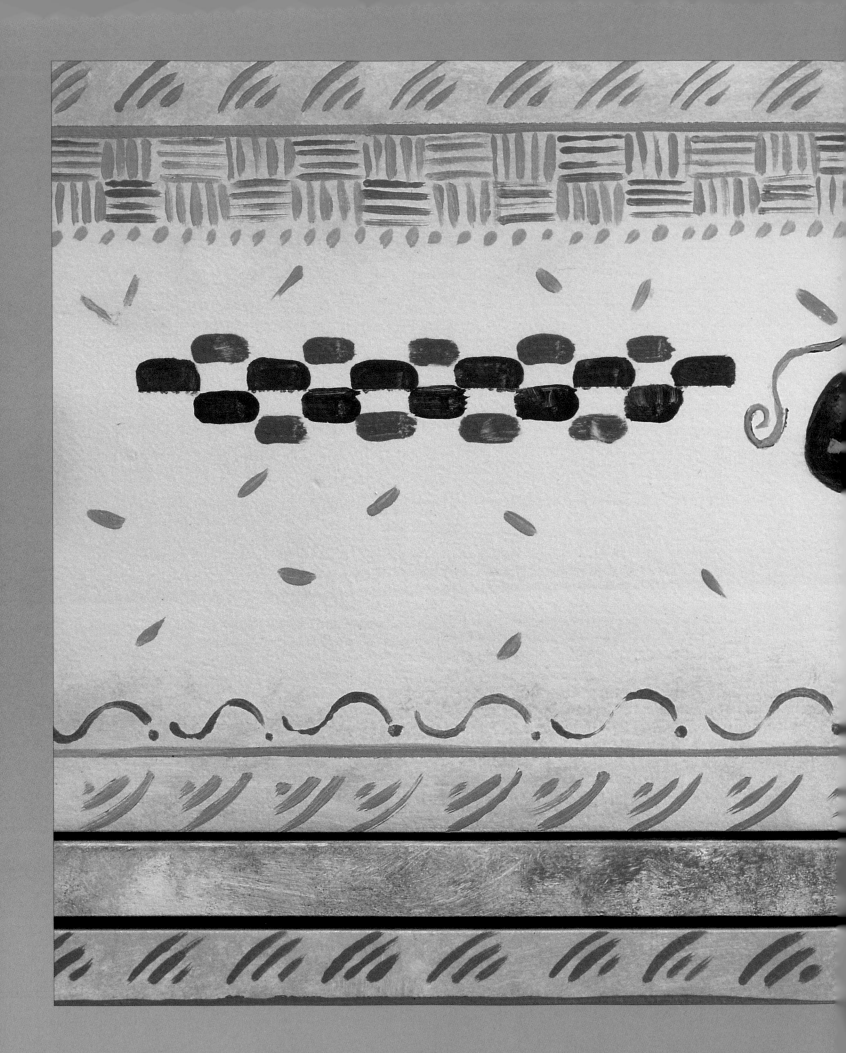

DRESSERS

Whether you're mad for Matisse, crazy for Klimt or pleased by Picasso, you can finish a dresser to suit your taste. Ornamental pieces with decorative moldings accommodate interesting, involved paint techniques. Plain fronts and smooth pieces are perfect for mounting large pictorial posters, giving any style a dramatic makeover. And don't just put a sock in it; a dresser treated to a unique, creative paint job needn't remain in the bedroom. Small-scale dressers are ideal for catching cast-offs in an entryway. Adding a small bookcase to the top of a dresser can transform it into a kitchen or dining room hutch.

Band Aid

BOLD BANDS IN NEUTRAL SHADES
REDEFINE A SIMPLE HIGHBOY

Loosely stroked-on bands of subdued color and oversized knobs of black
cut glass take this dresser to a new plateau, transcending the predictable
pattern of rigid awning stripes. This is a modern approach to striping,
moving toward the hand-crafted and away from machine-made stripes.

Read This First

This very fast, easy makeover works best on a piece with simple lines, a flat front with set-in drawers, and little trim or other detail. Many 1950s-vintage pieces are perfect for this treatment. A base-coat color is painted first, in the palest of your trio of colors. If your dresser has a plastic laminate finish, use melamine paint. (See *Melamine Paint,* page 27.) Wide painter's tape is used as a guide for painting the stripes, eliminating nearly all tedious measuring. The whole appeal of this piece is its obvious departure from perfection. It should fly in the face of convention and look like the painter had great fun painting it. It takes some discipline to allow this technique to become painterly – to keep yourself from straightening up and making your work too neat. The hand-painted, loosely-defined look of this technique can test one's patience, because the full effect isn't apparent until the very end. Hardware that makes a statement is a must. Choose outrageous colored plastic drawer pulls or oversized closet door pulls. Really showy hardware in wild colors and styles can be hard to find. Check sale bins for pieces that can be mixed or matched.

BEFORE

A usable wooden highboy of average quality and little personality. Add neutrals – taupe, off-white and black – with punch.

MATERIALS

- quart (litre) high-adhesion, water-based primer
- quart (litre) eggshell finish latex paint in a bone shade
- painting tools: 1½ in. (4 cm) wide paint brush, small roller, roller tray
- tape measure and pencil
- easy-release painter's tape, 2 in. (5 cm) wide (For narrow stripes, purchase narrower tape.)
- pint (.5 litre) acrylic (mars black) or latex (black) paint
- fine-point artist's brush
- pint (.5 litre) acrylic or latex paint, taupe
- quart (litre) non-yellowing, water-based varnish
- outstanding hardware
- *optional:* foam brush

1 *Painting the base coat*

Refer to *Painting Basics* (page 34). Prepare, prime and paint the dresser with two coats of the bone-colored latex paint. (If using colors other than the ones specified, use the palest color for the base coat.)

2 *Masking*

Paint the black stripes first. Begin by measuring the center of the dresser's front and top, marking points in several spots.

Use easy-release tape. Beginning at the top-back, lay the tape across the top and down the front of the dresser, with the center of the tape over the marks.

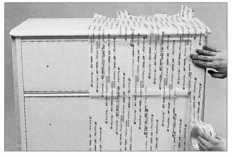

Lay another piece of tape next to the center piece, with the edges just touching but not overlapping. Continue laying strips until the full front and top of the dresser are covered. Do not worry if the tape doesn't stick perfectly to the surface.

3 *Painting black stripes*

Remove the pieces of tape on either side of the center piece. Continue, removing every second piece of tape.

Using black acrylic or latex paint, paint the black stripes. Thin the paint if necessary, so that it flows from the brush. Dip the paint brush into the black paint. Run the brush between two pieces of tape across the top and down the front, crossing the drawers, dividers and trim in one long stroke if possible. Avoid painting over the tape, using it only as a guide for painting between. Repeat, painting between all pieces of tape. The lines *should* be imperfect. Allow the paint to dry, then determine whether the stripes need a second coat. Remove the tape. Resist the urge to neaten the edges of the stripes.

4 *Painting taupe stripes*

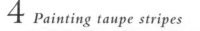

Using taupe paint and a fine-point artist's brush, paint freehand stripes next to the black stripes. These taupe stripes should look like a shadow, softening the overall effect of the black stripes. Lay the dresser on its back to make this stripe painting easier. (If your dresser is heavy, ask a friend to lend a hand.)

Optional: This 1950s-vintage dresser has grooved trim at the corners. This feature was highlighted by first painting the grooves with taupe. Then a foam brush was used to accent the raised portions in black.

5 *Striping the sides*

Repeat steps 2 and 3, taping the sides of the dresser and painting with taupe stripes.

6 *Varnishing*

To protect the paint and add richness to the color, varnish the dresser with non-yellowing, water-based varnish. (See *Varnishing*, page 48.)

Attach the new hardware.

Using tape as a painting guide need not be limited to the bold stripes demonstrated in this project. Shown above, decorative borders and linear motifs were painted in this manner, then sprinkled with fanciful dots and dashes, all in subdued pastels.
(See Peaches on Cream, page 215.)

Vanity Flair

GIVE THEM THE MOON AND THE STARS
WITH UNIQUE REVERSE-STENCILS

String a milky way of magical copper-gold stars and moons on a suedelike painted background to enchant a bedroom. These universally favored motifs, placed at random, give any dated furniture, especially dressers or vanities, an opulent and contemporary sensibility. The foil-like quality of a brushed-on metallic galaxy provides a stark, glowing counterpoint to a soft, sponge-painted background in hazy tones of smoke or neutral beiges.

Read This First

Traditional stenciling techniques give you a uniform, smooth coat of paint. To obtain a more brush-painted effect, use a reverse-stenciling technique. The color (copper) of the stenciled image is painted in position first. Then, self-adhesive cut-out images (decals) of moons and stars are stuck onto the copper paint. The base-coat color is painted and sponge painted over the moon and star decals and the surrounding area. Finally, the decals are removed to reveal brush-painted motifs that provide a perfect counterpoint to the soft, sponge-painted background. Sponge painting furniture differs from sponging a wall. The technique is similar, but the scale is much smaller. Try to find a natural or synthetic sponge that has small pores to give you a less ragged, more refined texture. And while the motif of the moon and stars is a universal favorite, ideal for this stenciling technique, many other simple shapes will work nicely too. (Patterns for the stencils are on page 207.)

BEFORE

A 1950s waterfall-style dresser set, but without the beautiful inlay of the better-quality dressers and vanities of its era. Instead, this set was covered in a peculiar bumpy finish made from a sprayed-on resinlike product.

MATERIALS

- quart (litre) high-adhesion, water-based primer
- painting tools: paint brush, small roller, roller tray
- easy-release painter's tape, 2 in. (5 cm) wide
- marker and scissors
- tubes of acrylics, iridescent copper and gold
- inexpensive, medium-sized square-tipped artist's brush
- quart (litre) eggshell finish latex paint, off-white (step 4)
- quart (litre) eggshell finish latex paint, taupe
- tubes of acrylics, raw sienna and yellow oxide
- flat containers for paints
- synthetic or natural sponge for sponge painting
- X-acto knife
- fine-point artist's brush
- quart (litre) non-yellowing, water-based varnish
- *optional:* pint (.5 litre) latex paint, slate blue
- *optional:* tubes of acrylics, Payne's gray and pthalo blue

1 Priming

Refer to *Painting Basics* (page 34). Prepare and prime, but *do not paint* the dresser.

2 Cutting reverse-stencil decals

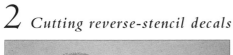

Trace the patterns on page 207 onto a piece of easy-release painter's tape. Cut five pieces of tape and layer them, sticking the pattern tracings on top. Cut out the patterns, through all layers of tape. Set the decals aside. You won't know exactly how many decals you will need until you apply them to the dresser.

3 Placing reverse-stencil decals

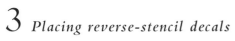

With the drawers in place in the dresser, paint sites for the moon and star motifs by brushing patches in a random pattern onto the dresser, using the square-tipped artist's brush and the copper and gold

acrylics. Rather than mixing the colors, take some paint from each tube directly onto the brush. Brushstrokes are desirable. Check that the patches are large enough to accommodate the moon and stars decals. Allow to dry.

One by one, stick the decals onto the copper and gold patches, until each patch has a decal. Cut more decals if needed.

4 Painting

Note: The instructions are for painting the background a tan shade. For a stormy-blue background, substitute the optional blue and gray paints. (See step 7.)

Refer to *Painting Basics* (page 34). Using the paint brush and roller and the off-white latex paint, paint the dresser with one coat of paint, painting over the moon and stars decals. Get as much coverage as possible with this coat. This will be the base coat. When sponge painting, the base-coat color is the one that shows the least. Allow to dry.

Note: If painting the interiors of drawers, give them a second coat. If you do not wish to sponge paint the dresser, apply a second coat of off-white paint and remove the decals when the paint is dry to the touch, but still soft. Go to step 8.

5 Sponge painting

Starting on the top, sponge paint the dresser in sections. Begin sponging when the latex paint is dry to the touch. Pour some taupe latex paint into a flat container. In another container, squeeze a mound each of raw sienna and yellow oxide acrylics. Glaze and extender may be added to the paint, if desired. (For information, see *Glaze* and *Extender,* page 28.) Tear off a chunk from the sponge, about the size of a tennis ball. Dampen it slightly with water, then dip it into the taupe paint. Saturate the sponge, then wring out some of the excess.

With a small pouncing motion, sponge the taupe over the surface, allowing about 50% of the base coat to show through. Always use a pouncing or patting motion. Avoid dragging the sponge.

While the taupe is still damp, dip the sponge into the raw sienna and yellow oxide acrylics, picking up both colors. Sponge these paints over the taupe.

Sponging with only a few pounces will create a coarse pattern. The more pouncing and sponging, the more subtle, blended and suedelike the effect, especially if you're sponging onto still-damp paint.

6 *Sponge painting, continued*

With the drawers in place in the dresser (or remove the drawers and line them up in order, so that the pattern is continuous), repeat step 5, sponge painting the drawers.

Remove the decals while the paint is dry to the touch but still soft. Use the point of an X–acto knife to lift an edge, and then peel off the decal.

Using a fine-point artist's brush, touch up any areas where the sponging may have seeped under the decals.

7 *Painting trim*

Optional: Tape off the sponge-painted areas and paint the trim with a base coat of slate blue latex paint. For a stormy-sky look, sponge paint the base coat with Payne's gray and pthalo blue acrylics.

8 *Varnishing*

Enrich the color and protect the paint with one or more coats of non-yellowing, water-based varnish. (See *Varnishing,* page 48.)

PATTERNS FOR REVERSE-STENCILING DECALS

Posterity

PLAYFUL, HISTORIC, ROMANTIC – POSTERS ADD MOOD AND DRAMA

Larger-than-life results start with a dramatic sense of scale.
An oversized poster, laminated to a dresser front, illustrates this concept
beautifully. Art posters capture any mood imaginable. Choose from
masters like Leonardo da Vinci or Rembrandt for rich sepia tones with warm
light. Draw on Miro, Mondrian or Picasso for a splash of color. Or look to
the ever-favorite impressionists for romance. The choices are unlimited.
Add background paint and detail, and watch your own masterpiece
fall into place with ease.

Read This First

Choose a dresser or cabinet that has a flat face, free of moldings and trim that will pucker the paper when laminated with a poster. A dresser with hardware is fine for this treatment. When poster shopping, take along measurements of the area to be covered, and choose a poster large enough to cover the full front of the dresser. It is easier to work with a poster that is too big than with one that is too small. Just assess how much image will be cut off and whether cropping and hardware will compromise the image. If the local poster shop doesn't have the size or subject matter you're after, try an art gallery's gift shop. Most art posters are printed on heavy paper, making them ideal for this treatment.

Don't be intimidated by the large scale of this project. Covering only a few large surfaces is quick, and the super-strong cellulose wallpaper paste now available makes the job easy. Once the base-coat color is painted, the découpage of the poster onto the drawers goes very quickly. If your dresser has a plastic laminate finish, use melamine paint for the base coat. (See *Melamine Paint,* page 27.)

BEFORE

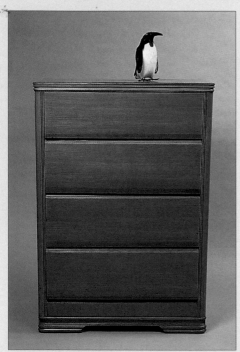

If you loved the 1950s, you can simply strip and refinish this dresser. If not, this dresser's flat front and simple lines make it an ideal candidate for a poster laminate treatment.

MATERIALS

- quart (litre) high-adhesion, water-based primer
- quart (litre) eggshell or satin finish latex paint in a color to coordinate with poster
- painting tools: paint brush, small roller, roller tray
- poster of a size to cover front of dresser completely
- easy-release painter's tape
- tape measure
- X-acto knife (with new blade) or utility knife
- ruler or other straight edge
- broad-tipped marker to match poster
- cellulose-based wallpaper paste
- mixing bowl or bucket
- soft, large brush
- household sponge
- quart (litre) non-yellowing, water-based varnish
- fine sandpaper (220 grade), tack cloth
- *optional:* pint (.5 litre) latex paint, white (step 1)
- *optional:* metallic leaf, adhesive and sealer

1 Painting

Refer to *Painting Basics* (page 34). Prepare, prime and paint the dresser with two coats of latex paint. Allow to dry. If the poster is a pale color or is printed on thin paper, all drawer fronts or other areas to be laminated should be painted white.

2 Cutting the poster to width

Lay the poster onto the cutting surface and tack it down with several pieces of easy-release tape. Measure and mark the width of the drawers, cropping the image attractively, if necessary. Instead of using a pen, use small pieces of tape, so that if one of the marks is wrong, the poster won't be defaced. (Old sewing proverb: Measure twice, cut once.)

Lay the ruler's edge along the marks and cut the poster with the X-acto knife (new blade, please), drawing the blade along the side of the ruler. When cutting the poster, draw the knife lightly along the cut several times. A single heavy cut is more difficult to control.

3 Cutting to fit drawers

Position the drawers in the chest, making certain they are all in their correct slots. Remove the top drawer and measure the face panel. Measure and mark the depth of the top drawer onto the top edge of the poster. Cut along the marks. Set the drawer and the poster piece aside, together.

Repeat for the remaining drawers, working from the top down.

Optional: If the poster is a medium to dark image, the bright-white cut edges of the poster can be distracting. Using a marker that closely matches the predominant color of the poster, run the tip quickly along the cut edges.

4 Wallpaper paste

Pour about 4 cups (1 litre) warm water into a small bucket or large bowl. Add the wallpaper paste according to package directions, allowing it to stand and thicken as required.

Apply paste to the drawer fronts in sequence from top to bottom to avoid any mix-ups. Using the large brush, paint the paste onto the front of the top drawer.

Apply paste evenly onto both sides of the poster piece. There should be no dry spots.

5 Laminating

Position the poster piece, right-side-up, onto the drawer front.

Begin by lining up one corner and a side edge, and then lay the poster carefully onto the drawer. When you laminate the drawer fronts, start at the same place every time (for example, the top right-hand corner).

Using a damp sponge, smooth the poster from the center to the edges, chasing air pockets out and making sure the paper is in contact with the drawer front.

Now you may notice two nasty things. First, the poster has stretched and hangs over one or two sides. Do not be concerned. The excess paper will be trimmed when it is dry. *Don't trim it damp.* Second, the paper has developed wrinkles. Leave these alone. As the paper dries, it will shrink and the wrinkles will flatten. If you try to flatten the wrinkles you will damage the poster.

Continue, pasting all sections of poster to the remaining drawer fronts. Allow to dry thoroughly.

Paste sections of poster onto any other sections of the dresser, as desired. Allow to dry.

6 Finishing

Using the X-acto or utility knife and the ruler, carefully trim any excess paper along the edges of the drawer fronts and touch up the cut edge with the matching marker.

To enrich color and protect the paint, apply three coats of non-yellowing, water-based varnish to the drawer fronts and any other areas that the posters have been laminated onto. After the second coat, sand the varnish lightly with fine sandpaper and wipe away all dust with a tack cloth. Apply the final coat. It is recommended that the full dresser be varnished. (See *Varnishing*, page 48.) Use the X-acto knife's point to cut openings at the predrilled hardware holes. Attach the hardware.

Optional: Apply gold, silver or copper metallic leaf to the trim of the dresser. (See *Mineral Rights*, page 279, steps 2 and 3.)

If you can't find a poster to fit your dresser, try laminating the drawer fronts with fabric. (See Office Romance, page 183.) Fabric is easier to apply than the stunning, professional-looking results would indicate. The huge choice of patterns and colors available makes fabric a natural substitute for a poster.

Découpage can be applied in many ways, aside from full coverage. Color reproductions of art, or photos from calendars or posters, can be laminated to furniture. These images are framed by faux-relief plaster (in reality, silicone caulking), which is later painted. (See Heaven Sent, page 221.)

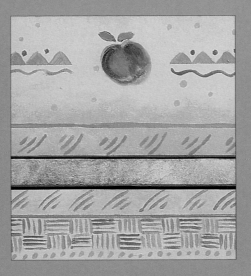

Peaches on Cream

A HAND-PAINTED TRIFLE OF BERRIES, BEES AND BRIC-A-BRAC

The drawer pulls came first. Spotted in a California specialty shop, they seemed to mix a sunny west coast sensibility with English country style. The rest of the painting simply fell into place, a decorative, freehand treatment consisting of charming and capricious motifs painted in soft, dusty pastels. Each of the designs is very simple, but in combination they form a wonderful potpourri. If the idea of a dresser in the kitchen or dining room seems incongruous, create a hutch by placing a small, shallow bookcase, painted in the same style, atop the chest.

Read This First

Choose furniture for this treatment that is simple yet chunky. The featured chest of drawers was selected for its overhanging top, rounded corners, flush drawers and funny, rounded feet. The drawer pulls can be hand painted with original designs, although porcelain or brass pulls work equally well. This technique consists of three stages. First the dresser is painted with a base-coat color. If your dresser has a plastic laminate finish, use melamine paint for the base coat. (See Melamine Paint, page 27.) Next, edges and corners are softened with a quick sponge painting. Then borders and designs are painted on each surface. The busy quality of the hand painting is what makes it appear difficult. In reality, it is a collection of simple patterns. If you have a collection of either latex or acrylic paint colors, this is the project for you. Otherwise, start your paint collection with this piece.

BEFORE

A nicely proportioned, solid wooden dresser with an interesting style. The top was scarred and stained – an ideal candidate for renovation.

MATERIALS

- quart (litre) high-adhesion, water-based primer
- quart (litre) eggshell or satin finish latex paint, pale cream
- painting tools: paint brush, small roller, roller tray
- synthetic or natural sponge for sponge painting
- tubes of acrylics (or substitute latex) in several different colors, pale-to-medium dusty tones: blue, brown, gray, olive green, orange, pink, purple, taupe, yellow
- paper towel
- fine-point artist's brush
- easy-release printer's tape, 1 in. (2.5 cm) wide
- chalk or light-colored pencil
- square-tipped artist's brush
- quart (litre) non-yellowing, water-based varnish

1 Painting

Refer to *Painting Basics* (page 34). Prepare, prime and paint the dresser with two coats of cream latex paint. Allow to dry.

2 Sponge painting

Start sponge painting with a 3 in. (7.5 cm) band of color (your choice) around the perimeter of the top, blending it out into the cream tone as follows. Thin the paint with water to a creamy, liquid consistency or add glaze (See *Glaze,* page 28.) Tear off a chunk of sponge about the size of a tennis ball. Saturate the sponge and squeeze it out.

Using a small pouncing motion, start sponge painting along the edge. As the sponge becomes drier, pat further into the center, fading the paint into the cream tone. If necessary, pick up excess paint with a damp paper towel.

Continue sponge painting the perimeters of flat surfaces and the crossbars between the drawers, using an assortment of colors. Also sponge paint the feet. Wash the sponge thoroughly between colors. Allow to dry.

Sponge paint around the perimeter of each drawer front with a different pale color. Position the drawers in the chest to observe how the various colors work together and whether there are exposed areas that require touch-ups. Remove the drawers. Make any needed touch-ups.

3 Painting borders

Now for the hand painting. Paint a border on each drawer front in a darker tone than the sponged paint. To do this, tape inside the perimeter on the face of each drawer with the 1 in. (2.5 cm) wide easy-release painter's tape. Use the tape as a guide for painting the border. Using the fine-point brush, paint a line close to, but not over, the inside edge of the tape. The line should look hand painted, not like a perfect stripe. Remove the tape.

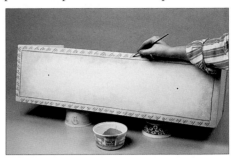

Add detail to the border by painting a series of three dashes, evenly spaced around the edge, inside the border.

4 Painting curlicues

Draw curlicues first in chalk or light-colored pencil. Thin the paint, if necessary, so that it flows from the brush. Using the fine-point artist's brush, paint the curlicue in one movement. Use the chalk line only as a guide. Trying to follow the chalk line exactly will make hesistant, cramped painted line. The lines should look hand painted.

Optional: The tree shown was copied from one of the drawer pulls. It consists of a stack of three quarter-moon shapes with a teardrop shape at the top. Add leaves along the sides of the curlicues by pressing the side of a fine-point artist's brush onto the surface at an angle to the line.

Optional: Add blue waves with dots along the top border and dashes along the bottom border. Paint small curlicues and dots onto the background.

5 *Painting sawtooth*

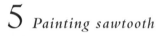

Tape the bottom line of the sawtooth. Using the square-tipped artist's brush, paint the sawtooth along the tape by holding the brush on an angle and drawing it down over the tape to create triangles. Remove the tape when the paint is dry to the touch, but still soft. Allow the paint to dry.

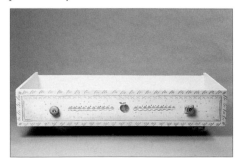

Optional: The peach in the center was copied from one of the drawer pulls. It consists of an apple shape painted in a soft orange, then highlighted in an orange-

brown shade on the "shoulders." Two green leaves complete the peach.

Add a row of X's along the top border, sprinkle random dots onto the background and paint wavy lines and dots to accent the sawtooth pattern.

6 *Painting checkerboard*

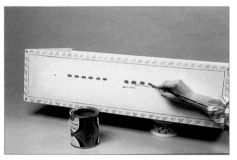

First, establish one line of checks. Tape the bottom line of the first row. Using the square-tipped artist's brush, paint brick-like dashes, spacing them evenly along the line. Remove the tape.

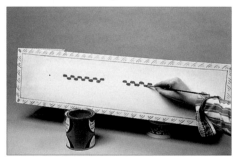

Paint two more lines of bricks above and below the first line, across the open spaces.

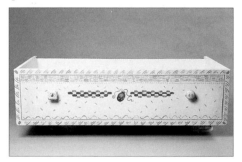

Optional: A strawberry was copied from one of the drawer pulls. Paint a strawberry-pink oval and highlight one side in deeper pink. Add seed dots in yellow or green. With quick brushstrokes, add leaves to the top and paint tendrils to each side.

Add basketweave along the top edge of the border, with dashes below it. Create lazy S's with dots along the bottom border and paint random dashes to fill the background.

7 *Painting the top*

Optional: Paint a motif in the corners. Here, trees were copied from one of the drawer pulls. (See step 4, second part.)

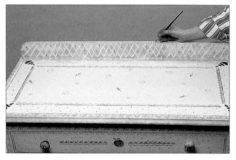

Add a second border to the dresser top. Paint dots between the borders and add stylized bumblebees, curlicues and stars to the center. If desired, add an overlapping diamond or lattice pattern in pale cream to the yellow backboard.

8 *Painting the sides*

On the dresser sides, paint corner curlicues and a cascade of dashes, stars and decorative borders with zigzags and triangles in a variety of colors.

9 *Varnishing*

To enrich color and protect the paint, apply one or more coats of non-yellowing, water-based varnish. (See *Varnishing*, page 48.)

Painting simple motifs, and lots of them, can give a beginning painter a feel for brush painting and the confidence to tackle a more advanced project like the folk painting shown above. (See Turning the Tables, page 293.)

Heaven Sent

DIVINE CHERUBS ARE FRAMED BY GILT-EDGED DECORATIVE PLASTERWORK

Every house has room for a little opulence, a lovely departure from the ordinary, with ever-popular angel paintings in the 19th century romantic style cut into pleasing ovals of various sizes and framed with a poetic frieze of faux-plaster relief. Combined with gold-burnished sage green paint, this heavenly treatment creates a moody yet surprisingly neutral effect.

Read This First

Silicone caulking, the kind used around windows and bathtubs, is the surprising modern material used to create decorative faux plaster work. Choose paintable caulking in a silicone-based product. Silicone has the best adhesion. Buy caulking that comes in a tube with a nozzle and fits into a gun – not the little plastic packages for bathtubs. Don't be intimidated by the gun. After a few practice tries, you'll have the hang of it. Pages from an oversized color calendar of Bouguereau paintings capture the high romance of angels. For découpage pictures, select posters or calendars. These pictures are usually beautifully printed on heavy paper. The heavy paper would normally render it unsuitable for découpage, but in this instance it will be edged in silicone to disguise the cut edge. This treatment should be limited to furniture other than tabletops, where the raised decoration would topple glasses and be harmed by wear and tear.

MATERIALS

- quart (litre) high-adhesion, water-based primer
- painting tools: paint brush, small roller, roller tray
- printed calendar or poster pictures
- access to photocopier
- scissors or X-acto knife
- pencil
- tape measure or ruler
- cellulose-based wallpaper paste
- sponge, rags
- tube of *paintable* silicone caulking, caulking gun
- wire or other narrow, sharp object
- cardboard or scrap piece of wood
- yardstick or other straight edge
- quart (litre) eggshell or satin finish latex paint, in a bone or sage green shade
- inexpensive square-tipped artist's brush
- fine-point artist's brush
- tube of acrylic (or substitute latex) for antiquing, burnt umber or deep olive green
- tube of acrylic, iridescent gold
- quart (litre) non-yellowing, water-based varnish

BEFORE

A 1950s dresser with simple lines and a highly lacquered finish that has seen its share of spills and cigarette burns. To refinish or to paint? The owner decided she'd rather go decorative than understated.

1 *Priming*

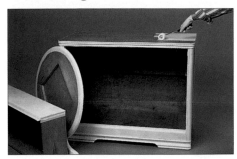

Refer to *Painting Basics* (page 34). Prepare and prime the dresser, but do not paint it. If your dresser has a mirror, remove it, but don't forget to work on it at each appropriate step.

2 *Cutting oval images*

Photocopy the pattern for the oval template (page 225), reducing or enlarging the pattern to fit the top and the drawer fronts of your dresser. Cut out the center of the oval pattern and trace the oval onto the calendar (or poster) image, making four very small marks on the edge of the picture at the cross lines. Cut out the calendar images along your line.

Mark the positions for the oval pictures on the dresser by measuring and lightly marking a cross at the center point of where a picture is desired. Match the four marks on the oval to the lines of the cross.

3 *Découpage*

Following the manufacturer's instructions, mix a small bowl of the wallpaper paste. Gently rub paste onto both sides of a paper oval, covering it thoroughly. Position the oval onto the dresser.

Using a damp sponge, smooth the image from the center outward, eliminating air bubbles and wiping away excess paste. Do not rub vigorously. The printed image may rub off.

Repeat for all ovals. Allow the paste to dry. You may see small wrinkles develop in the wet paper. Summon all your will-power and do not try to eliminate wrinkles. The paper will shrink as it dries, and the wrinkles will disappear. Trying to get rid of the wrinkles will damage the paper.

4 *Planning plaster relief*

Set the hardware in place but do not attach it. Pencil plaster-relief patterns onto the dresser, avoiding the hardware. These patterns will be followed with the caulking gun.

Keep the lines simple, with large loops, avoiding intricate patterns and tight curves that can be difficult to follow with the large caulking gun. Straight lines are good for borders.

If your dresser has a mirror, mark where it sits so that the area can be avoided.

5 *Testing the caulking*

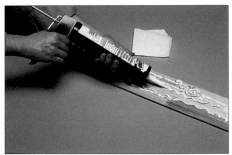

Cut off the tip of the plastic end of the caulking tube. Cut on an angle near the end, so that the hole in the tip is about ⅛ in. (3 mm) across. The tip can be recut later to a larger diameter, if desired. Insert a narrow sharp object, such as a piece of wire, into the tip and pierce the inside seal. (Some tips are removable for easy accessibility.) Load the tube of silicone caulking into the caulking gun and squeeze the trigger until caulking emerges from the tip.

On cardboard or a scrap piece of wood, do some test lines and squiggles to get a feel for the flow of the caulking. When applying caulking, drag the tip, creating contact between the caulking and the wood. No problem if you make a mistake. Scrape off the caulking while it is still damp and start again. Keep a rag handy on which to place the gun when you're pausing, since the caulking will continue to ooze.

Allow the caulking to dry. It will shrink as it dries. If the lines are too narrow and appear insignificant, recut the nozzle to a wider diameter.

6 *Caulking straight lines*

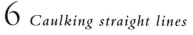

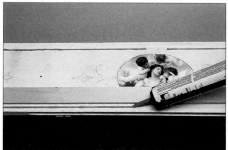

Remove the hardware from the drawer fronts. Do all straight lines first. Lay a yardstick along the line. Resting the tip of the nozzle against the dresser and the side of the nozzle against the wood, gently depress the trigger and make a line of caulking. At the end of the line, release the trigger and lift the gun off. Carefully remove the yardstick without touching the wet caulking. Let the caulking set.

The lines will not be perfect. They should be lumpy and somewhat uneven. A small point of caulking will be formed whenever the gun is lifted off, to be remedied later.

Finish caulking all straight lines.

7 *Caulking curves*

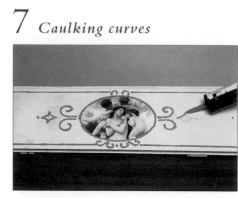

Caulking carefully around the pictures, cover the cut edge of the paper. Then, begin caulking along the curved lines. This job must be done freehand. Don't expect to follow the pencil lines exactly. They are only a guide.

As the caulking becomes dry to the touch, it is still wet inside. Using your fingers, press down any unwanted points. Allow the caulking to dry and harden.

8 *Painting*

Using a square-tipped artist's brush, paint around and over all the caulking details with the bone or sage green latex paint.

A fine-point artist's brush is useful for painting the caulking around the pictures.

Using a paint brush and a small roller, paint the rest of the dresser. Apply a second coat, if necessary, to achieve solid coverage.

9 *Antiquing*

To antique the dresser, use acrylic or latex paint in a similar yet much darker tone than the base coat. Use deep olive green for antiquing a sage green base coat, or burnt umber for a bone-colored base coat. Thin the paint to a watery consistency.

Brush the paint over a section of the caulking, working it into all details.

Allow the paint to pool in low spots. Wipe excess paint off high spots with a damp rag. Continue until all caulking has been antiqued. If desired, antique any trim or other details.

10 *Highlights*

To highlight the plaster-relief with gold, dip a brush into gold acrylic paint, wiping out the excess on a rag. Drag the brush lightly over the top ridges of the caulking, allowing paint to cling to the high areas.

Enrich color and protect the découpaged images and the paint job by varnishing the dresser with non-yellowing, water-based varnish. (See *Varnishing,* page 48.)

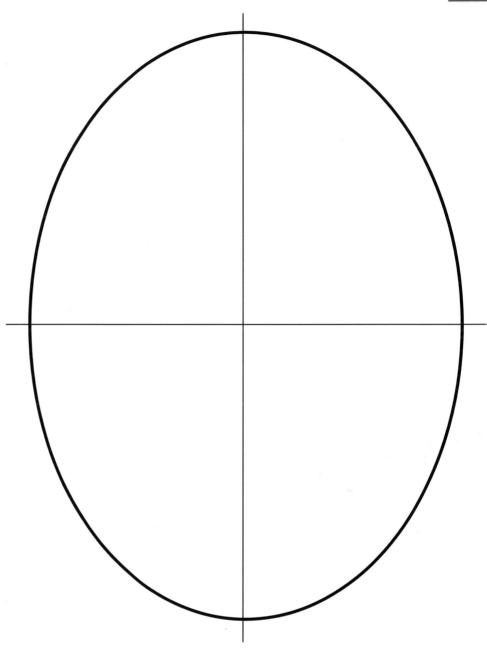

PATTERN FOR OVAL TEMPLATE

TABLES

Tabletops are to a furniture refinisher what a blank canvas is to an artist. The large flat area presented by a tabletop gives full reign to a decorator's creativity and allows the painter to make a statement. And with the range of easy-to-use, professional-looking treatments available, there's never been a better time to refinish a table. Crystal clear varnishes allow fragile materials such as paper or fabric to be laminated to a tabletop. Folk painting, block printing, faux marble and granite and a multitude of texturing techniques, even decorative tile mosaic, are within the reach of the hobbyist. Mosaics are fantastically tactile and a treat for the eye. If refinishing a dining set, treat the base and chairs as coordinates and minor players to the main attraction of the tabletop.

Lasting Impressions

A Simple, Striking School Of Block-Printed Fish

Country-blue fish on an off-white background perpetually swim the perimeter
of a generously proportioned round table. Each block-printed fish is unique
and decorative. Uncomplicated yet irresistible, the freshness of a block print
can never be matched by painting with a brush. A sawtooth border
completes a design that combines rustic simplicity
with a bold and stylish touch.

Read This First

This project utilizes one of the easiest paint techniques: block printing. Patterns are cut from an insole (the foam insert that goes into your shoe) and a potato, then easily applied. Printing with a foam insole may seem unusual, but the small regular pinholes give a decorative effect, and the composition of the insole makes it easy to cut, to carve details into and to manipulate. Dependable potato printing, in which a carved potato is used like a rubber stamp, is ideal for small designs and patterns. Before the block printing is done, the table is painted with a solid base-coat color of latex paint. If your table has a plastic laminate finish, use melamine paint. (See *Melamine Paint,* page 27.) Block printing can also be effective on natural wood that has been stained and varnished with one coat. Varnish again after the block printing.

BEFORE

Used for a stage set, this solid wood table, painted overpowering green in a heavy enamel, was chipped and peeling. It called for a simple, fresh treatment.

MATERIALS

- quart (litre) high-adhesion, water-based primer
- quart (litre) eggshell or satin finish latex paint, off-white
- 1 pint (.5 litre) latex paint, Wedgwood or linen blue
- painting tools: paint brush, small roller, roller tray
- access to photocopier, or paper and pencil
- permanent waterproof marker
- inexpensive foam insoles
- scissors, X-acto knife
- paper
- easy-release painter's tape
- inexpensive square-tipped artist's brush
- large potato
- sharp paring knife
- quart (litre) non-yellowing, water-based varnish
- *optional:* spray primer; low-luster acrylic spray primer

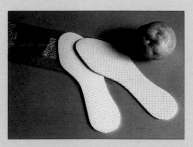

1 *Painting*

Refer to *Painting Basics* (page 34). Prepare, prime and paint the table and chairs with the off-white latex paint. Spray primer and paint may be used on the table base and chairs. (See *Spray Painting*, page 44.) The base of the table can be painted blue, if desired.

2 *Making the fish block print*

Photocopy the fish pattern (page 233) to an appropriate size for your table. (You could also trace the pattern using paper and pencil.) Keep in mind that the pattern must fit onto the insole. Cut out the pattern.

Position the pattern onto the foam side of the insole and trace around it (including the tab) with a permanent waterproof marker. The fish, when printed, will be swimming in the opposite direction of the pattern. (If you wish the fish to swim in the same direction as the pattern, place the pattern on the cloth side.)

Cut along the outline of the fish, including the tab. Draw the detail lines on the foam side of the fish.

3 *Adding detail*

Create scales, gills and other details in the fish. Using the X-acto knife, score two parallel cuts close together along the lines on the foam. Cut the foam, but don't cut through the fabric backing. Scrape the foam off the fabric backing between the parallel cuts. Remove a dot of foam for the eye. Score through the foam (not the fabric backing) at the base of the tab, so that it can bend back easily.

4 *Planning prints*

Cut several fish from paper and position them onto the tabletop in the direction they will print, spacing them evenly apart. Tape the paper fish lightly in place using easy-release painter's tape. Other tape may lift your paint.

5 *Test printing*

Test the fish print on some paper before printing the table. Using a square-tipped artist's brush, brush the blue paint onto the foam side of the fish, avoiding the tab. Place the fish foam-side-down onto the paper. Press gently all over the fabric side of the fish, being certain that it has made full contact. Lifting the tab, peel the fish from the paper.

Every print will be different. Applying more paint to the foam will make a darker print, with less detail. (Excess paint floods details, obscuring them.) Less paint gives a paler effect, with crisper detail. Make several test prints from one load of paint on the foam. Most block prints give better results after some use.

6 *Printing*

Begin to print the table. Apply paint to the foam. Then lift one paper pattern, placing the fish foam-side-down in place of the pattern.

Press fish evenly all over, then peel off. After several prints, paint may seep through the fabric backing. Although seepage is not a problem for the printing, be careful not to transfer paint from your hands to the tabletop.

Don't forget the chairs! Print as desired. Two fish, back-to-back on the seat or across the backrest, will coordinate the pieces.

7 *Making the potato print*

Make a sawtooth pattern around the table's edge. Use the paring knife to carve a solid W pattern (or use the pattern on page 233 as a guide) into a block of potato. To help you place the image when printing, cut away excess potato around the W, but leave enough attached to the back for a handle.

8 *Potato printing*

Make some test prints on paper. Brush some paint onto the W and press onto the paper, using a rocking motion.

Begin printing a continuous sawtooth around the edge of the table. Brush paint onto the W. Position the wide edge of the W against the outside edge of the table.

Press the image firmly down in a rocking motion toward the center of the table. Position each print tightly against the previous one to line up the pattern evenly.

When you are several sawtooth prints away from the end, you may wish to cut the W print in half and print each V individually. Overlap or spread the prints apart slightly to fill the remaining space as evenly as possible. Add sawtooth to the chairs if desired.

9 *Additional prints*

Add any further pattern or design, if desired. Here, a second potato print of three small leaves (see pattern, page 233) was added between the fish.

10 *Varnishing*

To enrich color and protect the paint, apply one or more coats of non-yellowing, water-based varnish to the tabletop, the chair seats and the backrests. (See *Varnishing*, page 48.)

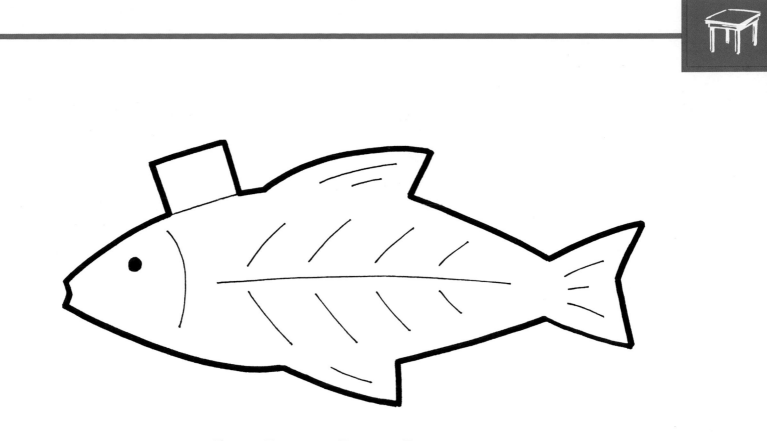

FISH BLOCK-PRINT PATTERN

SAWTOOTH POTATO-PRINT PATTERN

THREE-LEAF POTATO-PRINT PATTERN

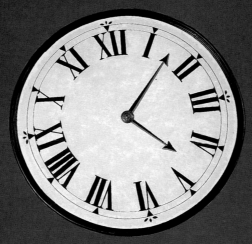

Times Tables

SIMPLE STENCILING CREATES
A TIMELY CLASSIC

Whatever the dimensions — from a lamp table to a full dining table — any
round table is suited to a traditional clock face composition. The neutral tones
and traditional Roman numeral clock face make this table treatment an instant
classic that fits virtually any room. This project is completed in
three simple stages. The difficult part is deciding what time
to set the clock's hands at, in perpetuity.

Read This First

After the base of the table is painted with a black base coat, three easy treatments complete the clock face – sponge painting, stenciling and some hand painting. If your table has a plastic laminate finish, use melamine paint for the base coat. (See *Melamine Paint,* page 27.) The sponge painting is very quick, giving the clock face an antiqued, parchmentlike appearance. Then Roman numerals are stenciled in black. Patterns for the stencils – a I, an X, a V, and a clock hand – are on page 239. The three numerals are all that are required because they will be sized and combined as needed. The paint with the fastest drying time for stenciling is acrylic paint. Cream paints, sold in craft stores, are the stencil paints with the consistency of shoe polish. If you choose them, remember that most require several days to dry. Spray paint can be used, but the overspray is a problem, requiring extensive masking for each numeral. This is a weekend project that renders impressive results for the time invested.

MATERIALS

- pint (.5 litre) eggshell finish latex paint, off-white
- paint brush, 1½ in. (4 cm) wide
- paper and easy-release painter's tape, for masking
- can of acrylic spray paint, black
- waterproof marker, black
- fine-point artist's brush
- sponge for sponge painting
- small quantity latex or acrylic paint, taupe
- chalk or pencil
- ruler and set-square or other right angle
- beam compass; or string, hammer and small nail
- stencil plastic (available at art supply and craft stores) or lightweight cardboard
- access to photocopier
- utility or X-acto knife
- tube of acrylic paint and square-tipped artist's brush, or cream paint and a stencil brush
- quart (litre) non-yellowing, water-based varnish
- *optional:* spray glue; scrap paper or dropsheet
- *optional:* small quantity black touch-up paint
- *optional:* large, flat brass button with a shank-back; power drill; white carpenter's glue
- *optional:* small quantity medium-gray acrylic paint

BEFORE

At first glance, a two-tiered table. In reality, a pleasing oak base with a mismatched top.

1 *Painting the base coat*

If possible, remove the top from the base of the table. (Recruit help if the table is large or heavy.) The top tier of this table was discarded because it was warped beyond repair.

Paint the tabletop with two coats of off-white latex paint. Allow to dry.

Mask the top of the table with paper and tape around the edge, inside the lip (if the table has one); or leave a 1 in. (2.5 cm) border. Turn the table over and, with the black spray paint, paint the underside of the tabletop. (See *Spray Painting*, page 44.) Allow to dry.

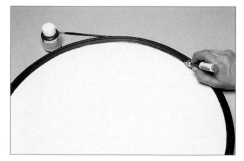

Turn the tabletop right-side-up and spray paint to the masked edge. Remove the masking. If the line of paint is wavy or uneven, draw a smooth line with a waterproof marker and fill in the gaps with a fine-point artist's brush and black paint.

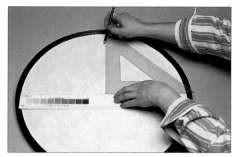

Spray paint the base black. Apply as many coats as needed for dense coverage. Allow to dry.

2 *Sponge painting*

Give the background of the clock face the look of parchment by sponge painting it with taupe paint. If desired, tape the edges to prevent sponging onto the black rim.

Thin the taupe paint with water to a liquid consistency, or add glaze. (See *Glaze*, page 28.) Tear off a chunk of sponge and dampen it slightly with water. It should be only slightly moist. Saturate the sponge with taupe paint and squeeze out excess. Using a patting motion, sponge the taupe paint over the off-white background, allowing about half the background color to show through. Avoid getting paint on the black edge. Remove tape and allow paint to dry. Make any needed touch-ups required.

3 *Planning the clock face*

Measure the center of the table and mark lightly with chalk or pencil. Divide and mark the table into quarters by laying a ruler across the center of the table, marking the halves. Then, using a set-square or other right angle, mark the top and bottom quarters.

Using a beam compass and a waterproof black marker, draw a line about 1 in. (2.5 cm) inside the edge of the circle.

A beam compass will give the best results, but if you don't own one try this low-tech method. Drive a small nail halfway into the center of the table. Tie string to the nail at one end and to a waterproof black marker at the other, at a correct distance to draw the circle. Holding the marker straight up, and maintaining tension on the string, draw the circle, carefully connecting the ends.

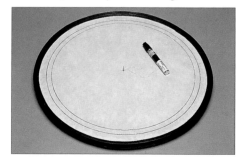

Repeat, drawing another circle about ¾ in. (2 cm) inside the first circle.

4 *Stenciling*

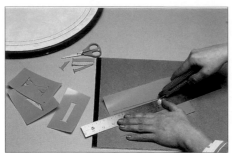

Photocopy the patterns (page 239) to the appropriate size, and trace them onto stencil plastic or lightweight cardboard. Cut them out, using a utility or an X-acto knife (sharp new blade, please).

Stenciling is easier and the results are cleaner if the backs of the stencils are sprayed with spray glue and allowed to dry for at least one hour, until lightly tacky. If the glue is too sticky, it will pull off background paint.

Mark the positions of numerals by measuring and dividing each quarter of the clock into thirds. Mark these divisions with pencil. Not all clocks have all twelve numerals. If you prefer, stencil only the XII, the III, the VI and the IX and use small decorative designs for the other hours.

Position a stencil with the top of the numeral on the curved line. (Numerals

read right-side-up from the center of the clock face.)

When stenciling, try to visualize the full numeral and work to center the numeral at the mark. For example, with the III, the center I would be at the mark, with the remaining I's on either side. Press the stencil in place, making a light bond. Using black paint – acrylic and a square-tipped artist's brush, or cream stencil paint and a stencil brush (a round brush with stiff bristles and a flat end) – fill in the stencil. Remove the stencil. Stencil the numerals in random order to avoid smearing wet paint.

Stencil the clock hands, starting at the center. Make sure to stencil the minute hand longer than the hour hand. Allow to dry.

5 *Decorative details*

Optional: In the centre of the table, drill a large, shallow hole for the shank-back of a large brass button. Press the shank into the hole, gluing the button in place with carpenter's glue. The brass button will cover the center of the clock where the hands join.

Optional: Using a fine-point artist's brush and black paint, add decorative triangles, floral motifs, diamonds or other motifs to the clock face.

Using a fine-point artist's brush and medium-gray paint, paint a narrow shadow along the bottom edges of the clock hands, giving them a three-dimensional appearance.

6 *Varnishing*

Protect the paint and enrich color on the clock face by applying non-yellowing, water-based varnish. (See *Varnishing*, page 48.)

Reattach the top to the rest of the table.

CLOCK NUMERAL AND CLOCK-HAND STENCIL PATTERNS

Make the clock-hand as long as necessary for your clock face.

Basketry

BASKETS ADD FRIVOLITY TO TINY TABLES

The texture and color of a basket add whimsy and a whole new purpose to
the classic, simple design of a tiny lamp table. A dependable lamp table is
an ideal pedestal for a basket, especially when finished to coordinate
with the surrounding decor. Three individual approaches — color-wash in
country blue, natural cane with accents of black, and wholly natural twigs —
show the versatility of this treatment. Load the finished table with
fruit or plants, or use it as an ingenious bread basket at your
next dinner party — no table space required.

Read This First

A knockdown table or one that can be easily taken apart is needed for this project. Choose a low-profile basket with a flat bottom to add a textured rim to the table, or select a chunkier basket complete with handle to create a plant stand. When you go on your basket hunt, take the tabletop along and check that it fits, easily, *flat inside* the base of the basket. After selecting the basket, decide on a treatment and choose spray paint or a faux finish for the base and top. The base and tabletop are painted with a base coat first. Then the basket is finished to coordinate, and the table is assembled. If your table has a plastic laminate finish, use melamine paint for the base coat. (See *Melamine Paint,* page 27.)

MATERIALS

For all tables:

These materials are required for all tables. They're also all you need for making the *Natural Plant Stand* (see photo, bottom right, page 240).

- basket to fit the tabletop
- fine sandpaper (220 grade), tack cloth
- 1 can spray paint or spray faux finish (for base), in an appropriate color (step 2)
- ruler or tape measure
- utility knife, heavy-duty scissors, or garden clippers
- corrugated cardboard
- white carpenter's glue
- stapler and staples, or screws and washers
- *optional:* masking tape

For a color-washed table:

See photo, top, page 240.

- 1 pint (.5 litre) primer or gesso (available at art supply shops)
- sponge or 1½ in. (4 cm) paint brush; rag
- small quantity flat latex paint, country blue (acrylic may be substituted)

For a brush-painted table:

See photo, bottom left, page 240.

- 1 can glossy acrylic spray paint, black
- pint (.5 litre) primer
- pint (.5 litre) eggshell latex, off-white
- tubes of acrylics: yellow oxide, burnt sienna, mars black
- rag or paper towel
- fine-point artist's brush
- *optional:* 2 plastic bags and tape
- *optional:* pencil
- *optional:* spray varnish

BEFORE

These inexpensive little knockdown lamp tables are sold at discount department stores.

FOR ALL TABLES

1 *Sanding*

With the table still in pieces, lightly sand the top of the table with fine sandpaper. Wipe completely clean of all dust, using a tack cloth. Legs may be sanded too, if finish is glossy.

2 *Spray painting*

Spray paint the base of the table with two or three coats as needed, following the manufacturer's instructions.

If making a *Color-Washed Table,* spray paint the base and top of the table a country-blue shade.

If making a *Brush-Painted Table,* spray paint only the table's base with glossy black. Do not paint the top.

If making a *Natural Plant Stand,* spray paint the base and top with faux-stone or granite spray paint in beige or gray. (See *Spray Painting,* page 44.)

Optional: To prevent paint build-up that can make assembly difficult, you may wish to tape the areas of the legs that slide into the center pole before painting.

3 *Cutting the basket*

Turn the tabletop upside-down and measure the diameter of the flange (the wooden circle in the center that the base screws into).

Cut a hole in the center of the basket, matching the diameter of the flange. If the basket has a loose, delicate weave, apply masking tape across the area before cutting.

Depending on the weight of the basket, use a utility knife, heavy-duty scissors or garden clippers for the cutting.

4 *Cardboard washer*

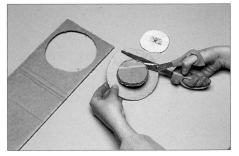

Cut a circle of corrugated cardboard, 4 in. (10 cm) larger in diameter than the flange on the underside of the tabletop. Cut a hole in the center of the cardboard circle to match the hole in the basket. Spray paint the cardboard if desired. Set the cardboard aside to be used when assembling the basket and table.

5 *Basket treatments*

To color-wash the basket, follow the steps for a *Color-Washed Table* (page 244). To brush paint the tabletop and basket, follow the steps for a *Brush-Painted Table* (page 245).

If you wish to make a *Natural Plant Stand,* move on to the next step, number 6.

6 *Attaching basket to top*

Apply carpenter's glue to the underside of the tabletop, avoiding the center flange. Place the tabletop upside-down on a support, like a small box. Position the basket upside-down, centering it onto the table-top, with the hole of the basket centered over the flange. The flange should show.

Place the cardboard grommet around the center flange. Staple the basket to the top. Be sure to use staples that will penetrate through the basket and into the tabletop.

If the basket is too thick for staples, use screws with washers. The washers will prevent the screws from pulling through the weave of the basket. Be certain the screws are long enough to penetrate the

washer and the basket and go *partway* through the tabletop.

7 *Assembly*

Assemble the base. Then screw the base into the tabletop.

COLOR-WASHED TABLE

Choose a rustic basket with a nubby weave in a light- to medium-colored cane.

A *Getting started*

Follow *For All Tables,* steps 1 to 4.

B *White washing*

Thin the primer or gesso so that it runs easily from a brush. Using a brush, sponge

or rag, prime the basket white, working it into all crevices. While working, use a damp rag to wipe the basket at random places, lifting the white in places to expose the natural cane on high spots. Allow to dry.

C *Blue washing*

Mix latex or acrylic paint to obtain a country-blue shade. Thin the paint to a soupy consistency. Work the blue paint over the basket as you did with the primer, using a brush, sponge or rag. While the paint is still wet, use a damp rag to lift the paint at random places from high spots, exposing both primer and natural cane. Allow to dry.

D *Finishing*

Follow *For All Tables,* steps 6 and 7.

BRUSH-PAINTED TABLE

Choose a basket with a flat weave. Inexpensive baskets of this type are readily available at stores in Chinatown. Particularly attractive are baskets with brass accents.

A *Getting started*

Follow *For All Tables*, steps 1 to 4, painting the base a glossy black. Do not paint the tabletop.

B *Painting the top*

Paint the tabletop with primer and two coats of off-white latex paint. Allow to dry.

Mix together the yellow oxide and burnt sienna acrylics. Thin the paint mixture with water to a watery consistency.

Dip a rag or paper towel into the paint and rub it lightly over the tabletop. This finish will be uneven and should coordinate with the basket. Allow to dry.

C *Painting the basket*

Optional: While the tabletop is drying, cut open two plastic bags. Place one over the outside of the basket, and the other on the inside. Tape the bags securely to the bottom edge of the basket's rim, leaving only the rim of the basket exposed. Spray paint the rim with two coats of glossy black. Allow to dry and remove the tape and plastic.

Using the fine-point artist's brush and mars black paint, paint freehand curlicues onto the tabletop. Thin the paint with water, if necessary, so that it flows easily from the brush. The curlicues should look hand painted, not perfect. Draw curlicues first in pencil, if desired, but don't attempt to follow your pencil lines too closely. Instead, use them only as a guide. Try to do the curlicue in one smooth motion. Add small dashes at odd angles around the curlicues. Allow to dry.

Paint a zigzag border and random dashes on the outside of the basket. Paint a zigzag border on the inside. Allow to dry.

D *Varnishing*

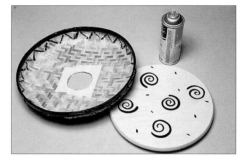

Optional: To protect the paint job, spray both sides of the basket and the tabletop with spray varnish. Allow to dry.

E *Finishing*

Follow *For All Tables*, steps 6 and 7.

Tabletop Rose Bower

MISTY ROSE STENCILS BEDECK
A WOODEN TABLE

Step into a pastel-painted Victorian rose garden. This impressionistic paint treatment is nostalgically English country and reminiscent of a turn-of-the-century lady's hatbox, with its hand-painted florals bordered by stripes and sprinkled with tiny blossoms. This adaptable table moves easily into an entryway or a bathroom, kitchen or bedroom.

Read This First

Choose furniture with an English-cottage feeling: simple wooden pieces with some trim, turned legs, or other gentle but not fussy detail. First, the table is painted with a solid base coat of latex paint. If your table has a plastic laminate finish, use melamine paint for the base coat. (See *Melamine Paint,* page 27.) Then flat areas are sponge painted and stenciled with rose and leaf motifs. A solid wood piece finished in this style can be antiqued if it is not primed before painting. (See *Cupboard Love,* page 53.) If pastels are too intense for your color scheme, step 7 shows how to apply a glaze over the paint for a muted look. Or try working in Victorian sepia tones of burgundy, slate blue and taupe. Four different stencils are used in this project, with many being layered. (Patterns are on page 251.) Choose acrylics or the cream paints made for stenciling. Acrylic paints are preferred for their fast drying times. If you use the cream stencil paints available in craft stores, expect each color to take several days to dry.

MATERIALS

- quart (litre) high-adhesion, water-based primer (or spray primer)
- quart (litre) eggshell finish latex paint, powder blue
- painting tools: paint brush, small roller, roller tray
- synthetic or natural sponge for sponge painting
- for sponging: latex and/or acrylic paints – pastel pink, pastel blue-green, off-white
- stencil plastic (available at art supply and craft stores (or lightweight cardboard))
- scissors or X-acto knife
- pink colored pencil
- for stenciling: tubes of acrylics (and an inexpensive square-tipped artist's brush), or cream stencil paints (and a stencil brush) – acid green, pastel blue-green, pastel pink, medium pink
- for hand painting: tubes of acrylics – yellow, off-white, deep blue, medium green, dark blue-gray
- fine-point artist's brush and medium-sized artist's brush
- easy-release painter's tape or masking tape
- quart (litre) non-yellowing, water-based varnish
- *optional:* spray glue; scrap paper, dropsheets

BEFORE

A pleasantly proportioned 1940s wooden table with turned spindle legs and gingerbread trim. When the flaking varnish is scraped down and the legs and trim are repaired, it becomes the perfect foil for a Victorian treatment.

1 *Painting*

Refer to *Painting Basics* (page 34). Prepare, prime and paint the table with two coats of powder blue paint.

Allow to dry. If you wish to antique the table, do not prime it. (See *Cupboard Love,* page 53.)

2 *Sponge painting*

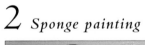

Mix each of the colors listed for sponging.

Use easy-release painter's tape or masking tape to mask off the area to be sponge painted.

Mix the pastel pink paint with water to a soupy consistency, or add glaze. (See *Glaze,* page 28.) Tear off a chunk of sponge and dampen it slightly with water. Then saturate it with paint. Squeeze out most of the paint.

Using a pouncing motion, sponge the tabletop (and any other sections that you wish), leaving about half the blue showing through. Make the coverage in some spots heavier, to resemble cloud formations. The base coat (powder blue) will begin disappearing, with each subsequent sponged-on color gaining prominence.

3 *Sponge painting, continued*

While the pink paint is still damp, sponge paint over it with pastel blue-green, allowing both pink and blue to show through.

Sponge paint a final coat of off-white, allowing the previous colors to glow through. Allow to dry.

4 *Preparing stencils*

While the sponge painting is drying, trace the rose and leaf patterns onto the stencil plastic (or similar material) and cut out the center shaded areas. The cutting can be done with scissors or an X-acto knife.

For easier stenciling, spray-glue the backs of the stencils. Let the glue dry at least an hour to a light tackiness. (If the glue is too sticky, it will lift the background paint.)

Try a few test stencils on paper before stenciling the table. Press the stencil onto paper and, using an artist's paint brush or a stencil brush (a round brush with stiff bristles and a flat end), paint the center of the stencil. A paint brush will give a hand-painted look with brushstrokes, while the stencil brush will give smooth color. Add freehand lines or details.

5 Stenciling

Using the *Rose in Bloom* stencil and a pink colored pencil, mark the positions of roses on the table. Set this stencil aside.

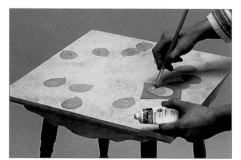

Using the *Large Leaf* stencil and acid green paint, stencil leaves around and overlapping the marked roses. Lay the stencil onto the surface, gently pressing it down for adhesion. Then paint the full opening to all edges. Carefully lift the stencil while the paint is still wet, and proceed to the next leaf. Be careful not to lay the stencil over wet paint. It's advisable first to stencil in corners of the table, adding more leaves in between as the paint dries.

Using the *Small Leaf* stencil and the pastel blue-green paint, stencil leaves adjoining the large leaves. Allow them to overlap the large leaves in some places, and in other places stop at the outline of the large leaves.

Using the *Rose in Bloom* stencil and pastel pink, stencil the roses where you marked them, covering parts of some leaves and painting around others.

Using the *Center Rose* stencil and the medium-pink paint, stencil centers on top of the roses. The centers can be stenciled on the roses in any direction. There is no particular way they must be lined up.

6 Hand painting

Mix a small amount of yellow into some off-white paint. Using a medium-sized artist's brush, paint random highlights onto the roses.

Paint short, curved outline strokes in and around the roses, using the deep-blue paint and a fine-point artist's brush. Paint random shadows and center lines onto the leaves, using a medium green and a fine-point artist's brush.

Create clusters of small dots in among the roses, using the dark-blue-gray paint and a fine-point artist's brush.

Paint the spindles on the legs, or add other details such as stripes, as shown here, with colors of your choice.

7 *Varnishing and glazing*

Enrich color and protect the paint by varnishing with non-yellowing, water-based varnish. If the colors are stronger than desired, glaze them to reduce their intensity by adding a very small amount of off-white paint to the varnish, mixing thoroughly. Brush onto the table as you would with pure varnish. (See *Varnishing,* page 48.)

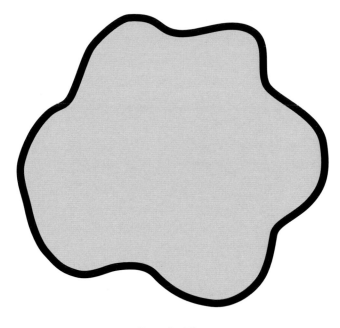

Rose in Bloom

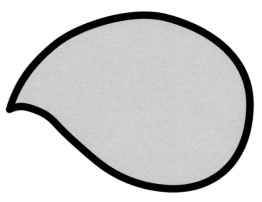

Large Leaf

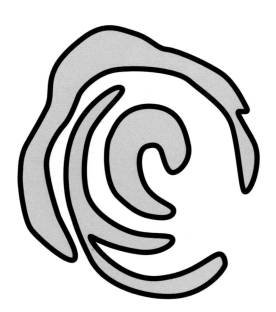

Center Rose

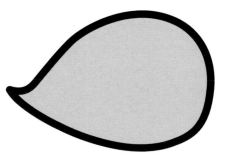

Small Leaf

Material Pleasures

FABRIC PANELS ADD DRAMA WITH TEXTURE AND COLOR

There is no better way to dramatically change the mood and appearance of a piece of furniture than to introduce fabric into the renovation equation. Coordinating paint and fabric covers the decorating bases of color, pattern and texture. The extensive selection of fabric — in a variety of weaves and a full range of colors, designs and patterns to suit any mood — means easy-to-make, impressive renovations. Shown here are two very different results from the same treatment, both with fabric panels replacing glass.

Read This First

This treatment is straightforward. The base of the piece of furniture is painted to coordinate with the fabric. If your table has a plastic laminate finish, use melamine paint. (*See Melamine Paint,* page 27.) While the paint dries, the fabric is laminated to a plywood board with spray glue, then varnished for protection. Spray glue allows only one chance to position the fabric onto the plywood when laminating. If this prospect makes you nervous, use wallpaper paste. (See *Office Romance,* page 183.) The panel is then assembled with the painted furniture. Purchase plywood that is the correct thickness for the opening. Cut it yourself,

or have it cut to fit the opening in the piece of furniture. Many lumberyards offer this service. The fit should not be tight, allowing space for the fabric to wrap over the edges. The plywood should be good one side, which means there should be no knots or roughness on one side of it. Good both sides, which is much more expensive, is not required. Check that the plywood is not warped. Purchase enough fabric to cover the plywood piece with a 2 in. (5 cm) overlap on all sides. When choosing the fabric, check how the pattern will fit the panel. Select relatively smooth fabric of a medium weight.

BEFORE

Left, a sorry coffee table with scuffed wood-grain melamine over particleboard and missing glass. *Worth saving? We thought we'd try.* **Right,** *a charming butler's table, complete with spray-painted gold glass and crumbling, flaking varnish.*

MATERIALS

- quart (litre) high-adhesion, water-based primer
- quart (litre) latex paint, in a color to match or coordinate with the fabric (eggshell or satin finish)
- plywood, good one side, cut to fit panel
- fine sandpaper (220 grade), tack cloth
- fabric to cover plywood, with at least 2 in. (5 cm) extra on all sides
- iron, scissors
- easy-release painter's tape, 2 in. (5 cm) wide
- spray glue (or cellulose-based wallpaper paste)
- dropsheet
- quart (litre) non-yellowing, water-based varnish
- *optional:* saws to cut plywood (step 2)
- *optional:* dressmaker's pins
- *optional:* wood trim and finishing nails
- *optional:* contrasting paint for trim
- *optional:* screws or white carpenter's glue, thick phone book, tools for attaching panel
- *optional:* braid, hot-glue gun

1 *Painting*

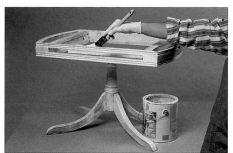

Refer to *Painting Basics* (page 34). Prepare, prime and paint the table with two coats of the latex paint.

Paint the piece of plywood on both sides with primer. Priming one side may cause warping, especially if the plywood is thin.

Note: Plywood may be primed and painted before or after cutting it to size.

2 *Plywood*

If it's not already cut, cut the plywood to the correct size or shape. For curves, use a jigsaw or scroll saw. Straight cuts should be made with a table saw. Lightly sand the cut edges and the top (the smooth side), removing any bumps. Even small bits of debris will dimple the fabric. Wipe with a tack cloth.

3 *Cutting fabric*

Iron the fabric, then lay it wrong-side-up on a flat surface.

Center the plywood onto the design of the fabric.

Note: If it is difficult to position fabric on its wrong side because the design is faint, turn the material over. Center the plywood on the right side, marking the corners with pins. Then turn the fabric to the wrong side, position the plywood inside the pins and remove the pins.

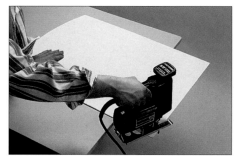

To mark a uniform overlap of fabric and supply a cutting line, tape the easy-release painter's tape onto the fabric, around the perimeter of the plywood. On a curved edge, use several short pieces to conform to the curve. Cut the fabric along the *outside* edge of the tape. Don't remove the tape.

4 *Laminating fabric*

Remove the plywood from the fabric, keeping the tape in place. Read the instructions on the spray glue for making a permanent bond. Usually they say to coat one surface well and bond the items while the glue is still "aggressively tacky." Place the fabric right-side-down onto a dropsheet to catch any overspray, and spray the fabric with the spray glue.

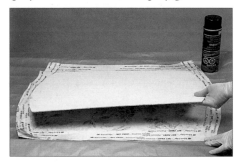

Place the smooth side of the plywood onto the glued area of the fabric, inside the taped edge, by placing the point of one corner in position, lining up the adjoining side and slowly lowering the plywood onto the fabric.

Optional: Using spray glue for laminating gives you only one try at positioning the fabric. If this idea is too scary, use wallpaper paste. (See *Office Romance*, page 183.)

5 *Laminating edges*

Turn the board over with the fabric attached. With clean hands, start in the center and work toward the edges, smoothing the fabric onto the plywood.

Turn the plywood and fabric upside-down again. Remove the tape. Cut across the corners so they will meet neatly when they are folded over. If the plywood has a curved edge, cut V shapes into the excess fabric so it will conform and lie flat when folded to the back of the plywood.

Working in sections, spray one fabric edge at a time with the spray glue, then pull the edge gently but firmly onto the back of the wood and smooth it down. Continue until all sides are glued down. Allow to dry.

6 *Varnishing*

To seal and protect the fabric, apply a coat of the water-based varnish and allow it to dry. Apply a second coat and allow it to dry. (See *Varnishing,* page 48.)

Using a fine sandpaper, *lightly* sand the second coat of varnish. Wipe clean with a tack cloth. Don't be alarmed by the cloudy appearance of the varnish.

Apply two more coats of varnish, sanding and wiping between coats. By now the surface of the fabric should be smooth and completely covered and protected by the varnish. Apply more coats if you wish.

7 *Details*

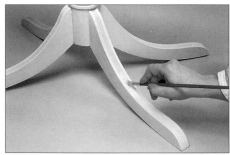

Optional: Highlight wood trim with contrasting color. Attach trim or other details, and paint as desired.

8 *Finishing*

If the bottom of the panel is visible, paint the exposed plywood on the back of the panel in the same color as the table.

Attach the panel to your piece of furniture. The coffee table panel was inserted from below with wood pieces screwed into the table for support.

The top of the butler's table can be simply set in, or glued in place with carpenter's glue. If gluing, place a telephone book on the tabletop until the glue is dry.

Note: If the fit of the panel shows gaps, you may wish to glue braid around the edge. Use a hot-glue gun. *Be careful not to burn your fingers, especially if you are not experienced with a glue gun.* The glue becomes hot enough to cause deep burns, and the glue sticks and keeps burning. Tuck and glue the ends of the braid between the panel and the edge.

Sheer Delight

GAUZY, PRINTED FLORAL VINES ENTWINE OVER PAINTED TRELLIS

Muted glazes layer pink springtime roses, purple and blue morning glories, and dusty-green foliage. These block-printed floral vines trail and weave their way through lattice over a subdued, neutral ground. Create a fresh and lovely painterly garden for a sunny solarium or a foyer, bedroom, bathroom or dressing room. This is a very modern approach to romance.

Read This First

Several simple techniques are used on this table, the sum of them more impressive than the parts. First a base coat of latex paint is applied. If your table has a plastic laminate finish, use melamine paint. (See *Melamine Paint,* page 27.) The base-coat paint is then textured by smooshing – lifting a deeper, similar shade of paint with a crumpled plastic bag. The lattice is taped and spray painted, and the floral patterns and leaves are block printed. The blocks for printing are made from cut-and-scored foam. You could purchase precut designs available in craft stores, but you'd save a small fortune by making your own from the patterns provided (pages 264 and 265). Once you become accustomed to block printing, you will find that nearly any piece of furniture deserves a touch of romantic decoration.

MATERIALS

- quart (litre) high-adhesion, water-based primer
- quart (litre) eggshell finish latex paint, in a pale bone shade
- easy-release painter's tape, 2 in. (5 cm) wide
- pint (.5 litre) glaze, paint pot
- pint (.5 litre) eggshell finish latex paint, light taupe
- small roller or a paint brush
- several grocery-sized plastic bags
- dropsheets or paper
- tape measure and pencil
- marker
- spray paint, pale gray
- fine-point artist's brush
- green pencil crayon or chalk
- thin flexible foam (used for children's crafts and available at art supply and craft stores)
- access to photocopier, or tracing paper and pencil
- scissors, X-acto knife
- inexpensive, medium-sized square-tipped artist's brush
- acrylic glazes (or mix acrylics and glaze, or substitute transparent acrylic paint), dark green, blue-green, light green, pink, red, orange, purple and blue
- quart (litre) non-yellowing, water-based varnish
- fine sandpaper (220 grade), tack cloth
- *optional:* small quantity medium-gray acrylic or latex paint
- *optional:* extender
- *optional:* metal polish for hardware

BEFORE

A well-proportioned dropleaf table with several desirable features – solid base, brass feet, and drawers with decorative hardware. But flaking varnish, cigarette burns and deep scars put it beyond the strip-and-finish category. An intricate paint job hides the imperfections.

1 *Painting*

Refer to *Painting Basics* (page 34). Prepare, prime and paint the table with two coats of the pale bone latex paint.

2 *Smooshing*

Create a soft, textured background by smooshing the tabletop. Position the leaves of the table in the up position. Tape the edges of the tabletop, using the easy-release painter's tape. Mix the taupe latex paint with glaze in a paint pot. Stir well. Extender can be added. (See *Glaze,* page 28; *Extender,* page 28.) Using a small roller or a paint brush, apply paint to a small section of the top.

Press a crumpled plastic bag onto the paint and remove it, lifting the taupe paint off and revealing the base coat in a crinkled pattern. Turn to a clean side of the plastic bag and recrumple as needed.

Continue, changing to a new plastic bag when the old one becomes gooey. When the full tabletop is textured, allow to dry.

3 *Measuring for lattice*

Drop the leaves of the table and mask around the top, protecting the base and the leaves of the table with dropsheets or paper. Measure the width of the tabletop.

Mark the width measurement along one side of the tabletop, beginning at a corner.

4 *Masking lattice*

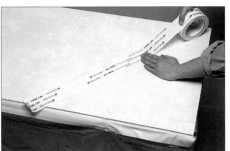

Lay a strip of easy-release painter's tape across the table, beginning at the measured mark on the side and crossing to the opposite corner. The bottom edge of the tape should run beside the mark and bisect the corner, forming a 45-degree triangle.

With a marker, mark this tape "First Strip."

Lay more tape strips side-by-side across the table, with each strip just touching the previous one. Continue, until the entire tabletop is covered with tape strips.

Remove the tape strips on either side of the first strip. Continue, removing every second strip. These strips can be reused later.

5 *Spray painting lattice*

Spray paint the tabletop with one or two coats, following the manufacturer's directions. (See *Spray Painting,* page 44.) Remove the tape strips when the paint is dry to the touch. Allow to dry thoroughly.

Repeat steps 3, 4 and 5, starting at the same end of the table but this time laying the tape in the opposite direction, across the spray-painted lines. Apply the spray paint. Allow to dry.

6 *Shadows*

Optional: To give the lattice depth, mix a small quantity of medium-gray paint, either acrylic or latex. Using a fine-point artist's brush, paint shadows on one side of the lattice lines where they cross other lines.

7 *Drawing vines*

Raise the table leaves into the up position. Using the pencil crayon or chalk, lightly sketch the direction of branches and vines for roses on one table leaf, and for morning glories on the other table leaf. The vines should begin at opposite corners of the table and follow a curvy S shape, then bend around and overlap on the lattice. Draw generous curves to accommodate the leaves and floral patterns. Add branches to fill space.

8 *Cutting block prints*

Transfer the patterns (pages 264 and 265), including tabs, by tracing or photocopying them. Trace the patterns onto the foam. Cut out the foam block-print shapes with scissors or an X-acto knife.

Using an X-acto knife, score along the lines inside the blocks. Try not to cut right through the foam. The scored lines will print darker, giving detail to the print.

9 *Printing*

Do some test prints on paper. Using a medium-sized, square-tipped artist's brush, paint glaze onto the surface of the foam block. Press the block face-down and apply even pressure over the surface. Lift off by pulling gently on the tab. Try using one color. Then try painting patches of several shades of one color on a single block. The block can be used several times with one load of glaze, producing interesting variations in the intensity of the print.

With the table leaves in the up position, begin printing the morning glory leaves in a variety of greens on one table leaf and onto the lattice, following the chalk lines for the vines. Overlapping the morning glory leaves gives wonderful depth to the pattern. Allow room for blossoms.

Continue, printing the rose leaves. Wash out the blocks and set them aside.

Add blossoms and buds, with morning glories in shades of blue and purple and with roses in shades of pink, red and/or orange. When the floral prints are complete, add the *Sepal Leaf Cluster* print at the base of the rose and morning glory blossoms.

IO *Freehand painting*

Using a fine-point artist's brush and glaze or acrylic paint, paint the vines and branches in a green/brown tone. (Mix green with some pink or purple to get green/brown.) Load the brush with thinned paint, and paint in a long sweeping motion. Do not worry about painting directly onto the lines. Use the lines only as a guide.

Add more leaves or blossoms where desired.

II *Varnishing and finishing*

Enrich color and protect the paint job by varnishing with two or three coats of non-yellowing, water-based varnish. Sand lightly with fine sandpaper and wipe with a tack cloth between each coat. When varnish is dry, use an X-acto knife to cut along the crease where the table leaves meet the table. Lightly sand any excess varnish with fine sandpaper. If sanding clouds the varnish, touch up these areas with another coat. (See *Varnishing,* page 48.)

Polish brass feet or other hardware, and attach the hardware.

PATTERNS FOR FOAM BLOCK PRINTS

Rose, Full Bloom

Rose, Profile Bloom

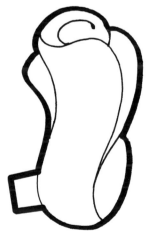

Rosebud

Rose Leaf

Sepal Leaf Cluster

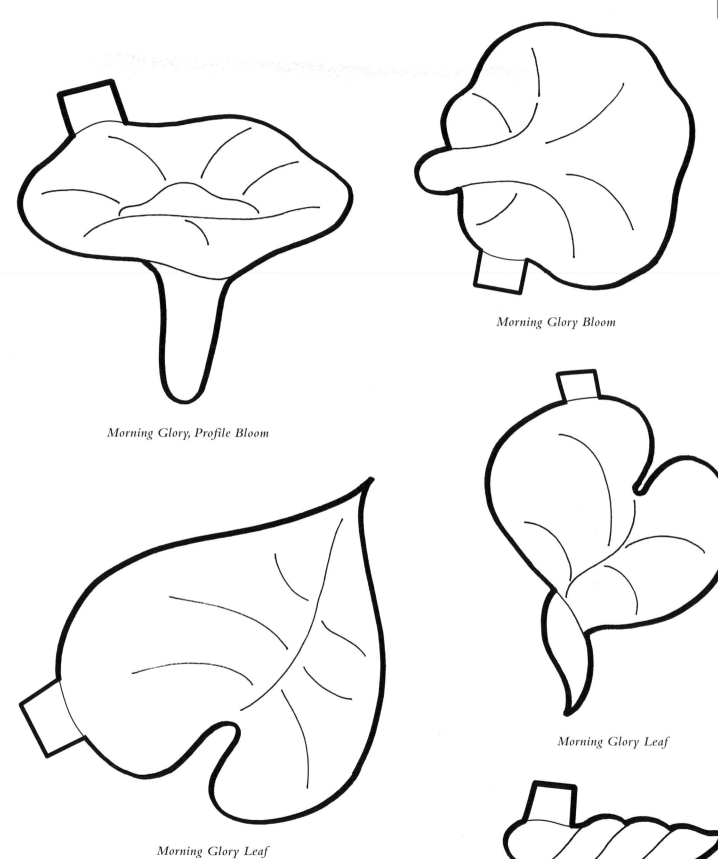

Morning Glory Bloom

Morning Glory, Profile Bloom

Morning Glory Leaf

Morning Glory Leaf

Morning Glory Bud

Ivy League

SET AN AMBER-STAINED TABLE
WITH IVY TRIMMED IN COPPER

Mix some natural elements – natural wood burnished by a honey
stain, trailing vines laden with leaves in rich summer greens, and
copper ore weathered to a glorious patina. These are the types
of elements meant to be combined. They offset each other
while creating harmony in texture and tone, resulting in
a remarkable piece of furniture.

Read This First

Choose a wooden table that is unpainted, or one that has a thoroughly stripped wooden tabletop. The tabletop is stained, and stain must be applied to raw wood. (The table's base can be made of any material.) A copper border is then painted and patinated. The vines and ivy leaves are block printed with a roller – a fast, easy method – and additional leaves are added at random for spontaneity. Then the whole top is varnished. The base of the table is painted deep teal green with latex paint. If your table base has a plastic laminate finish, use melamine paint. (See *Melamine Paint,* page 27.) Finally, the table is assembled. Although each phase of the process is simple and straightforward, the results are outstanding. The copper (often called copper topper) for the border and the patina (choose blue or green) can be purchased at art supply or craft stores. Purchase the compatible primer-sealer as well.

MATERIALS

- quart (litre) high-adhesion, water-based primer
- quart (litre) eggshell finish latex paint, deep teal green
- paint brush, 1½ in. (4 cm) wide
- ½ pint (250 ml) amber stain
- quart (litre) non-yellowing, water-based varnish
- ruler or tape measure
- easy-release painter's tape
- small boxes or plastic containers for supporting tabletop
- paint-on ground copper; compatible liquid patina (blue or green); clear, compatible primer-sealer
- 4 in. (10 cm) roller with sleeve
- several sheets of paper
- pair of inexpensive foam insoles
- pen or pencil
- scissors, X-acto knife
- spray glue; scrap paper or dropsheet
- light-colored pencil or piece of chalk
- fine-point artist's brush
- acrylic glazes (or mix acrylics and glaze, or substitute transparent acrylic paint), deep green, medium green, light green
- square-tipped artist's brush

BEFORE

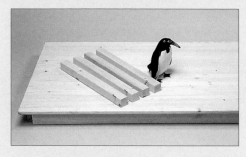

A knockdown table of unpainted solid wood. The possibilities for creative finishing are endless.

1 *Painting*

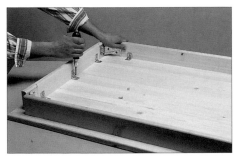

If the tabletop has a base attached, use the appropriate tools and remove it, if possible.

Refer to *Painting Basics* (page 34). Prepare, prime and paint the base and the legs deep teal green. Allow to dry. If your table is wooden and you wish to antique the base, do not prime it before painting. (See *Cupboard Love*, page 53.)

2 *Staining and varnishing*

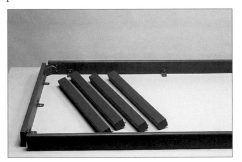

Stain the tabletop on both sides with the amber stain. Stain the underside first, then stain the top and sides. (See *Staining Wood*, page 46.)

Apply a coat of non-yellowing, water-based varnish (or the clear primer-sealer for the copper) to the underside, the top and the sides of the tabletop. The varnish will protect the stained wood, making it easy to wipe off any marks you might make while working. (See *Varnishing*, page 48.)

3 *Copper border*

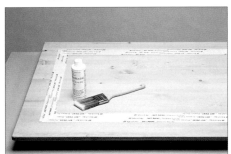

Measure and mask off a 3 in. (7.5 cm) wide border around the edge of the table-top with easy-release painter's tape. Mask an equivalent border on the underside of the table. The underside will be done first. Support the tabletop, upside-down, on small boxes or plastic containers.

Paint the border and the edges with the ground copper (copper topper). When the copper topper is dry to the touch, turn the table over and paint the border on the top. Read the manufacturer's instructions for the copper and apply a second coat, if recommended. Allow to dry.

Pour some patina blue (or green) into a small container. Brush the patina onto the copper on the underside of the table. Allow it to start turning color, then turn the tabletop over and apply the patina to the remaining copper on the top side and the edges.

The patina will begin coloring the copper very quickly; however, it must cure fully before being coated with primer-sealer, often taking three days. Read the manufacturer's instructions. Allow the patina to cure fully, then coat the copper border with clear, compatible primer-sealer. Allow to dry and remove all tape.

Apply a coat of primer-sealer to the patinated copper border on both sides of the tabletop. Do the underside of the table first. Coating the full tabletop will prevent a ridge of sealer from forming along the edge of the border. Allow to dry.

4 *Cutting patterns*

Trace the pattern for the *Small Ivy Leaf,* below. Set it aside. Cut a piece of paper the width of the roller sleeve and the right length to wrap around the sleeve.

Determine how many ivy leaves you will need. Cut out the traced ivy leaf. Trace around the leaf, onto the paper that fits around the roller. Make several tracings, creating a pattern of leaves along the length of the paper. Set this paper aside.

SMALL IVY LEAF

PATTERN

5 *Cutting block prints*

Lay the cut-out leaf pattern on the cloth side of an insole and trace around it. Continue tracing the pattern until you have the required number of ivy leaves. Cut out the leaves with scissors.

Using the X-acto knife, score veins into the leaves, cutting the foam – but not all the way through the cloth backing. As each leaf is finished, lay it *foam-side-down* onto the roller-sized piece of paper. You may wish to position the leaves as you originally placed and indicated them, or you could turn the paper over (to eliminate your original layout) and rearrange the pattern.

6 *Gluing block prints*

Position the roller-sized paper (with the ivy leaves on it) onto some scrap paper to catch any overspray from the glue.

Tape the edges down. Read the instructions on the spray-glue can for making a permanent bond. Most say to attach surfaces when the glue is "aggressively tacky," which means to spray, wait about two minutes, and then bond the surfaces. Check that the leaves are foam-side-down, then spray with glue.

Position the roller sleeve straight, at one end of the paper. Slowly roll the sleeve over the paper, picking up the foam leaves. Assist by lifting the leaves with your fingers if necessary. Don't worry if some glue becomes attached to the roller fuzz. It will dry. Continue until all leaves are securely glued to the roller sleeve. Set aside.

7 *Painting vines*

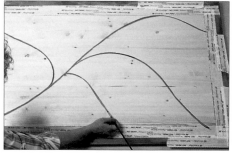

Using easy-release painter's tape, mask off the copper border. With a light shade of colored pencil or a piece of chalk, draw vines onto the center of the table. Make the lines gently curved so they will be easy to follow with the roller. Thin some medium-green paint or use a glaze to paint the vines. The paint should flow freely from a fine-point artist's brush. Paint the lines quickly, using your sketched lines only as a guide. Allow to dry.

8 Printing

Do some roller-print tests on paper before rolling the table. Apply paint to the foam leaves by painting them with a square-tipped artist's brush and several shades of green glaze, or transparent acrylic paint thinned with water. For greater depth and interest, try painting more than one shade of green on a leaf. Avoid getting paint on the roller fuzz. Lay the roller on the paper and apply pressure as you roll. Generally the block prints are better and crisper, with more detail, after some use.

Begin to print the table. Start at the edge of the table and roll into the center, following a vine. Try to keep the vine in the center of the roller as you roll, stopping at the junction of another vine or at the table edge. Continue adding paint to the foam and printing until all vines have leaves.

9 Finishing touches

Optional: If your pattern appears too regular for your liking, add some random large ivy leaves. Trace the *Large Ivy Leaf* pattern (this page), including the tab. Transfer it to the cloth side of the insole and cut out the shape. Score veins into the foam side and score between the tab and the leaf. Use this foam leaf as a single block print.

Apply paint to the foam side except for the tab, and apply the print to the tabletop, pressing it evenly. Remove the foam leaf by lifting it by its tab. Add leaves along the vines, as desired. These larger leaves can overlap the smaller ones.

Optional: Using the fine-point artist's brush and some paint or glaze, paint freehand tendrils randomly along the vines. A narrow border may also be masked and painted along the edge of the copper border.

10 Varnishing

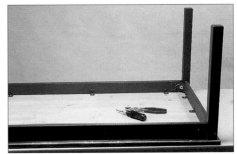

Enrich color and protect the stained wood and your paint job by varnishing the tabletop and edges with two coats of non-yellowing, water-based varnish. (See *Varnishing,* page 48.) Allow to dry.

11 Finishing

Reassemble the base of the table with the top.

LARGE IVY LEAF PATTERN

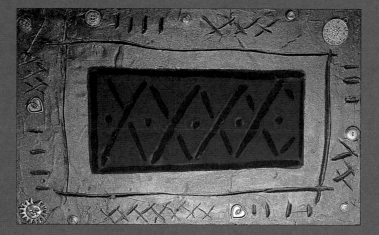

Sterling Qualities

SILVER AND MICA PUT
FIRE INTO THE IRON

Ignore the gold rush. Silver and its cousins — iron, aluminum, pewter and
chrome — create accents with both a presence and a cool neutrality. A small
wooden end table gets a novel twist when the very convincing antiqued silver
leaf makes it look too heavy to lift. Topping this table: gel infused
with mica, scored with freehand designs and impressed with
pewter medallions and silver buttons.

Read This First

This project produces unusual and daring results. Each of the stages to completion is straightforward. It's the combination that is startling. For this treatment, choose a table that is small and has a recessed top with a lip around it, possibly one that has a missing glass insert. First you spray paint the table a deep base color. If your table has a plastic laminate finish, use melamine paint for the base coat. (See *Melamine Paint,* page 27.) Over this color, apply silver leaf. Along with the silver leaf, use the compatible adhesive and sealer made by the same manufacturer — and buy enough to do the whole base of the table.

When the silver leaf is complete and antiqued, the mica-gel top is applied to the recessed tabletop. This is a very thick gel mixed with mica, which gives it a black iridescence. Gels with other additives are also available, but buy the heaviest consistency available. The density of the gel lets you carve and embed it with medallions and coins, which enhance the tone-on-tone nature of the piece. If desired, instant iron can be added to the table center and rusted to perfection, providing an unexpected touch of rust-red. Purchase these materials at art supply and craft stores.

BEFORE

An ordinary wooden end table. At second glance: some attractive lines, and interesting scored trim that deserves highlighting.

MATERIALS

- low-luster acrylic spray paint, 1 can each of deep green and black
- silver leaf, adhesive and sealer to cover the entire base of the table (Buy compatible products.)
- paint brush, 1 in. (2.5 cm) wide
- small, stiff-bristled house-painting brush
- mica gel or other heavy-consistency colored or textured gel (enough to cover and fill the top of the table)
- narrow and wide paint scrapers
- silver medallions, silver buttons, coins, or other flat objects
- wiping cloth
- *optional:* tubes of acrylics, pthalo green and Payne's gray
- *optional:* rags or paper towels
- *optional:* instant iron, instant rust (available at art supply and craft stores); fine-point artist's brush

1 *Spray painting*

Refer to *Painting Basics* (page 34). Prepare your table (*Preparation,* page 36). Then turn to *Spray Painting* (page 44), and spray paint the table with the black and green spray paints. Spray each color in sections, overlapping the colors. These variegated colors will show through cracks in the silver leaf when it is applied, giving it a rich appearance. Allow the spray paint to dry.

2 *Silver leaf*

The silver leaf should be applied to the base and around the rim of the top, but not on the top (the gel will be applied there).

Following the instructions on the jar, use the 1 in. (2.5 cm) paint brush to apply the adhesive for the silver leaf to a section of the table. Allow the adhesive to cure for the time specified. The adhesive will remain very sticky.

Remove a sheet of silver leaf from the folio. Lay it onto the adhesive. Don't worry if it tears or cracks as it is applied. In fact, such fissures are desirable. Burnish the silver leaf with your fingers, making sure the leaf is in contact with the adhesive.

Tear away any loose large sections of silver leaf at the edges of the adhesive and reserve them. Using the small, stiff-bristled house-painting brush, brush vigorously over the silver leaf, flicking away any small excess pieces. This is a surprisingly messy job, producing fairy dust all over your work area.

Continue applying adhesive and silver leaf in sections until the full table is covered except for the top. Leave cracks and small gaps open, but patch any large gaps.

3 *Antiquing*

Optional: Antique the silver leaf to make the silver richer and to kill the brightness. In a small tub, mix together some pthalo green and Payne's gray paint to make a deep-green-black tone. Thin with water until the paint is a watery consistency. Start in an inconspicuous section of the table. Paint a section of the silver leaf with the thin paint.

Allow the paint to sit for about two minutes, then wipe away excess paint with a slightly dampened rag or paper towel. Leave a fine film of paint on the silver leaf, and leave paint in depressions and recessed areas. Continue, until all silver leaf has been antiqued. Allow to dry. Then paint all silver leaf with sealer.

4 *Mica gel*

Apply the mica gel to the tabletop. Using the narrow paint scraper, scoop a blob of gel from the jar and plop it onto the tabletop. Continue until the jar is emptied. Spread the gel with the wide paint scraper, achieving an even depth of gel. The gel will shrink somewhat as it dries, so apply enough gel to make it nearly as thick as the recessed top.

When spreading the gel, avoid the temptation to try to make it completely smooth and flat, because that's impossible. Instead of fighting the natural textures that form from folding and smoothing the gel, continue working it until it is a satisfying overall texture.

5 *Embedding medallions*

While the gel is still very wet, press medallions or other flat objects into the surface. The medallions can create an uneven surface, so you may wish to keep them near the edges of the tabletop, where they're not likely to topple glasses of red wine.

While the gel is still wet, look over the tabletop. Add or remove medallions and adjust the texture of the gel. If necessary, use a damp cloth to clean off any excess gel on the lip surrounding the top.

While the gel is still wet, use the narrow paint scraper to carve patterns or designs into the gel. Don't worry if you goof. Simply smooth out the gel again (removing and cleaning off the medallions if necessary) and start over.

Allow the gel to dry, two to three days.

6 *Rusted iron*

Optional: Add instant iron and instant rust. Using instant iron, paint the center section of the tabletop, following the directions on the jar. Allow to dry overnight.

Using a fine-point artist's brush, paint a design on the iron with the liquid instant rust. Apply a second coat if necessary. Allow to cure and dry. Some instructions on instant iron and rust suggest coating with a sealer, but sealer can obscure the effect of the rust and will also diminish the iridescent quality of the mica and the medallions. Try a test on paper or cardboard to see if you like the results before sealing the tabletop.

If your table has a top that is not recessed or is otherwise not suited to a studded-gel treatment, consider combining cut-out appliqués of sheet metal with stenciled motifs in metallic leaf. (See Art in Craft, page 189.)

Mineral Rights

FAUX MARBLE, GRANITE AND GOLD
FORGE A MINER'S PALETTE

Gilded and polished stone, applied by the hand of an artist, is no longer
dismissed as a copy. Re-creating the aura of natural stone and ore has become an
art form unto itself. Hand-crafted faux-stone finishes should not be confused
with machine-printed melamines and other manufactured finishes. While
printed finishes are frauds, hand-rendered stone, marble, granite, or metallic
leaf treatment has a *trompe l'oiel* effect, fooling the eye for a second,
then allowing the onlooker to appreciate it for what it is —
a carefully crafted, often tongue-in-cheek replication.

Read This First

Faux-stone finishes should be executed in plausible places such as flat surfaces on bureau tops, tabletops or desktops. Some less likely surfaces are acceptable – door panels, columns, or window sills. But a complete dresser would never be made from stone – after all, it would be rather difficult to move. If you marbleize an entire dresser, chair or desk, do it with a sense of humor. In this project, first the set is painted with a base-coat color and the stone effects are applied over it. If your table has a plastic laminate finish, use melamine paint for the base coat. (See *Melamine Paint,* page 27.) The granite effect is achieved with a spray product widely available at paint stores. The normally lumpy spray is water soluble when dried and not practical for tabletops. The technique shown here, however, of sanding and varnishing the granite spray, produces a finish that is glasslike, waterproof and durable. The marbling technique can be as subtle or as bold as you wish. (Real marble comes in a staggering variety of color combinations, with veining that changes hue and intensity from piece to piece.) Antiqued gold leaf trim adds a warm and rich frame for the cooler stone treatments.

BEFORE

A shopworn, yet interesting dining set with its elaborate table base, layers of trim and King Arthur's Court chairs. The hexagonal expanse of the tabletop is a good setting for faux stone with gold leaf accents on the trim.

MATERIALS

- low-luster acrylic spray paint, forest green
- dropsheets
- easy-release painter's tape
- gold leaf and compatible adhesive and sealer
- inexpensive square-tipped artist's brush, ½ in. (1.25 cm) wide
- small paint brush
- rag
- *optional:* tubes of acrylics, burnt umber and/or burnt sienna

For faux granite:
- paper or plastic to cover table areas
- faux-granite spray and finishing spray lacquer (often available in kit form)
- quart (litre) non-yellowing, water-based varnish
- fine sandpaper (220 grade), tack cloth

For marbling and veining:
- pint (.5 litre) latex paint, deep green
- small quantitites of acrylic or latex paint: medium-pale green, medium-dark green, off-white
- rectangular household sponge
- 2 flat plastic containers (to fit sponge)
- stir sticks or similar items
- small quantity extender and glaze (See *Extender,* page 28; *Glaze,* page 28.)
- medium- to large-sized feather
- quart (litre) non-yellowing, water-based varnish
- fine sandpaper (220 grade), tack cloth

1 *Painting the base coat*

Refer to *Painting Basics* (page 34). Remove the tabletop if possible. Prepare the table (and chairs), spread out dropsheets, and spray paint the edges of the tabletop. (See *Spray Painting,* page 44.)

Spray paint the table's base and the chairs. If the table has a center leaf, keep it separate from the table – but don't forget to work on it at each appropriate step. Apply two or more coats to every piece to achieve dense coverage. Allow to dry.

2 *Gold leaf*

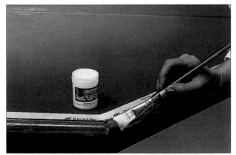

Decide which areas of trim or detail should be gilded. Using the easy-release painter's tape, mask the edges of the trim, unless the sections are easy to paint without masking (raised or isolated portions, for example). Using the inexpensive artist's brush, follow the manufacturer's

instructions and paint on the gold leaf adhesive. Allow to cure, according to instructions. The adhesive will remain highly tacky.

Remove the tape. Lay a sheet of gold leaf onto the adhesive. Burnish it with your fingers, pressing it into recessed areas with a toothpick or the point of a paint-brush handle. Tear off any large pieces of excess leaf and reserve them. Repeat until all adhesive is covered with gold leaf. Small cracks in the gold leaf are desirable.

Using a small paint brush (fairly stiff bristles are preferred), flick away all excess gold leaf – a surprisingly messy job, spreading fairy gold all over the place.

Apply gold leaf to the chairs and the table base. To apply gold leaf to finials or rungs, paint on the adhesive. Then wrap a sheet of gold leaf around, working the gilt into crevices or details. Cover any bare spots with scraps of gold leaf.

Paint sealer over all gold leaf sections and allow it to dry.

3 *Antiquing*

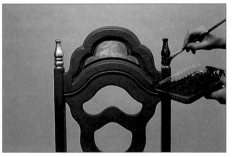

Optional: To make the gold richer and subdue the brightness, antique the gold leaf. Mix a small quantity of burnt umber and/or burnt sienna acrylics with water to create a watery consistency. Paint a section of gold leaf with the brown paint.

Wait for about two minutes. Wipe the section with a slightly damp rag, removing the excess. A thin film should remain, toning down the bright quality of the leaf and enriching the color. Allow the antiquing to dry. Then paint with a coat of sealer.

To make cushions for the finished chairs, see *Seating,* page 153.

4 *Faux granite*

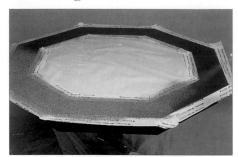

Using the easy-release painter's tape, mask off the area to receive the faux-granite treatment. Spread dropsheets and cover the rest of the table with paper or plastic taped in place. Allow no gaps.

Spray the masked-off section with the faux-granite spray, achieving a solid coverage. Allow to dry. It will be bumpy and speckly.

Use the spray lacquer that comes with the spray granite and spray the faux granite thoroughly, following the directions on the can. Allow to dry.

Paint a coat of the non-yellowing, water-based varnish onto the faux granite. Allow to dry.

Using fine sandpaper, *very lightly* sand the granite. Sanding will smooth some of the bumps. Don't be alarmed if the granite appears cloudy from the sanding. Use a tack cloth to wipe the surface completely clean of all dust. Then apply another coat of varnish. The granite should be fairly smooth. More varnish, which will give the granite a completely smooth surface, will be applied later. Allow to dry. (See *Varnishing,* page 48.)

5 *Marble base coat*

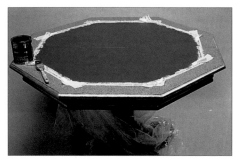

Remove all tape and paper from the tabletop, leaving the dropsheet on the table base for protection. If the table has a center leaf, place it into the table. Determine which areas will be marbled. Mask around these areas with easy-release tape. Paint the marble sections with a base coat of deep-green latex paint. Allow to dry.

6 *Marbling*

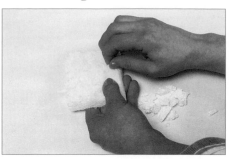

Lightly dampen the household sponge. Create a cratered moonscape – the more cratered, the better – on one side of the sponge by pulling small, irregular chunks out of the surface. Set the sponge aside.

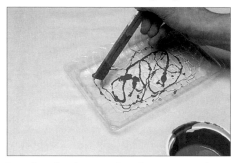

In a flat plastic container large enough to accommodate the sponge, use a stir stick or other implement to drizzle ribbons of extender and glaze in a random pattern. (See *Extender,* page 28; *Glaze,* page 28.) Then drizzle medium-pale green and, on top of that, medium-dark green. Thin the paint with water if necessary. Neither of these colors should be as dark as the deep-green base coat.

Hold the still-damp sponge flat, crater-side-down, and dip it into the drizzled paint. Don't squish it or move it in any way that will mix the paint. Lift the sponge and dip again in another section of the flat container.

7 *Veining*

Pat the paint side of the sponge onto the base coat of the tabletop, making a curved path of color. When patting, never drag the sponge. Use only an up-and-down motion. Work over the path, patting lightly outward from the center. The more patting, the more soft and graduated the color will be. Continue in this manner, creating several lighter pathways of color that gently blend into the base coat.

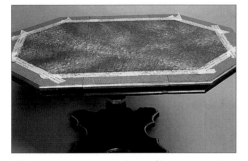

This process creates the softly textured-looking background colors of the rock formation. Stand back from the table and squint to see a pattern emerge. When working across the table's center leaf, try to balance the design so that, when the center leaf is removed, the pattern will match fairly closely. If the center leaf will be a fairly permanent fixture, it is more important that the design match from the table to the leaf and across it. But if it will seldom be used, concentrate on matching the design with the center leaf removed. (Ideally, the design will match both with and without the center leaf.) Remove the leaf and lightly touch up the pattern to make it match across the division.

Do the veining with the center leaf out of the table and the table closed. Drizzle small, equal amounts of extender, glaze and off-white paint into a flat container. Don't mix.

Take the feather and dip a length of the feathery edge into the container, allowing the feather to pick up both paint and extender.

Starting at an edge close to you, place the feather lightly onto the table and push it away from you. As you push, make your hand tremble in small jerking movements.

Don't give in to the urge to drag the feather toward you. If you do, the veining will look very regular and phony. As you progress, the edge of the feather will break up into segments, producing multiple lines in various widths, all following the same motion. This look is desirable. For best results, push the feather using the left hand (if you are right-handed), and vice versa.

For a natural appearance, remember that most veining should radiate from one point, breaking into branches that in turn create additional points of origin for more veins. Stand back regularly to see the overall pattern of the veining. Veining can be as subtle or as bold as you'd like.

Place the center leaf into the tabletop. Join the veins from one side of the leaf to the other, using the feather and paint mixture.

8 *Varnishing*

To protect the paint, enrich the color and impart a deep, glasslike finish, give the tabletop, including the granite, three coats of non-yellowing, water-based varnish. Sand lightly with fine sandpaper and wipe with a tack cloth between each coat. Varnish the center leaf separately. (See *Varnishing,* page 48.)

Mad for Mosaic

CRAZY PAVING DISHES UP THREE FASCINATING TABLETOPS

Mosaic's history is cemented in Greek and Roman times, when magnificent pictures and designs were created from tiny tiles. But contemporary mosaic patterns, whether pictorial or abstract, can be created with combinations of whole or broken tiles, cutlery, marbles, jewelry, beads — even antique picture frames and lockets. Mosaics today not only mix texture, color and pattern, but also combine unlimited creative potential with hard-wearing permanence.

Read This First

Apply mosaic to a stable wooden tabletop, or cut a piece of plywood to fit the table. Many lumberyards will cut wood to your specifications, even circles. With its small irregular pieces, mosaic eliminates the precision work of cutting and fitting tile. The tile and crockery are smashed with a hammer (great therapy), and the pieces are placed to fit. Adhesives and grout are easy to use and virtually foolproof.

When collecting tile and other bits and pieces, decide ahead approximately which colors and textures you want. But be flexible. The serendipity of finding mismatched yet compatible pieces is inspiring. And don't worry if items aren't all exactly the same thickness. Some leveling can be done at the adhesive stage. Purchase *sanded floor grout,* not wall grout, in a color to complement the tile. Mosaic uses far more grout than tile, because the mosaic pieces are small, so buy at least double the recommended amount. Once the tile and grout choices are made, purchase paint in a coordinating color to paint the table's base. To tile a countertop or table with full tiles, not mosaic, see *The Cupboard Was Bare* (page 105, steps 10 to 14).

MATERIALS

- fine sandpaper (220 grade) and tack cloth to degloss existing tabletop
- *if the table needs a top:* plywood, good one side, cut to fit your table (step 1); jigsaw, table saw; beam compass (or string, hammer and nail); pencil or pen
- primer and paint (step 2)
- tiles, crockery and other collectible items (marbles, glass beads, etc.)
- towel or rag
- hammer
- tile adhesive (either ready-mixed or the dry, mix-it-yourself kind)
- tongue depressor or similar disposable utensil
- sanded floor grout in the color desired (at least double the quantity specified on the package)

- small pail or bowl for mixing grout
- dropsheet
- rubber or plastic kitchen spatula
- plastic scrub pad or coarse rag, cloth
- *optional:* steel wool (for wrought iron)
- *optional:* power drill and large-diameter bit
- *optional:* bins for sorting tile pieces
- *optional:* grout sealer

BEFORE

Left, a table for two, in canary yellow with plenty of rust, needs some TLC.
Center, an interesting side table with that old tired look. But closer examination reveals elegant
lines, with the lip around the tabletop providing a perfect edge for mosaic.
Right, this new, small and rather expensive occasional table came with four quarry tiles set into
its top, one of which broke in transit. A new surface was needed.

AFTER

Left, a glossy-black border and fiddlehead pattern provide a sophisticated counterpoint to
earth-tone tile. The pattern is created from narrow border tile which, with its
consistent width, is excellent for composing linear designs.
Center, small, square, patterned accent tiles are arranged in a center block, with more smashed and
used as a border detail. Coordinating pieces of white tile fill the gap.
Right, this crockery mosaic combines plates, marbles, beads — and even the handle of a fork.
Crockery mosaics, because of their busy nature, are best when showcased
on a small table.

1 *Preparing the tabletop*

If your table has a top, sand it well to remove any loose or flaking varnish and to degloss any shiny areas, so that the adhesive will stick. Use a tack cloth to clean off all dust.

If the table has no top, cut one to size from plywood of the required thickness, ¼ in. (6 mm) if set into a small table, ½ in. (1.25 cm) for medium-sized tables, and ¾ in. (2 cm) for dining-sized tables. Many lumberyards provide a cutting service. If you're cutting the top, use a jigsaw for odd shapes or a table saw for straight edges. If the tabletop is circular, draw the circle with a beam compass. If you don't have a beam compass, hammer a small nail into the center of the board. Tie a string to the nail and, at the correct radius from the center, tie a pencil or pen. Holding the string taut and the pencil or pen straight up and down, draw a circle.

Cut along the line with a jigsaw.

Optional: Paint the underside of the tabletop (the good, smooth side of the plywood) with a coat of primer, then a coat of paint. Allow to dry.

2 *Painting*

If your table is wooden, prepare, prime and paint the base with either latex or spray paint. (See *Painting Basics,* page 34.) If your table has a plastic laminate finish, use melamine paint. (See *Melamine Paint,* page 27.)

If your table is wrought iron, clean it thoroughly, removing as much rust as possible with steel wool, and spray paint it with rust-covering spray paint. (See *Spray Painting,* page 44.)

Whatever type of table you have, do not paint the area to be tiled.

3 *Smashing tile*

Place the tile (or crockery), covered with a towel or rag, on a hard surface such as a concrete floor. Breaking tile on wood or another resilient surface is far more difficult.

Hit the tile (or crockery) with the hammer. After a few tries, you'll know how hard you need to hit to break things up. If you prefer to do your smashing without covering the materials, allowing greater control over the size of the pieces, *you must wear safety goggles.*

Continue breaking up the pieces of tile until they are a uniform, fairly small size, about an inch (2.5 cm) across. Sorting different color groups into different bins can help in the design process. Use care handling the broken pieces. Not only are the edges sharp, but the glaze on crockery and tile is actually glass. Small slivers of the glaze may break off and are difficult to see.

4 *Planning mosaic*

Plan your design. One by one, lay the tile and crockery pieces onto the tabletop, fitting the pieces onto the space. Leave a narrow gap, ⅛ to ¼ in. (3 to 6 mm), between each tile. This gap will later be filled with grout.

If making a crockery mosaic, set the pieces at random, or create some order by positioning like pieces together to form a block of color or perhaps a whole or partial shattered plate. Arrange all the pieces of the design in place, including any beads, marbles, jewelry and cutlery.

If creating a tile mosaic, mix both color and texture to create pattern. The design can be pictorial (sunflower, moon, stars, cat silhouette, rosebud) or abstract (pinwheels, zigzags, checkers, curlicues). Whole tiles can be worked in among the broken pieces, and borders can be formed.

5 *Gluing mosaic*

Use ready-mixed adhesive, or mix a small quantity of the dry adhesive with water according to the manufacturer's directions. Mix more as required. The adhesive should be the consistency of peanut butter.

Using a tongue depressor or similar stick, apply adhesive to the bottom of a mosaic piece. Cover the full underside of the mosaic piece, then put it back in its place on the tabletop. As you place it back, give it a little twist to ensure full contact of the adhesive with the tabletop. (If working on a crockery mosaic, glue all pieces except marbles and beads. See step 6.)

Start at one side or in a corner. With large surfaces, it's easy to lose track of which pieces have been glued. Place a ruler or stick across the table and work up to the stick. Then move the stick further along and work up to it again. Continue until all tiles are glued.

Keep the mosaics as level as possible. Add extra adhesive to the thin mosaic pieces in order to bring them up to the height of thicker ones. Allow the adhesive to dry and cure, a process that takes one or two days. Check the package directions for drying times.

6 *Gluing marbles and beads*

If working on a crockery mosaic, glue down everything except marbles or glass beads. Allow the adhesive to dry and cure. Using a power drill and a large drill bit, drill holes through the tabletop where the marbles are to be placed. Drill slowly and carefully, trying not to dislodge other pieces. If a piece pops off, glue it back on. Test the marble in the hole. It should sit lower than it did before, more level with the other mosaic pieces. If it is still too high, redrill the hole with a larger drill bit.

Spread some adhesive around the rim of the drilled hole, then place the marble or glass bead into the hole. Light from the drilled hole should illuminate the glass. Allow the adhesive to dry and cure.

7 Grouting

If you are applying mosaic to a large tabletop or a countertop, place the top onto its base now. Moving a large mosaic tabletop separately after grouting may cause grout to crack. Make sure the screws are the correct length and will not disturb the mosaic pieces.

Mix a small amount of grout. (A large batch will begin to dry while you're working.) It's easiest to work on small sections, unless two people are working together. Place four cups of warm water into a small pail or bowl. Add grout to the water until it has the consistency of heavy sour cream mixed with sand. If the grout is too wet, it will form hairline cracks when it dries. Too dry, and it will dry before you can work with it. Mix well. If the package directions call for slaking (allowing it to sit undisturbed), you must let the grout mixture sit for the required time.

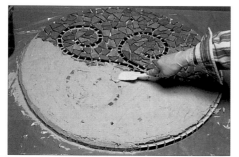

Work over a dropsheet. This is a very messy job, resulting in a lot of grout crumbs and grout sand. Using a rubber or plastic kitchen spatula, spread grout over a section of the tiles, forcing it into the spaces between the tiles. If your table has a lip around the edge, fill up to the lip.

Fill all spaces, up to and including tiles attached to the cut edge of the plywood.

8 Removing excess grout

While the grout is still wet, sprinkle a dusting of dry grout onto the surface. This dusting will absorb some surface dampness, making the surface grout easier to remove.

Do not use any water in this step. Using a dry plastic scouring pad or a coarse rag, rub the surface of the tabletop, removing the excess grout and exposing the surface of the mosaics. The grout should fill the spaces between the tiles and be very close to level with the tops of the mosaic pieces.

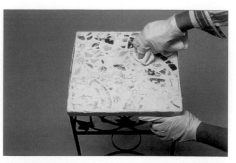

It is tempting to use water to wash off the grout, but water is the enemy of grout. It will create hairline cracks as the grout dries.

Once the surface grout has been removed, wipe the surface of the mosaic clean with a slightly damp cloth.

Never put leftover grout down the drain or into a toilet, unless you like to keep your plumber busy. Instead, place all left-over grout into household garbage. Allow the grout to dry and cure while the table remains in place – don't move it. This stage will take two days.

9 *Finishing*

If the tabletop has not been reunited with its base, reattach it now.

If desired, apply grout sealer (available at tile stores) onto the grout. This product prevents the grout from absorbing stains.

Turning the Tables

FOLK PAINTING CREATES A VERSATILE SEASONAL SCENE ON A DROPLEAF TABLE

Folk painting is a timeless art form, combining naiveté with representations of everyday life. These settings focus on country scenes, domestic activities and depictions of small-town life. Whether stark and simple or full of activity and detail, folk painting portrays an aura of a simpler, cozier time. This table, painted with summer on one leaf and linked by sky to autumn on the other leaf, portrays country seasons with a twist. For the experienced painter, allow us to serve as inspiration for your own creation. For the novice, detailed instructions make painter-perfect results.

Read This First

For this technique, choose basic, plain furniture with simple lines. While a limited amount of ornamental detail can enhance your work, overly refined and fussy pieces will compromise the painting style. Folk painting is an ideal camouflage for a beaten-up finish. The complex pattern and the texture of the paint distract from the damage. The flat nature of folk art, which does not require proficiency in painting perspective, puts it within the grasp of the novice. Indeed, the best folk art is that which is the most unaffected and childlike.

There are two stages to painting a piece of furniture in this style. A basic paint job of primer and latex paint (or spray paint, if preferred) is required. If your table has a plastic laminate finish, use melamine paint for the base coat. (See *Melamine Paint,* page 27.) The folk painting is applied over the base coat of paint. An array of colors is required. This is an ideal project for anyone with a collection of acrylics, or for someone wishing to start a collection.

BEFORE

A nicely proportioned Duncan Phyfe-style dropleaf table. Missing its brass feet, and with its top scarred and battered, it was a great buy at a used furniture store.

MATERIALS

- quart (litre) high-adhesion, water-based primer
- quart (litre) latex paint, eggshell or satin finish, Oxford green (Use acrylic-based spray paint if you prefer.)
- painting tools: paint brush, small roller, roller tray
- access to photocopier
- scissors
- chalk or white colored pencil
- tubes of acrylics: titanium white, burnt umber, mars black, pale pink (or red mixed with white), Payne's gray, pthalo green, burnt sienna, Prussian blue, various greens, browns, yellows and reds
- square-tipped artist's brush, ½ in. (1.25 cm) wide
- fine-point artist's brush for detail
- easy-release painter's tape
- quart (litre) non-yellowing, water-based varnish
- *optional:* paste wax, buffing cloth

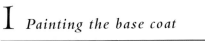

1 *Painting the base coat*

Refer to *Painting Basics* (page 34). Prepare, prime and paint the full table Oxford green. If you prefer, use acrylic-based spray paint. (See *Spray Painting*, page 44.) If your table is wooden and you wish to antique it, don't prime it before painting. (See *Cupboard Love,* page 53.) Reassemble the table when dry.

2 *Painting the cow*

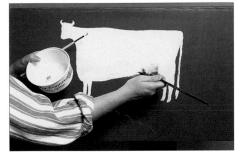

Place the table on a small but sturdy box or table. The area to be painted should be at eye level; you should be able to walk around the table, reaching it from all sides. (Recruit some help to lift the table.)

Photocopy the cow (page 298) to fit your table. Cut it out. Place it in position, centering it on a leaf of the table, and trace around it with chalk or white colored pencil.

Mix some titanium white acrylic paint with a small amount of burnt umber (to kill the brightness). Using the square-tipped artist's brush, paint the full silhouette of the cow. Allow to dry. Add a second coat if needed.

Draw outlines of Holstein spots onto the cow and paint them in with mars black.

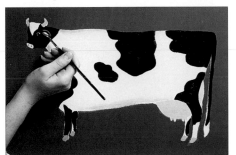

Mix white with black to make a light gray. Paint a soft gray line in the white portions of the cow, near the edge of the silhouette, to make the cow appear three-dimensional. Save some gray. Using the fine brush, outline the eye and ear, and paint the hooves and horns gray.

Using pale pink mixed with a small amount of burnt umber, paint the udder, nose and ear.

3 *Painting scenery*

Draw the outline of hills, barns, trees and houses in white chalk. Tape the edges of the tabletop using the easy-release tape.

To paint a dark undercoat on the hills, use Payne's gray and begin to paint from the base of each hill up, blending into pthalo green. Thin the pthalo green and paint it as a semitransparent glaze. Paint up to the cow, defining her legs and body. When the paint is dry, redraw any objects that have been covered.

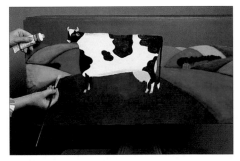

Using a variety of greens (and some browns if desired), paint each hill or field a different tone, painting around houses, trees and other such scenic objects. Use the paint directly from the tube, with very little water; you'll achieve a rich scumbled effect, with hints of the base coat showing through. Lines can be left unpainted along the edge of each hill to create divisions.

Use a square-tipped brush to paint around the cow and tidy up her outline.

4 *Painting details*

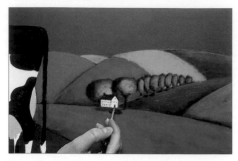

Decide the direction from which the sun is shining. Paint the shadowed side of all trees pthalo green. Paint the sunny side a bright green. Paint the shadowed side of a house light gray or beige, and paint the sunny side bright white. Roofs and windows can be black. Add shadows on the ground next to the shady sides of trees and structures, anchoring them to the ground.

Add rows of crops on some of the hillsides. These can simply be lines, dashes or rows of dots that follow the contour of the hills. Use contrasting colors for crops.

Add any other details you wish: lakes, streams with fish, roads, hay wagons, farm animals, fences, tractors, people – whatever captures your imagination.

5 *Painting the horse*

Turn the table around. On the remaining table leaf, photocopy the horse (page 299) and draw the outline of the horse, as you did for the cow. Fill the silhouette of the horse with Payne's gray. Paint over the gray, almost to the edges of the silhouette, with burnt umber, leaving an edge of the gray showing. Add form and highlights with burnt sienna. Draw the background hills.

Paint the mane, tail and hooves black, and outline the eye in light gray.

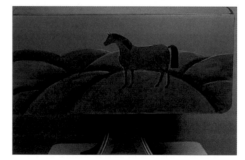

Tape the sides of the tabletop. Paint a base coat on the hills, using Payne's gray at the base and blending into burnt umber at the tops. The burnt umber and Payne's gray can be thinned with water and applied as a glaze. Redraw any details that were painted over.

6 *Painting additional details*

Paint the hills, painting around trees, barns and other details, as you did on the cow painting, but use a warm fall palette of yellows, dull greens and browns. Add details as you did for the cow painting, keeping in mind the sunny and shady sides of the objects and the fall tones and colors.

Add more fall details if desired, such as burning leaves, pumpkins, scarecrows, harvest baskets, a church, a mill, a stream, hay bales or wagon rides.

7 *Painting the sky*

Get someone to help remove the table from its perch. Position both table leaves in the up position and draw clouds on the sky. Look at them from both sides, to be sure they don't look upside-down from one side.

Mix white with a small amount of brown and/or pink (to subdue the brightness) and paint the clouds.

Mix half a tube of titanium white and a third of a tube of Prussian blue. Paint the sky blue up to the clouds, allowing the green base coat to show through around the clouds by leaving a small edge unpainted. Drop the leaves of the table, and use blue to paint exposed edges between the table's top and its leaves. Allow to dry.

8 *Varnishing*

Enrich the color and protect the paint job. Position tape in the grooves where the leaves meet the tabletop and place the leaves in the up position. Varnish the tabletop with two coats of non-yellowing, water-based varnish. Allow to dry, and remove the tape from the grooves. Then very lightly sand off any excess varnish. If sanding leaves the varnish cloudy, apply another light coat to the area. (See *Varnishing,* page 48.) Keep the leaves in the down position until the paint and varnish have cured. Then, to help prevent sticking, apply one or two coats of paste wax in the grooves where the leaves meet the tabletop.

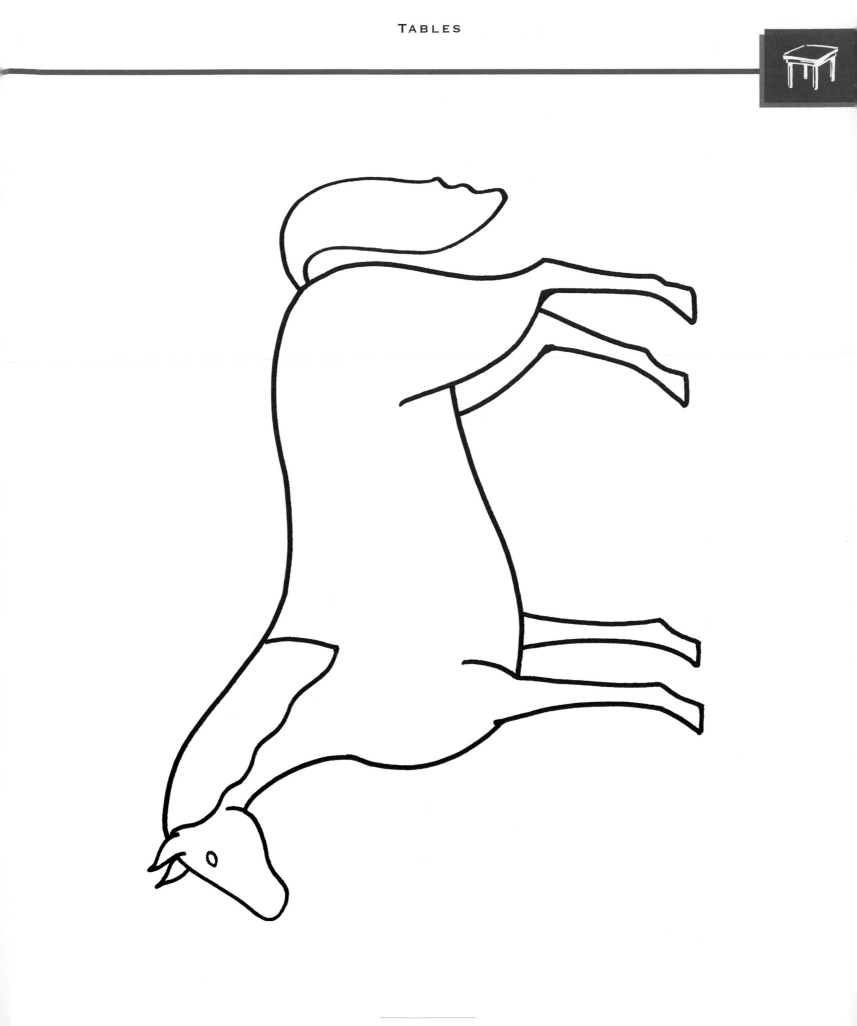

Index

adhesives (also see découpage):
  carpenter's glue (about), 16
  carpenter's glue on fabric découpage, 187
    (step 9)
  hot glue (about), 16
  hot glue on a chair halter, 138 (step 7)
  hot glue on cushions, 166 (step 9), 167
    (step 10)
  hot gluing braid, 167 (step 10), 257 (step
    8)
  mucilage (about), 16
  mucilage for crackle, 65 (steps 1–2)
  spray glue (about), 17
  spray glue on block prints, 59 (step 3), 270
    (step 6)
  spray glue on cushions, 156 (steps 3–4),
    165 (steps 3–4)
  spray glue on stencils, 238 (step 4), 249
    (step 4)
  spray gluing fabric to plywood, 256 (steps
    4–5)
  tile adhesive with full tiles, 112 (step 12)
  tile adhesive with mosaic, 289 (steps 5–6)
  wallpaper paste (about), 17
  wallpaper paste for découpage, 77 (step
    3), 179 (steps 2–3), 211 (steps 4–5)
  wallpaper paste and fabric, 185 (steps 3–9)
antiquing (also see patina):
  by sanding paint (about), 53–54
  by sanding (application), 55 (steps 4–6),
    101 (steps 2–5)
  on crackled varnish, 111 (step 9)
  on faux plaster, 224 (step 9)
  on faux stucco, 84 (step 6)
  on gold leaf, 72 (step 6), 174 (step 6), 281
    (step 3)
  on silver leaf, 275 (step 3)

baskets added to tables, 242–245
block printing:
  block printing (about), 25, 230, 260

block printing fish, 231 (steps 2–6); 233
    (pattern)
block printing roses and morning glories,
    262 (steps 8–9); 264–265 (patterns)
block printing single ivy leaves, 271 (step
    9); 271 (pattern)
block printing using foam, 262
block printing using a foam insole, 59,
    231, 270–271
potato printing, see potato printing
roller block printing (about), 25, 43, 58,
    268
roller block printing ivy, 270 (steps 4–8);
    270 (pattern)
roller block printing leaves, 59 (steps
    2–5); 60 (pattern)
brushes and applicators (also see each tech-
    nique):
  block prints (about), 25, 43, 58, 230, 260,
    268
  brushes (about), 24, 40–41
  kits (about), 32
  rollers (about), 25
  special applicators (about), 32
  sponges (about), 25
  stenciling materials (about), 33
  texturing materials (about), 25
brush painting (also see folk painting, free-
    hand painting):
  brush painting (about), 40
  brush painting a flat area, 41 (step 1), 55
    (steps 2–3), 101 (steps 2–3)
  color blocking on a chair, 149 (step 1)
  color wash on a basket, 244 (steps B–C)
  copying a fabric pattern onto cane, 137
    (step 3)
  cutting in, 41 (step 2)
  detail and freehand brush painting, 41
    (steps 2–3)
  dry-brush painting, 191 (step 2)
  painting with templates, 119 (steps 2–3)

roller painting (about), 42–43 (also see
    rollers and roller printing)
  spindles, 120 (step 4)
  stripes (about), 198, 199 (steps 2–5)
  varnish, 48–49

cabinets, 50
cane on chairs:
  alternatives to cane, 124, 136, 161
  painting on cane, 137 (step 3)
  removing seat, 125 (step 1), 137 (step 1)
  replacing cane seat by weaving, 161–163
chairs, 114
choosing furniture, 12
color washing:
  on a basket, 244 (steps B–C)
  over partial stripping, 126 (step 7)
compass (beam compass or alternative), 237
    (step 3)
corners:
  cutting, 166 (step 9)
  fabric laminated to a desk, 186 (step 6)
  notching, 165 (step 3)
  notching for laminating, 256 (step 5)
  sewing, 159 (step 4)
  stapling, 160 (step 6), 166 (step 8)
crackle:
  crackled paint (about), 63–64
  crackled varnish (about), 106
  crackling and antiquing varnish, 111
    (steps 8–9)
  crackling paint, 65 (steps 1–2)
  gum Arabic for crackling varnish (about),
    106, 111 (steps 8–9)
  mucilage for crackling paint (about), 16
cushions, see seating
cutlery for ornamentation, 148–150

decals, see templates and decals
decorations, see ornamentation
découpage:
  découpage (about), 70, 76, 178, 222

découpage (continued)

découpage (preparation), 179 (step 1), 211 (step 1)

full-coverage fabric découpage, 182–187

grape leaves, 96 (steps 6, 8)

ovals with silicone faux plaster, 223 (steps 2–3)

photocopies of fabric, 77 (steps 1–4)

posters (about), 210

posters (application), 211 (steps 2–6)

random découpage, 179 (step 2)

stamps on gold leaf, 71 (steps 4–6)

wrapping paper découpage, 179 (steps 3–4)

deglossing agents:

compounds and TSP (about), 18

emery cloth, garnet paper, green sandpaper (about), 19

sanding for deglossing, 37 (step 5)

sanding on new unpainted wood, 47 (step 1), 143 (step 1)

sanding paint for antiquing, 55 (steps 4–6), 101 (steps 2–5)

sanding stripped wood, 109 (step 4)

sanding varnish, 49 (step 3)

sandpaper (about), 18

tack cloth (about), 19

desks, 168

distressing (*also see* crackle):

distressing (about), 190

on faux stucco, 83 (step 4)

on paint, 191 (step 2)

dragging, 170–175 (*also see* texturing)

dressers, 194

extender, see paint additives

fabric dyes as stain, 140–144

fabric treatments:

adding braid for finishing, 257 (step 8)

covered plywood panels for tabletops (about), 254

covering a full desk, 182–187

covering plywood panels, 255 (steps 3–6)

for cushions, *see* seating

halters for chairs (about), 136

halters for chairs, 137–138 (steps 4–7)

sewing piping, 159 (step 4)

shirred curtain, 78 (steps 6–7)

weaving webbing, 161

wrapping chairs (about), 130

wrapping chairs (preparation), 131 (steps 1–2)

wrapping chairs, 132 (steps 3–8)

fixing furniture:

cane chair (about), 136

cane seat (about), 124

choosing furniture, 12

filling holes with wood filler, 37 (step 3)

filling screw holes, 109 (step 5)

fixing loose parts, 37 (step 4)

inserts for tables (fabric covered), 253–257

installing a window in a wardrobe door, 78 (step 5)

reattaching a backrest cushion, 167 (step 11)

reattaching a seat cushion, 160 (step 7)

removing loose varnish, 37 (step 5)

removing an old cushion, 131 (step 1)

tools (manual and power), 20–21

folk painting (*also see* brush painting, freehand painting):

folk painting a rural scene (about), 293–294

folk painting a rural scene, 295–297; 298–299 (patterns)

folk painting trees and fruit, 110 (step 7)

freehand painting (*also see* brush painting, folk painting):

borders, checker squares, curlicues, fruit, sawtooth, 216–219

on cane, 137 (step 3)

curlicues and zigzags, 245 (step C)

details on stenciled roses, 250 (step 6)

freehand brushwork, 41

motifs on a chair, 149 (step 2)

motifs, shadows on a clock face, 238 (step 8)

tendrils, 271 (step 9)

vines, 263 (step 10), 270 (step 7)

gel:

gels (about), 28

mica gel for a tabletop (carved and studded), 276 (steps 4–5)

gesso as faux stucco, 82–83 (steps 2–4, 6)

glaze and glazing (*also see* paint additives):

glazes (about), 28

glaze added to paint for dragging, 173 (step 3)

glaze added to paint for marbling, 282 (step 5)

glaze added to paint for ragging on, or off, 110 (step 6)

glaze added to paint for sponge painting, 205 (step 5)

gold paint highlights on faux plaster, 225 (step 10)

paint used as glaze to antique gold leaf, 72 (step 6), 174 (step 6)

paint used as a glaze to antique silver leaf, 275 (step 3)

paint and varnish glaze to subdue color, 251 (step 7)

premixed glazes for block printing, 262 (steps 9–10)

thinned paint color wash on a basket, 244 (steps B–C)

thinned paint color wash on partial stripping, 126 (step 7)

glue, see adhesives

gold leaf, see metallic leaf

granite, faux treatment:

granite, faux (about), 279–280

on a table base, 243 (step 2)

waterproof treatment for a tabletop, 282 (step 4)

grout:

choosing grout, 107 (materials)

grouting mosaic, 290 (steps 7–8)

grouting tile, 113 (step 14)

handwriting:

handwriting on bedstands, 89 (steps 2–3, 5)

handwriting quotations (about), 88

insoles for block printing, see block printing

iron and rust (paint-on), 276 (step 6)

kits (about), 32, 64

knockdown furniture:

bedstand painted multiple colors, 100

chair stained multiple colors, 142

table for adding a basket, 242

table for staining and painting, 268

lattice (masking and spray painting), 261 (steps 3–5)

leaves (*also see* natural properties):

leaves (about), 94

pasting leaves to furniture, 92 (step 1), 96 (step 6)

marbling (*also see* texturing):
marbling (about), 279
marbling (application), 282 (steps 5–8)
metallic leaf (*also see* sheet metal):
metallic leaf (about), 22, 70
adhesive and sealer for metallic leaf, 22
antiquing gold leaf, 72 (step 6), 174 (step 6), 281 (step 3)
antiquing silver leaf, 275 (step 3)
complete coverage (gold leaf), 71 (steps 2–6)
complete coverage (silver leaf), 275 (steps 1–3)
metallic leaf for a border, 174 (step 6), 281 (steps 2–3)
metallic leaf on finials, 281 (steps 2–3)
stenciling with metallic leaf, 191 (step 4)
metallic paint and patina (*also see* sheet metal):
metallic paint and patina (about), 23
copper paint and patina for a border, 269 (step 3)
iron paint, 276 (step 6)
rust patina, 276 (step 6)
mosaic (*also see* tiling):
mosaic (about), 286
gluing mosaic, 289 (steps 5–6)
grouting mosaic, 290 (steps 7–8)
planning, 288 (steps 3–4)
preparation, 288 (steps 1–2)

natural properties:
branches (about), 100
branches (cutting and attaching), 102 (steps 6–8)
branches (sealing for drying), 101 (step 1)
grapevines (about), 94
grapevines (attaching and arranging), 95 (step 5)
grapevines (soaking), 95 (step 2)
leaves (about), 94
leaves (drying), 95 (step 1)
leaves (laminating to furniture), 92 (step 1), 96 (step 6)

ornamentation:
baskets added to tabletops, 242–245
beads and silverware, 149 (steps 3–7)
branches as hardware, 98
button to finish a clock face, 238 (step 5)
faux decorative plaster, 222–225

gel studded with medallions, 276 (steps 4–5)
leaves on furniture, 94–96
mosaic, 284–291
silicone caulking faux plaster, 220–225
wooden bow on a wardrobe, 79 (step 8)

paint (*also see* paint additives, varnish):
acrylic wall paint (about), 27
acrylics for folk painting, 292–299, 110 (step 7)
acrylics for stenciling, 33, 236, 248
artist's acrylics (about), 27
faux-granite paint, 243 (step 2), 282 (step 4)
gesso for faux stucco, 83 (steps 2–4, 6)
glazes for block printing (about), 28, 262 (steps 8–9)
latex (about), 26
melamine paint (about), 27
primer/sealer (about), 28
rust-covering spray paint, 45 (step 3), 131 (step 2), 288 (step 2)
specialty paints (about), 32–33
spray paint (about), 27
spray varnish, 90 (step 5), 150 (step 5), 245 (step D)
stencil cream paints, 33
varnish (about), 29
paint additives (*also see* glaze and glazing):
extender (about), 28
extender in marbling, 282 (step 6)
extender in texturing, 173 (step 3)
gel for a tabletop, 276 (steps 4–5)
glaze (about), 28
medium and gel (about), 28
painting basics:
painting basics (about), 34
brush painting, 40–41
preparation, 36–37
priming and painting, 38–39
roller painting, 42–43
spray painting, 44–45
staining wood, 46–47
varnishing, 48–49
work area (setting up), 36
painting tools (about), 24–25, 32–33
patina (*also see* antiquing):
patinas (about), 23
etching metal for patina, 192 (step 5)
patinating copper paint, 269 (step 3)
patinating iron with rust, 276 (step 6)

patinating sheet copper, 192 (step 5)
patterns:
block print, fish, 233
block print, ivy, 270–271
block print, leaves, 60
block print, morning glory, 265
block print, rose, 264
decal pattern (reverse stencil), moon and stars, 207
folk painting, cow, 298
folk painting, horse, 299
oval template, 225
potato print, diamond-eye, 67
potato print, three-leaf and sawtooth, 233
stencil, clock face hands and numerals, 239
stencil, rose and leaves, 251
photocopies:
découpage photocopies (about), 76
découpage photocopies (application), 77 (steps 2–4)
photocopy transfer (about), 88
transferring photocopies 89 (steps 4–5)
plaster, faux treatments:
faux stucco (about), 82
faux stucco on a jam cupboard, 83 (steps 2–4, 6)
plaster figure added to a door, 83 (step 5)
silicone faux plaster (about), 222
silicone faux plaster on a dresser, 223 (steps 4–10)
posters for découpage, 210–212
potato prints:
potato printing (about), 25, 64
potato printing, 65 (steps 3–5), 232 (steps 7–9)
potato print patterns, 67 (diamond-eye); 233 (three-leaf and sawtooth)
sawtooth border, 66 (step 5), 232 (steps 7–9)
preparation for painting, 36–37
primers and sealers:
primer/sealer (about), 28
primer application (about), 38–39
shellac on cross-grain cuts when staining, 47 (step 1)
shellac on wood knots, 39 (step 1)
sealer for cut branches, 101 (step 1)
sealer for metallic leaf, 22
sealer for metallic paint (about), 23
when not to apply primer, 54–55, 101 (step 2), 120 (step 4), 249 (step 1)

priming and painting, 38–39

ragging (*also see* texturing):
    ragging on, and off, 110 (step 6)
    ragging a straw color, 245 (step B)
repairing furniture: see fixing furniture
rollers and roller painting:
    rollers (about), 25
    roller painting (about), 42–43
    block printing ivy with a roller, 270 (steps 4–8)
    block printing leaf pattern with a roller, 59 (steps 2–5)

sanded paint (*also see* deglossing agents):
    for antiquing, 55 (steps 2–4), 101 (steps 2–5)
    revealing undercoats of paint, 191 (step 2)
    sanding on partial stripping, 126 (step 6)
sandpapers, 18–19 (*also see* deglossing agents):
sealers: see primers and sealers
seating:
    backrest cushions, 164–167
    basic seat cushion, 155–157
    batting, foam and dust-cover cloth (about), 153
    cutting foam (about), 153
    cutting plywood for seating, 156 (step 1)
    piped seat cushion, 158–160
    woven seat, 161–163
selecting furniture: see choosing furniture
sewing: see fabric treatments
sheet metal:
    sheet copper (about), 23, 190
    cutting, patinating, applying sheet copper, 192 (step 5)
shellac: see primers and sealers
silicone caulking for faux plaster, 222–224 (*also see* plaster, faux treatments)
silver leaf (*also see* metallic leaf):
    silver leaf (about), 273–274
    antiquing silver leaf, 275 (step 3)
    applying silver leaf, 275 (steps 1–2)
smooshing, 261 (step 2) (*also see* texturing)
sponge painting (*also see* texturing):
    sponges (about), 25
    background for a clock face, 237 (step 2)
    background for découpage, 179 (step 2)
    background for hand-painted motifs, 217 (step 2)
    for marbling, 282 (step 6)

    for reverse-stenciling, 205 (steps 5–7)
    three colors on tabletop, 249 (steps 2–3)
spray glue, see adhesives
spray painting:
    spray painting (about), 44
    base coat for a chair, 119 (step 1)
    base coat for mosaic, 288 (step 2)
    base coat for silver leaf, 275 (step 1)
    base coat for small tables, 243 (step 2)
    bentwood chair, 137 (step 2)
    border treatment, 245 (step C)
    covering rust, 45 (step 3), 131 (step 2), 288 (step 2)
    faux granite, 243 (step 2), 282 (step 4)
    lattice, 261 (steps 3–6)
    spray primer, 39 (step 1), 45 (step 2)
    table and chairs, 281 (step 1)
staining:
    staining wood (about), 46–47, 268
    block printing ivy on stained wood, 270 (steps 4–9)
    fabric dye stains, 140–145
    staining wood (application), 47, 269 (step 2)
    staining for antiquing, 55 (step 5), 101 (step 5)
    staining wood trim, 95 (step 3)
stamps (postage) for découpage, 71 (steps 4–6)
stapling:
    staple gun, manual and power (about), 20–21
    carpet staples for attaching grapevines, 95 (step 5)
    stapling baskets to tabletops, 244 (step 6)
    stapling cushions, 157 (steps 5–6), 160 (steps 6–7), 166 (steps 6, 7, 10)
    stapling halters for chairs, 137 (step 4)
stenciling:
    stencil materials (about), 33, 236, 248
    clock face (about), 236
    clock face, 238 (step 4)
    clock face (patterns), 239
    cutting stencils, 238 (step 4), 249 (step 4)
    gluing stencils, 238 (step 4), 249 (step 4)
    metallic leaf, 191 (step 4)
    reverse-stenciling (about), 204
    reverse-stenciling (application), 205 (steps 1–4)
    Victorian roses, 249 (steps 4–5)
    Victorian roses (patterns), 251

stripes:
    loose stripes (about), 198
    painting loose stripes, 199 (steps 2–5)
stripper and stripping paint:
    paint stripper (about), 30
    partial stripping, 124–126
    protective gear (about), 31
    stripping hardware, 108 (step 2)
    stripping to raw wood, 106–109
    stripping for repainting (about), 54, 124
    stripping tools (about), 31
stucco, see plaster, faux treatments

tables, 226
tape and taping:
    tape (about), 17
    cutting guide, 255 (step 3)
    guide for a border, 217 (step 3)
    guide for painting patterns, 217 (steps 3–8)
    guide for stripes, 198, 199 (steps 2–5)
    masking off a border, 269 (step 3)
    masking for texturing, 173 (step 2), 282 (step 4)
    painting lattice, 261 (steps 3–5)
templates and decals:
    decals (about), 204
    templates (about), 118
    decal patterns (moon and stars), 207
    decals used for reverse-stenciling, 205 (steps 1–4)
    painting with templates, 119 (steps 2–3)
    patterns for templates (tulips), 120
texturing (*also see* sponge painting):
    dragging (about), 172
    dragging a desktop, 173 (steps 2–5)
    faux granite, 282 (step 4)
    marbling (about), 280
    marbling a tabletop, 282 (steps 5–8)
    masking areas for texturing, 173 (step 2), 282 (step 4)
    materials (about), 25
    ragging on, ragging off, 110 (step 6)
    ragging a straw color, 245 (step B)
    scumbling by stripping paint (about), 123
    smooshing, 261 (step 2)
    veining marble, 283 (step 7)
tiling a countertop (*also see* mosaic):
    cutting tile, 112 (step 11)
    grouting tile, 107 (materials), 113 (step 14)
    laying and gluing tile, 112 (step 12)
    planning, 112 (step 10)

tiling a countertop (continued)
    trim, 113 (step 13)
tools:
    manual tools, 20
    painting tools (about), 24–25, 32–33
    power tools, 21
    protective gear, 21

varnish (*also see* primers and sealers):
    varnish (about), 29
    varnish (application), 48–49
    glazing with a paint-varnish mixture, 251
        (step 7)
    oil-based varnish (about), 29

oil-based varnish for crackle (about), 106
oil-based varnish for crackle (application), 111 (steps 8–9)
on block printing, 232 (step 10), 271 (step
    10)
on decorative paint, 120 (step 5)
on découpage, 78 (step 4)
on découpage (posters), 212 (step 6)
on fabric, 187 (step 10), 256 (step 6)
on handwriting, 90 (step 5)
on leaves, 96 (step 8)
on marbling, 283 (step 8)
on photocopy transfers, 90 (step 5)
on reverse stencils, 206 (step 8)

sanding varnish, 49 (step 3)
spray varnish, 90 (step 5), 150 (step 5), 245
    (step D)
on stain (commercial), 47 (step 3), 49
    (steps 1–3)
on stain (fabric dyes), 144 (step 6)
on stripped wood, 109 (step 4)
on texturing (dragging), 175 (step 7)
waxing varnish, 49 (step 3)
vines, see natural properties

weaving a chair seat, 161–163